THE FLYING
SIKH

The Story of a WW1 Fighter Pilot –
Flying Officer Hardit Singh Malik

To my Mother, June

THE FLYING
SIKH

The Story of a WW1 Fighter Pilot –
Flying Officer Hardit Singh Malik

STEPHEN BARKER

AIR WORLD

AIR WORLD

THE FLYING SIKH
The Story of a WW1 Fighter Pilot –
Flying Officer Hardit Singh Malik

First published in Great Britain in 2022 by
Air World
An imprint of
Pen & Sword Books Ltd
Yorkshire – Philadelphia

ISBN 978 1 39908 329 4

Typeset by SJmagic DESIGN SERVICES, India.

Printed and bound in the UK by CPI Group (UK) Ltd, Croydon, CR0 4YY.

Pen & Sword Books Limited incorporates the imprints of Atlas, Archaeology,
Aviation, Discovery, Family History, Fiction, History, Maritime, Military, Military
Classics, Politics, Select, Transport, True Crime, Air World, Frontline Publishing, Leo
Cooper, Remember When, Seaforth Publishing, The Praetorian Press, Wharncliffe
Local History, Wharncliffe Transport, Wharncliffe True Crime and White Owl.

For a complete list of Pen & Sword titles please contact

PEN & SWORD BOOKS LIMITED
47 Church Street, Barnsley, South Yorkshire, S70 2AS, England
E-mail: enquiries@pen-and-sword.co.uk
Website: www.pen-and-sword.co.uk

Or
PEN AND SWORD BOOKS
1950 Lawrence Rd, Havertown, PA 19083, USA
E-mail: Uspen-and-sword@casematepublishers.com
Website: www.penandswordbooks.com

Contents

Foreword

On the battlefields of Europe, as the First World War raged, around 1.3 million Indian soldiers served in ghastly conditions, far from their homes, fighting a war which was not their own. Some 74,000 of these brave troops lost their lives. Among the contingent of Indian troops was Hardit Singh Malik. In his later life he became well-known as a senior civil servant and diplomat, eventually serving as High Commissioner to Canada and Ambassador to France. His distinguished war years, though, during which he served as the only Sikh in service with the Royal Flying Corps, have been unjustly neglected.

With *The Flying Sikh*, Stephen Barker seeks to bring the fascinating story of Malik's military service to a wider audience. Covering Malik's early years through his studies at school and university and then eventually coming to his role as a crack fighter pilot on the aerial front lines of the First World War. Beyond painting an insightful portrait of this interesting and accomplished man's own life, Barker delves into various angles of the history of Britain's relationship with colonial India: the alienation sometimes felt by Indian students in Britain, the long battle to allow Indians to serve in Britain's army, and more.

It is only in recent years that the long-overlooked history of India's massive contribution to the First World War has finally begun receiving part of the attention it deserves. There is still a great deal of research to be done on the issue. With this book, the author has contributed an important piece of scholarship to the shamefully small body of work on the subject, and I wish him the best in bringing it to a wide audience.

Dr Shashi Tharoor,
1 September 2021
Delhi

Acknowledgements

I have been very appreciative of the support of members of Hardit Singh's family, particularly Santhya Malik and Vinita Tripathi. Santhya was particularly helpful in tirelessly answering my queries in relation to her grandfather's life and for enabling publication of images from the family archive for which I am very grateful.

I am very thankful to Dr Shashi Tharoor for the generous Foreword. I could think of no one better and am honoured that he felt able to do so. I've often wondered if he knew that his speech decrying Colonialism to the Oxford Union in May of 2015 would reach such a wide audience? It certainly reached me several days later.

During the planning and writing of this book over the last few years, a number of individuals have become involved in the process. I am immensely grateful to all who did so, for this is a book which required a detailed understanding of a number of subjects outside my own First World War military specialism. Included among them were: Dr Priya Atwal, Shrabani Basu, Robin Boston, Jill Bush, Christy Campbell, Professor Santanu Das, John Dimmock, Sophy Gardner, Professor Adrian Gregory, Mark Haselden, Bernard Lewis, Amandeep Madra, Conor Reeves, Poppy Kamel Sall, Sukhdeep Singh and Richard van Emden.

I'm very appreciative of the support received at the following institutions: the Asian & African Studies department of The British Library; The National Archives and the Imperial War Museum, all in London. I am also grateful to the following individuals: Peter Devitt and Bryan Legate at the RAF Museum, London; Corine Arnaud at the Musée D'Art et D'Histoire du Cognac; Geraldine Galland at the Martell Archive in Cognac; Virginie Alauzet at the Croix Rouge Française, Paris; Celia Pilkington at the Inner Temple Archives, London; Paul Jordan and Michael Partridge at the Eastbourne College Archives; Jon Filby, Phil Barnes and Nicholas Sharp at the Sussex County Cricket Club Museum and Archive, Hove; Tara Finn at the Foreign and Commonwealth Office; Dr Bethany Hamblen at Balliol College, University of Oxford and Alison Metcalfe at the National Library of Scotland.

This book was written at the height of the Covid-19 pandemic in 2020 and the closure at times of some of these institutions, only served to emphasise their fundamental importance.

Literary Agent Anuj Bahri in Delhi has played a central role in the publication of this book. I am indebted to him.

I'm grateful for the support of John Grehan and Ken Patterson, both associated with Pen & Sword Books.

If all else failed, I knew that members of the 'The Aerodrome' forum (theaerodrome.com) would have an answer. Many thanks to all those who contribute, and whose collective patience, wisdom and generosity were greatly appreciated.

Finally, thank you to my family for their support, but particularly to my mother June for her continued interest in, and enthusiasm both for the project and wanting to find out more about the life of HS Malik. Last but not least, thank you to Yvonne Barker for her encouragement throughout the development of this book, especially during the long days of 2020. I have appreciated the support of both more than I can say.

Buckingham,
January 2021

Dramatis Personae

Royal Flying Corps and Royal Air Force

Captain William George "Billy" Barker (1894–1930) was a Canadian fighter ace and Victoria Cross recipient. He remains the most decorated serviceman in the history of Canada to this day, earning the VC, DSO and bar, MC and two bars. He was credited with bringing down fifty enemy machines during the First World War. Barker died in 1930 when he lost control of his biplane trainer during a demonstration flight.

Major-General William Sefton Brancker (1877–1930) was one of the most influential officers during the early days of the RFC. In 1917, he served briefly as the commander of the Palestine headquarters and then its Middle East headquarters. He was promoted to major-general in 1918, becoming Controller-General of Equipment in January of that year and Master-General of Personnel in August 1918. He was knighted on 1 January 1919 and retired from the RAF almost two weeks later. He was granted the rank of Air Vice-Marshal in 1924. Brancker was killed in an airship crash in 1930.

Lieutenant-General Sir David Henderson (1862–1921) was the senior leader of British military aviation during the First World War, having previously established himself as the leading authority on tactical intelligence in the British Army. He served as the commander of the RFC in the field during the opening year of the First World War. In 1915, Henderson was back in London as Director-General of Military

ix

Aeronautics, having been superseded by General Trenchard. After the war Henderson was the first Director-General of the League of Red Cross Societies.

India Office

Sir Joseph Austen Chamberlain (1863–1937) served as Chancellor of the Exchequer (twice) and was briefly Conservative Party leader before serving as Foreign Secretary. Chamberlain returned to office in Herbert Asquith's wartime coalition government in May 1915, as Secretary of State for India, but resigned as a consequence of the disastrous Kut Campaign in July 1917.

Lieutenant-General Herbert Vaughan Cox (1860–1923) was a British officer in the Indian Army. He was promoted to the rank of lieutenant-general in January 1917 for distinguished service in the field and then became Military Secretary to the India Office, where he remained until his retirement in January 1921. In 1919, he was appointed to the Esher Committee to look into Indian Army administration and organisation. He was promoted to general in 1920, and knighted in the 1921 Birthday Honours.

Edwin Samuel Montagu (1879–1924) was a British Liberal politician who served as Secretary of State for India between 1917 and 1922. Montagu was a 'radical' Liberal and the third practising Jew to serve in the British cabinet. He was primarily responsible for the Montagu-Chelmsford Reforms which led to the Government of India Act of 1919, committing the British to the eventual evolution of India towards dominion status.

Government of India

Frederic John Napier Thesiger, 1st Viscount Chelmsford (1868–1933) was a British statesman who served as Viceroy of India from 1916 to 1921, where he was jointly responsible for the creation of the Montagu–Chelmsford Reforms.

The University of Oxford

Francis Fortescue Urquhart (1868–1934) was educated at Beaumont College, Old Windsor, and Stonyhurst College, before becoming a student at Balliol College, Oxford. He acquired the nickname 'Sligger' as an undergraduate. He was lecturer in history and a Fellow at Balliol, later becoming Dean. Urquhart was the first Roman Catholic to have acted as a tutorial Fellow in the University of Oxford since the sixteenth century.

Notes on the Text and Abbreviations

Where possible, I have included the content of letters, telegrams, minutes and reports verbatim, enabling the reader to study the documents as they were written and to interpret for themselves. Some of the most important items have been included as appendices, the better to access in their entirety and to enable understanding. I have reproduced all of this material as it was written originally, including the inconsistencies of grammar, spelling and rendering of proper nouns, titles and headings.

Whilst I recognise the colonial connotations of nineteenth century transliteration, I have retained the original spelling to avoid confusion and to stay as close to the primary materials as possible, hence Kolkata is rendered Calcutta and Mumbai as Bombay, for example.

Some places in Europe have also changed the spelling of their names e.g., Ichteghem is now rendered 'Ichtegem'. Similarly, I have employed the version in common usage in the early twentieth century.

Throughout the text, use is made of '1914-19' as shorthand for the Great War, to reflect not only the signing of the Versailles Treaty, but also the inclusion of the Jallianwala Bagh Massacre and the ratification of the Government of India Act 1919, in December.

Reference to the 'Government of India' (GOI) is used as shorthand in the text for references associated with the Viceroy of India, the Viceroy's Army Department and the Imperial Legislative Council.

The word 'cabinet' is used as shorthand in the text for references associated with the Imperial War Cabinet in London.

In terms of orthography, compound ranks of British Army officers were invariably hyphenated, prior to about 1980, e.g., Lieutenant-General. I have recorded these ranks as they were written at the time.

In spite of the guidance and assistance that I have received, I accept that any errors made in this book are my own. Every effort has been made to trace the copyright holders of illustrations used. Where it has not been established the author would be grateful to anyone who believes that they do hold such a copyright to get in touch with the publishers.

Underlined words in their first usage are to be found in the Glossary.

Abbreviations

AIR	Air Ministry papers
CAB	Cabinet papers
GOI	Government of India
ICS	Indian Civil Service
IOR	India Office Records
OTC	Officer Training Corps
TNA	The National Archives
WO	War Office
RAF	Royal Air Force
RFC	Royal Flying Corps
RNAS	Royal Naval Air Service

Introduction

'H.S. Malik was about the handsomest and best
dressed *sardar* I have met.'

Kushwant Singh

On a warm afternoon in June 2018, whilst working at a 'Digital Collection Day' at the King's High School in Warwick, I decided to start writing this book. The event was one of those run by the University of Oxford, part of the 'Lest We Forget' programme associated with the First World War Centenary, aimed to capture the memories and stories of participants before they were lost to history. A colleague drew my attention to a photographic album brought in by a member of the public, Mark Haselden, the grandson of Eric Haselden, who flew with 141 Squadron during 1918. The album had been compiled by Eric and is beautifully preserved.

One of the photographs caught my eye immediately, at its heart was an oversize sign in the shape of a teapot, an advertising hoarding as it turned out, larger than any of the nineteen men surrounding it, some of whom were wearing Royal Flying Corps (RFC) uniforms. All were looking into the camera, some smiling, others rather more sternly. The image also attracted my attention for another reason: in the background was the figure of a man I recognised instantly. Having attempted to identify individual soldiers believed to be concealed in grainy Great War snapshots for over twenty-five years, I had become rather sceptical about such recognitions, but on this occasion, there was no doubt. The familiar face of Hardit Singh Malik looked calmly towards the camera, his right hand resting on a nearby shoulder and the other linked through that of the airman to his left. I later came to know the full story of the photograph's significance, but there and then in Warwick that day, I knew it had been taken at Biggin Hill, one of those names synonymous with the Royal Air Force (RAF).

INTRODUCTION

Lieutenant Hardit Singh Malik would be the only Indian on active service with the RAF when the Armistice came on 11 November 1918. He was one of a handful of recruits from South Asia who had managed to enlist on behalf of the Empire whilst living in Britain. His education and career in the RFC and subsequently the RAF, in the ten years after 1909, would underpin what was to be, by any standards, a successful and fulfilling life. With significant achievements to his name in the spheres of diplomacy and sport and fortified by family and by friends made around the world, his was a name which came to earn the utmost respect. According to Khushwant Singh, the greatest of Indian writers, he would become the most distinguished Sikh of his time.

I'd come across Hardit Singh's story for the first time in the mid 2000s, but it was whilst working with the Soldiers of Oxfordshire Museum at Woodstock that I became somewhat more familiar with his achievements. Whilst curating exhibitions for the Great War Centenary, I dug a little deeper into the story, referencing his University of Oxford connections in local displays and presentations. Having obtained copies from India of Hardit's own autobiography *A Little Work, A Little Play*, which had been published posthumously in 2010, and Somnath Sapru's *Sky Hawks* published in 2006, I believed initially that there was little more to be said. However, an impromptu visit to the National Archives in London in 2013 gave tantalising glimpses of another narrative and made me think again. This was confirmed by the work of the journalist and author Christy Campbell. Further exploration at the British Library; Balliol College, Oxford; the Imperial War Museum and RAF Museums, London, convinced me that there was more to say. My interest was cemented, when as part of a University of Oxford working group producing an exhibition late in 2017, Hardit's story was chosen to be represented. The interpretation aimed to highlight the roles of men and women associated with the city during the First World War and whose stories resonated to this day.

It wasn't the first time that his flying career was portrayed during the Great War Centenary in Britain. Organisations as diverse as The Royal British Legion, United Kingdom Punjabi Heritage Association (UKPHA), Historic England and the RAF Museum all sought to bring the story to a wider audience during 2014-19. Similarly, a multiplicity of articles about Hardit appeared in newspapers, magazines and online outlets in India and other places around the world, a number of these publications highlighting his role as the forerunner of those who serve today in the Indian Air Force. His part in the war was commemorated on stamps, reinterpreted by a children's author and featured in several books about the Indian Army in the First World War – most notably Shrabani Basu's *For King and Another Country.*

At the heart of some of the coverage, particularly in Britain, was the use made of Hardit's story as a symbol of India's contribution to the Empire during the Great War. In the last twenty years or so, increasing emphasis has been given to the involvement of India during 1914-19, by both academic and popular historians. Museums, libraries and archives followed not far behind, producing exhibitions which highlighted the part played not just by India, but also soldiers and non-combatants from the Caribbean, China and Africa for example – typified by the recently installed galleries at the Imperial War and National Army Museums.

Whilst the contributions made by former dominions of Empire and India were well known in Britain by historians and those with a specific interest in the war, conversely, amongst the public at large, they were not. As *British Future's* own research indicated however, by 2018, knowledge of the participation of Empire troops in the war, inspired by the centennial commemorations, had increased awareness among Britons, with a striking seventy per cent of respondents having greater knowledge of Indian soldiers in particular, up from forty-four per cent in 2014.[1] Throughout this centenary period, I noted how often members of the public commented on their unfamiliarity with the scale of the Indian contribution in terms of resources, finances, supplies and personnel. They were particularly surprised to learn that the scale of Indian recruitment – 1.5 million combatants and labourers - was twice the size of the next largest contingent of Empire from Canada, and usually drew the rejoinders – 'I never knew' or 'everyone should know about this!'

As an airman, Hardit Singh's story offered an unusual and alternative perspective for those wanting to portray Indian participation in the conflict. The subsequent narratives employed by curators and writers included not only RFC and RAF themes, but also those associated with other aspects of Hardit's identity: his Sikh faith, Punjabi heritage, sporting talents and later professional life as a civil servant, diplomat and ambassador. The best

---

1. Buckerfield, L. & Ballinger, S., *'The People's Centenary – Tracking public attitudes to the First World War Centenary 2013-2018'* (British Future: London, 2019), p. 5

of these representations was typified by the *Empire, Faith & War* virtual exhibition which highlighted the role of Sikh participation in the war, within the larger context of the Indian Army.[2] With so many accounts of Hardit's story across a range of media there seemed little purpose to add to them. What else was there to say about a man who had written his own autobiography?

In the first instance, there was sufficient previously unexploited material at the British Library in London to add greatly to what was already known. This important documentary evidence offered new perspectives about how his part in the war was viewed by the British authorities, but also how Hardit himself reflected on the events at the time.

Writing this book also presented the opportunity to set Hardit's experiences within the context of the war as a whole, explaining in detail, where he was going, what he was doing and why he was doing it. I have tried to give to the reader a sense of the world in which he lived and its impact upon him. I also wanted to give a uniform account of the period 1894-1921, giving due prominence to the entirety of his lived experiences by augmenting what had previously been well documented, whilst highlighting for the first time what had not. One of the joys of working on this book was the opportunity to explore further small details described by Hardit in *A Little Work, A Little Play*, which would often lead to moments of unlooked for insight or illumination.

An important part of contextualising Hardit's own experiences was making relevant and appropriate connections to the political events associated with the campaigns for Indian independence and various challenges to British authority during his formative years. The unrest in the Punjab in 1907, the assassination of Sir Curzon Wyllie in 1909 and the Jallianwala Bagh Massacre ten years later were all touched upon briefly in the autobiography and have been amplified here. Without reference to these and the other related significant events and personalities during this period, it is difficult not only to understand Hardit's world, but to make sense of the ways in which that political environment affected him personally.

This book also gave an opportunity to provide a counterpoint to a number of myths and inaccuracies about his story, which have developed since his

---

2. *'Empire, Faith & War'*, - as of 23 September 2020 - empirefaithwar.com

death in 1985, mainly about his experiences during the war. I will refer to one only – he was never a German prisoner!

When writing, I was conscious of what Vedica Kant referred to as the 'complex and intertwined histories that bound India and its colonial master Great Britain during the Great War'.[3] The deeper questions asked by many historians about both this relationship and the meaning of 'commemoration' during the recent centennial, enabled previously neglected global perspectives of the war to come to the fore. This greater emphasis on the international nature of the conflict allowed a space in which stories of the Indian contribution were not only able to be told, but were given a more willing ear than ever before. Against this background, the memorialisation of those Indians who fought for an imperial cause over a hundred years ago was an uncomfortable reminder to some people in India today of a difficult past, one that many would rather forget.[4] Others viewed the *sepoys* who fought on behalf of the British Empire as having been on the 'wrong' side, having fought *for* rather than *against* the colonial authorities.[5] This may partly explain Hardit's seeming reticence about committing to paper his memories until later in life, yet typical of veterans in all eras who begin to recount their experiences of war only in advanced age. We should be grateful that he did, for there are so few diaries and memoirs from those who participated in the war on India's behalf, a time when so many were illiterate or who lacked the resources necessary to have their works published for a wider audience. Hardit's experiences were entwined with India's story during the conflict, rather more than he realised and are well worthy of further study.

The complexities and ambiguities of India's Great War participation is actually *the* very reason for our continued interest, so great was the scale of impact the period had on Indian history.[6] Though this war was made in Europe, and did itself not lead directly to decolonisation, it signalled the beginning of the end, for after the Jallianwala Bagh Massacre, any further illusions about the nature of British rule had been shattered.[7] During

---

3. Kant, V., *'India and the First World War'* (Roli Books: New Delhi, 2014), p. 17
4. Ibid.
5. Ibid.
6. Ibid., p. 18
7. Das, S., *'India, Empire and First World War Culture'* (Cambridge University Press: Cambridge, 2018), p. 408

1914-19, many nationalist leaders, notably Gandhi himself, progressed from advocating support for the war at its outset, to actively rousing the independence movement by its end, after which there was no going back.

I believe that Hardit Singh's story is rather more important than perhaps he, a modest man, realised. As a western educated Indian flying officer, his experiences bore witness not only to the challenges of being an Indian serving amongst Europeans, but also offered a unique perspective of the RAF in its embryonic stages and in which so few Indians fought during the war. None of the other South Asian airmen or indeed soldiers who managed to enlist in the armed forces whilst living in Britain have bequeathed to us any significant autobiography. Although *A Little Work, A Little Play* was written by Hardit in his dotage and care needs to be taken therefore with his recollections of detail and interpretation, this in no way devalues its potential as an important historical source. For as historian Santanu Das reminds us, there is no homogeneous Indian war experience and one of the joys of researching Hardit's war was understanding just how unique his perspective was.[8]

Yet, in one way, he is typical of the one and a half million of his countrymen who experienced the war at first hand – he was changed by his experiences and what he had seen. After the end of the Great War, many of his *sepoy* compatriots developed political consciousness and large numbers would take up the cause of the growing nationalist movement in the years that followed. One of the most difficult challenges when writing has been to assess how Hardit's political outlook evolved before 1922, for he was always diplomatic at the time, using language as carefully as one would expect as an embryonic member of the <u>Indian Civil Service (ICS)</u> and later the diplomatic corps. Nonetheless, it's clear that he was a proud Sikh and a proud Indian. The main personal legacy of the war that he *was* willing to share, often very powerfully and movingly, was the impact that it had upon his spiritual and religious life.

Inevitably, this book draws upon some of Hardit's experiences described in his autobiography *A Little Work, A Little Play* and to a lesser degree the work and interviews of Somnath Sapru and others. Taken together, the combined texts represent a full and comprehensive account of his life until the autumn of 1921.

---

8. Ibid.

Hardit Singh never wanted to write an autobiography but was persuaded to do so by his wife Prakash and their children. He began work on the draft in the 1960s and then having completed it, set it aside. In 2010, his daughter had the manuscript published in India. Both *A Little Work, A Little Play* and Sapru's *Sky Hawks* have to date only been available to readers in the subcontinent and I hope that this publication will act as a catalyst for further reprints in Britain and elsewhere, for it is a story which deserves to be told widely.

This book's narrative begins in Rawalpindi in 1894, for the reason that education and upbringing are significant in all our lives but seem particularly so for Hardit in shaping the man that he was to become. It ends with his return to India following the end of his ICS probationary year at Oxford in the autumn of 1921. Although these years of his life were instrumental in what followed, it is for another to recount Hardit's rich professional life as a diplomat and ambassador.

Chapter 1

Rawalpindi
1894–1909

'I sigh for distant Albion's shore,
The more I sigh, the will is more.
Whose glens are green, whose people white,
Afar extends whose terrestrial light.'

Surya Kumar Bhuyan

Hardit Singh Malik was born in the small hours of 23 November 1894 in the city of Rawalpindi, located on the western side of the Punjab, part of what was then India, but is now Pakistan. It was a setting which would shape his childhood and early adolescence.

The District of Rawalpindi in the late nineteenth century, was bounded on the northern side by the Hazara District of North-West Frontier Province, on the eastern by the River Jhelum, which divided it from Kashmir territory, and on its western side by the River Indus, which separated it from the Peshawar and Kohat Districts. The area formed a roughly drawn quadrilateral with the Murree Hills jutting from its north-east corner, the range extending south-westward along the eastern side of the district to within a few miles of Rawalpindi itself. The valleys between the spurs of the Murree Range were covered with a diverse growth of trees, particularly silver fir, blue pine and wild cherry, which unite to form dense forests and the resulting views looking upwards from the plains below remain one of extreme beauty to this day.

The area's climate is cooler than in the hot Punjab plains to the south-east, its monsoon season lasting only a couple of months and the close proximity of the hills lowers the temperature during the succeeding months, even when there is no rain on the plains.

1

In the past, the district was considered to be a favourite first posting for newly arrived soldiers from Britain, owing to this agreeable environment, though the cold winters remained very severe, with a trying east wind prevailing in January and February.[9]

The area had been dominated by the British after the surrender of the Sikh army in 1849, following its defeat in the Battle of Gujrat. Yet, Sikh chieftains had ruled since the 1760s, when Gujar Singh Bhangi had marched from Lahore to defeat the last and most celebrated independent Mughal chief Mukkarab Khan. In 1810, the great Ranjit Singh had assumed power of the Rawalpindi region, controlling it as part of the prodigious Sikh Empire, until it passed under British rule. Nevertheless, during the 1857 *sepoy* rebellion, the district's peoples remained loyal to the British.

The city of Rawalpindi itself, stood on the Grand Trunk Road, one of Asia's longest and oldest routes, forming a significant transport network which ran back from Peshawar to Calcutta via the capital Delhi, and enabling the city to develop rapidly in size and importance during the latter half of the 1800s. It also enjoyed improved communications with other parts of India when a connection was established to the mainline by the extension of the North-Western Railway to Peshawar.

By 1909, almost half of the city's population was Muslim, over a third Hindu, with smaller communities of Sikhs, Jains and Christians. Onion domes, chhatris, spires and minarets dominated the skyline of the late Victorian city. Its burgeoning wealth at this time stimulated a plethora of temple building, evidence too of the growing population. Western religious practices had been introduced for the first time in Rawalpindi in 1856, when the American United Presbyterian Mission was established. In time, its founders built a church, maintained the Gordon Mission College and established three large high schools, two of them for girls. The founding of the Mission College in particular would have important implications for Hardit Singh's education over fifty years later.[10]

Rawalpindi stood on the Leh River, a muddy, sluggish stream flowing between precipitous banks and separating the ancient city on the eastern bank

---

9. Hunter, W.W., '*Imperial Gazetteer of India*' (Clarendon Press: Oxford, 1908), p. 263

10. See Wagner, K.A., '*The Skull of Alum Bheg*' (Hurst: London, 2017) for details of Andrew Gordon's proselytising activities during the Indian Rebellion of 1857-58, through his letters and memoirs.

to the north, from the <u>cantonment</u> and <u>Civil Lines</u> on the western bank to the south. The former was almost entirely occupied by the Indian inhabitants, whilst the latter was dominated by the British, both parts kept detached, managed and administered separately, as a matter of colonial policy. The cantonment had become a major centre of military power after an arsenal was established there in 1883, coming to define Rawalpindi's nature during the Raj. At its eastern end lay a fort, which enclosed an arsenal within its walls. Lying adjacent to the cantonment were the Civil Lines, the residential neighbourhoods developed solely for senior British civilian officers and their families. There would have been very strong disapproval of any Indian coming to live in these areas, the lives of Indians and British being kept very much apart. [11]

During the First World War, the district would recruit more *sepoys* for the Indian Army than any other, with greater financial assistance from the British government being channelled into the area in return. By 1921, the cantonment and Civil Lines would overshadow even the city - one of seven in the Punjab in which over half the population lived there.

It was here in Rawalpindi, that Hardit Singh grew up in the old family home, now long gone, which was shared between four brothers, their families and servants. The dwelling was the most noticeable amongst the narrow streets of their *mohalla,* a little more elegant, a little better maintained perhaps and rather more spacious that those around. Nevertheless, its entrance was situated at the end of a dark *gali,* which led to an even gloomier side street devoid of sunlight even at the height of summer. A gateway entrance adorned with roughly hewn figures and cement mouldings added a touch of the ornamental, notably absent elsewhere. Other decorative flourishes set the entrance apart too – windowpanes of coloured glass, which for a brief moment in time each day reflected the overhead rays of the sun, penetrating the dark passage beyond.

In short, it was a home which reflected the increasing wealth, status and aspirations of the extended Malik family. Their *mohalla* was occupied by lower middle-class Sikh and Hindu families headed by aspirant fathers for the most part: engineers employed at the Railway and Carriage Works, or shopkeepers specialising in the sale of rice, hardware, tea and salt. There were fitters from the gasworks, clerks from the armoury and weavers employed at the great tent factory close to the river. Muslims lived in the

---

11. Malik, H.S., '*A Little Work, A Little Play*' (Bookwise: Delhi, 2011), p.16

neighbouring *mohalla* and relations with Hindus and Sikhs were cordial, though religious and cultural differences precluded greater familiarity.

One of the brothers whose family shared the home was Mohan Singh Malik and his wife Lajwanti Bhagat. Their marriage would produce three sons, the oldest Teja, born in 1886, Hardit followed in 1894 and finally Iqbal in 1902. Their father was a small, thickset, yet commanding man whose charismatic character garnered the respect of those who knew him. He was considered to be a person of principle, earning the esteem of others with his physical and moral courage. Notably generous, Mohan was judged to be resourceful, and audacious in the scale of his ambitions, enabling his family to prosper through his enterprise and oftentimes fearlessness. He valued independence and hard work above all, tenets he imparted to his sons persistently. He made his wealth as a contractor, taking on commissions to support the building of the expanding rail network in Rawalpindi, constructing bridges and taking on other capital projects. In turn, he invested in land purchases and bought property to develop, and in so doing became one of the most well respected and wealthy notables in the district. As a result, he rose to become the city's Municipal Committee President, aiming to improve local amenities and oppose corruption wherever possible.

Hardit's brothers both became eminent in their own ways, the elder, Sir Teja Singh Malik would graduate from University College London in 1910, going on to join the Central Public Works Department in Delhi and enjoying an illustrious career. After becoming the chief engineer in the capital, he would become responsible for the government buildings, some of the best known landmarks of New Delhi. The most notable structures on which he worked were the Viceroy's House, now Rashtrapati Bhavan, and the Secretariat buildings. The two chief architects were Edwin Lutyens and Herbert Baker of course, but among the dozen or so engineers, there was only one Indian and Teja Singh Malik received a knighthood on his retirement.

Hardit's younger brother Iqbal Singh also enjoyed a distinguished career in railway management, but he is best remembered as a golfer, one of the earliest Indians to win his home golf championship. He achieved it first in 1950 at the age of forty-eight, and then followed up that success on two more occasions.

In Hardit's home, emphasis was placed on religious devotion and prayer, particularly by his mother Lajwanti Bhagat, a softly spoken, gentle woman of seemingly unlimited patience. Although apparently timid from the outside, she held strong moral views about the way a life was to be led, able to guide her sons and on occasions her husband when the need arose. Hardit would later say of her:

> She was a fine, noble person, very gentle, but with a quiet strength. She was never aggressive and had a profound influence on my character. The spiritual content there has been in my life, which has meant so much to me, I owe largely to her deep faith.[12]

Mohan Singh would often spoil Hardit with expensive gifts, something frowned upon by his mother, who instead encouraged in him an interest in the spiritual side of life. With tenderness, she also steered her beloved Mohan away from the partying and drinking occasionally associated with some of his increasingly numerous civic duties, inspiring instead the habits of religious ritual. This transformation was completed when regular visits were made to the Maliks' home by various _sants_ of the Sikh faith, most notably Sant Attar Singh in 1906. Hardit described the impact of this visit on his father as 'both instantaneous and profound'.[13]

Yet it was from his father that Hardit learned the value of independence and discipline, the former emphasising to his son by word and through action the importance of personal integrity and respect for others. So, while the young Hardit enjoyed the service of a servant, an elderly retainer whom he revered, it was made clear to him that such a privilege carried responsibility and that personal independence was important. Although not a bibliophile himself, Mohan Singh's favourite book was _Self Help_ by Samuel Smiles. His sons were made to read Smiles' work, to learn it by heart, its pages a reminder to be self-reliant in order to ward off any inclination towards idleness. It's worth taking a moment to say a little more about Smiles' writing, for his philosophy was important in Hardit's upbringing.

Samuel Smiles was a Scottish author and government reformer, famous particularly during the latter half of the nineteenth century. His greatest achievement _Self-Help_ is said to have reflected the spirit of the age. It also

---

12. Malik, H.S., _'A Little Work, A Little Play'_, p. 5
13. Ibid., p. 10

proved to be a best seller – with more than a quarter of a million copies sold by the time of the author's death in 1904. Smiles emphasised the importance of character, thrift, and perseverance in the lives of ordinary people and also acclaimed the significance of civility, independence and individuality. What follows is a typical assertion from *Self-Help,* one representative of a book which would play a part in shaping the nature of Hardit's character:

> Biographies of great, but especially of good men, are nevertheless most instructive and useful, as helps, guides, and incentives to others [...] They eloquently illustrate the efficacy of self-respect and self-reliance in enabling men of even the humblest rank to work out for themselves an honourable competency and a solid reputation.[14]

Mohan Singh had received very little formal education, but as a self-made man, he believed that he knew the value of learning and particularly the type of teaching which would best prepare his sons for life. More importantly, he enjoyed a level of wealth which enabled him to make educational choices on their behalf. Since Mohan believed that the local schools offered a relatively inferior education, he decided that Hardit would be tutored alone at home.

Initially taught by the Morris', an <u>Anglo-Indian</u> couple who ran a nearby kindergarten, during the secondary school years that followed, he was privately taught by professors from the local Gordon Mission College. Professor Satya Nand Mukarji, a Bengali whose family had long been settled in the Punjab, taught mathematics. A cultured, sensitive, yet strict disciplinarian, Mukarji rose to become Principal of St Stephen's College in Delhi between 1926 and his death in 1945. Hardit's other teacher was Ponsonby, an Anglo-Indian Christian from Sri Lanka who taught English. Ponsonby was also an understanding and principled man who produced the best of results from the teenager. Both tutors taught English, but it was Ponsonby who engendered a love of the language and its literature, which stayed with Hardit throughout his life. He developed a love of poetry, but particularly the tales of chivalry and adventure by authors such as Walter

---

14. Smiles, S., *'Self-Help with Illustrations of Conduct and Perseverance'* (John Murray: London, 1859)

Scott, G.A. Henry and Philip Meadows Taylor, which heightened an already romantic nature.

Mohan Singh also fostered his son's natural love of sport, arranging coaching from Master Sandhe Khan of the Gordon Mission College, as Hardit made clear later in life:

> As a youngster, I was only interested in games for which I had a natural gift and liking, encouraged wisely by my father who arranged expert coaching for me in cricket and tennis, enabling me to attain a proficiency in both, unusual for a boy even before his early teens as I was then. Similarly, I was shaken out of an indifference to studies common to boys of my age and background by contact with two of the best tutors available, engaged by a far seeing father, thanks to whom again I gained a proficiency in English and Mathematics which was beyond the normal for a boy of my age.[15]

In spite of not taking part in formal schooling, Hardit enjoyed a happy childhood, playing sports, flying kites, learning to ride well – a skill of great value when in Europe and throughout his time in the diplomatic service in India.[16] He also enjoyed visits to Rawalpindi's bazaars with other boys, taking pleasure in the stalls selling freshly made street foods, along with spices, fruit and vegetables. Yet Hardit was forbidden the treats and delicacies by his parents, usually obeying their warning not to linger too long for fear of mixing in bad company and the lure of other temptations down the dark *galiaan*.

Hardit's childhood might have been a lonely one being educated away from his peers, yet with the encouragement of his parents and tutors and through contacts at the Mission College, he found that his innate charisma and enthusiasm bound other children to him. In this way, he formed sporting teams of his own, helping to organise fixtures and events, and in doing so, found that he was able to compete with allegedly more experienced and proficient players, often among the British community.

---

15. Sapru, S., *'Sky Hawks'* (Writers Workshop Books: Calcutta, 2006), p. 221
16. All candidates for the ICS had to pass a compulsory horse riding test in those days.

Hardit's parents were both practicing Sikhs, equally devout in their faith, following his father's religious reawakening. There was an air of piety at home, prayers being said regularly throughout the day by his mother, whilst his father would make recitations from the scriptures of the <u>Guru Granth Sahib</u>. Hardit remembered the depths of his father's devotion:

> He would stand and say *ardas* before leaving the house, especially when he was about to do something he considered important. The *ardas* conclude with the beautiful words, "Tera bhane sarbet ka bhala*"*, which means "May it please you Lord that good may come to all." From time to time, father would bring home a *sant* or holy man who would conduct our prayers [...] sometimes they would stay with us and this would mean a great deal of religious activity.[17]

When a young child, the significance of these visits escaped Hardit's attention and he took little interest, sport being his one, true religion at that time. Yet the arrival of Sant Attar Singh in the Maliks' Rawalpindi home for the first time had a profound impact, leaving a lasting legacy.

Sant Attar Singh of Mastuana, is arguably the most charismatic figure in the story of modern day Sikhism. Born in 1866, he became an apprentice at the local village monastery in his youth, acquiring an aptitude in Sikh religious texts and philosophical treatises. He developed a profound faith, becoming absorbed in reciting hymns from the Guru Granth Sahib. At the age of seventeen, he enlisted as a gunner in the Royal Artillery, later being transferred to 54 Sikhs stationed at Kohat. There he received initiation in the cantonment *gurdwara* and continued his study of the scriptures. He became involved in the <u>Singh Sabha movement</u>'s concerns about the evangelising activities of Christians from the 1890s onwards. He came to believe that the restoration of the purity of Sikh belief and custom, the rejuvenation of Sikh society and of promoting Western education among Sikhs were of paramount importance. Through his extensive tours of the Punjab and his often resounding and always memorable recitations before frequently large crowds, he created a new and reinvigorated faith within the Sikh community. In spite of being illiterate, many who met him

---

17. Malik, H.S., *'A Little Work, A Little Play'*, p. 9

were impressed by his calm, spiritual manner and some would be drawn into Sikhism as a result. To receive baptism at his hands was considered especially commendable and new *gurdwaras* sprang up in several places following such ceremonies. It was therefore a great honour for the Malik family to welcome him into their Rawalpindi home.

The first meeting with Attar Singh had a significant effect on Hardit, who described how the old man 'gave an impression of serenity and self-possession, yet radiated a unique dynamism which flowed from his prayers and meditations'.[18] When Attar Singh left Rawalpindi, Hardit was permitted to abandon his lessons and sports to follow the old man's journeys across the Punjab. He gave Hardit his *kara*, the bangle worn by the devout, and which the teenager would treasure for the rest of his life.

The beginnings of the boy's spirituality and devotion to the Sikh faith began in the three years before his departure for England, awakened by the old man and nurtured by his parents, who asked Attar Singh to bless Hardit at his leaving: 'Sir, be kind to our son. Give your protecting hand to him and confer your blessings on him.'[19]

Hardit and Attar Singh maintained contact until the latter's death in 1927, the Sant's biographer recording some details of their final meeting:

> As soon as he came back to India, Hardit Singh went straight to Sant Ji to pay his respects. His belief that it was due to the Grace of Sant Ji that he was saved during the war, became most strong. Tears were flowing from his eyes and his voice was choked due to emotion.[20]

It is hard to overstate how important Attar Singh was in the formation of the young Sikh's spiritual maturity, giving him a sense also of the history and traditions of his faith and furnishing him with an inner strength. In an interview given in 1972, Hardit reflected on this transformation:

> Fate or destiny came in when, quite by accident, I came into contact at an early age with one of our great saints to whom

---

18. Ibid., p. 10
19. Doabia, H.S., *'Life Story of Sant Attar Singh Ji'* (Singh Brothers: Amritsar, 1992), p. 78
20. Doabia, H.S., *'Life Story of Sant Attar Singh Ji'*, p. 80

I became devoted and that contact gave spiritual content to my life, which has made it so full and rich. Had I not met this great man and become attached to him before I left for England at the age of fourteen my life would have been very different.[21]

Mohan Singh also played a significant secular role in Rawalpindi as well as a religious one, enabling him to exercise authority and influence in the city during the first decade of the 1900s. As one of the leading citizens, an honorary magistrate and President of the Municipal Committee, Mohan frequently met with the principal British military and civil officials on rather formal and sometimes difficult occasions. He was well respected by these administrators, yet conflict could sporadically break out, complicated by the unjust balance in the relationships between Indians and Britons.

Yet at some point during this period, Mohan and his family moved into the Rawalpindi cantonment. The change to 40 Edwards Road, made possible perhaps by, and to reflect, Mohan's eminent roles within the community and indicative of his growing wealth, possibly also reflected the age-old desire for greater privacy for his immediate family.[22]

Many of the institutional practices of the British, enabled them to maintain a distance and detachment from their Indian neighbours, preserving their standing and underlining the extent of their control and assumed superiority. Such customs were symptomatic of the way that the British had controlled India since the days of the East India Company army victories in the mid-eighteenth century. For example, Indians were expected to remove their shoes when visiting a British official before being ushered into his presence. This was greatly resented, though it was usually only those Indians who had lived and worked in Britain who actively refused to do so, knowing that such rituals were absent amongst the British at home and therefore finding the practice particularly humiliating. Indians were also expected to avoid riding on the main roads of the cantonment, nor did they share railway carriages with British people – compartments often being marked 'for Europeans only'- which led to numerous incidents across India, as Hardit himself would discover in 1919.

---

21. Sapru, S., *'Sky Hawks'*, p. 221
22. 40 Edwards Road in Rawalpindi is now 40 Bank Road, though the Malik home is long gone.

Nonetheless, he was privileged to witness at first-hand how his father managed successful exchanges with British officers, Mohan speaking good English and his charismatic personality and endless contacts enabling good working relationships with all but the stoniest faced official. In the years immediately before departing for Britain, Hardit, with equally well-spoken English, experience of joint Indo-British sporting events and an occasional observer of his father's political activities, developed some knowledge and understanding of the subtleties of British society, culture and officialdom.

During these formative years, the movements for Indian independence from British rule began to gain traction. Hardit's initial encounter at first-hand with these freedom movements came in 1907, when the celebrated nationalist leader Lala Lajpat Rai arrived in Rawalpindi from Lahore. Rai was a political activist, a lawyer and member of the Indian National Congress who became best known as one of three nationalists who came to prominence in the first two decades of the twentieth century, the other two being Bal Gangadhar Tilak, and Bipin Chandra Pal. They were known collectively as 'Lal Bal Pal' and the three played a key role in advocating the demands of the Swadeshi movement which supported an embargo on all imported items, particularly from Britain. The origins of the movement lay in the anti-Partition agitation in Bengal from 1905 and specifically the boycotting of Manchester cotton goods for which Bengal provided the richest market in the world. The main outcome of this campaign was the fusion of nationalist, economic and working-class protests into a relatively unified whole against the Government of India (GOI), for arguably the first time, and certainly since the Rebellion of 1857.[23]

From 1900, there was increasing unrest in the Punjab, the beginning of a period of discontent, which in one form or another, would end with the massacre at the Jallianwala Bagh in April 1919. What brought Lala Lajpat Rai to Rawalpindi in 1907 were two land reforms being introduced by the Punjab Government. The Land Alienation Act of 1900 was intended to ameliorate the lot of the peasant classes who were on the brink of serious agitation owing to alleged economic exploitation, whilst on the other hand the provincial government wanted to give some 'relief' to them. However,

---

23. Chandra, B., *'India's Struggle for Independence'* (Penguin Books: Delhi, 1989), p. 214

the bill was opposed by Indian leaders and the press, claiming that it had no part to play in improving the lot of the peasantry, while at the same time damaging the prospects of the professional and mercantile classes.[24]

The Colonisation Bill of 1906 provided for the transfer of a person's property after his death to the government if he had no heirs. In turn, the government could sell the property to any public or private developer. This was completely against the social conditions prevailing in the region and was rejected by all sides.[25] There were other causes for the unrest during March and April of 1907: a recent increase in land revenues, rising taxation and a particularly virulent plague outbreak all added to Punjab's recent woes.[26] The unrest was unlike any previous protest in the province, as the Punjab Government had for the first time aggravated a significant portion of the whole population, albeit by uniting a myriad of different causes.[27] Public meetings were organised across the region, headed on occasions by Lala Lajpat Rai, most notably at Lahore, Faisalabad and Rawalpindi. As a result, a number of public meetings took place in Hardit's home city attended by many thousands of people. At one of them, held on 21 April, between eight and ten thousand protestors were in attendance, including a significant number of railway workers who had their own grievances with the Punjab Government.[28] The main speaker was a radical revolutionary from Lahore, Ajit Singh, who allegedly made a seditious speech, according to the local District Magistrate, a man called Agnew.[29] Three lawyers, key members of the organising committee of the 21 April public meeting, were called to appear before Agnew on 2 May. Lala Lajpat Rai arrived in the city the day before in support of the three men.

---

24. Cassan, G., '*British law and caste identity manipulation in colonial India: the Punjab Alienation of Land Act*', Paris School of Economics (PSE), Laboratoire d'Economie Appliquée (LEA-INRA) and Centre de Sciences Humaines de Delhi (CSH), 12 January 2010, pp. 3-5

25. Mazunder, R.K., '*The Indian Army and the Making of Punjab*' (Orient Longman: Delhi 2003), p. 203

26. Ibid.

27. Barrier, N.G., '*The Punjab Disturbances of 1907: The Response of the British Government in India to Agrarian Unrest*' Modern Asian Studies, Vol. 1, no. 4, 1967, pp. 353–383

28. Hansard, H.C., Deb 06, May 1907 vol. 173, cc. 1331-2

29. Rai, L.R., '*The Story of My Deportation, 1908*' (Digital Library of India: Delhi, 2015), p. 40

A large crowd of over twenty thousand people assembled in the court compound that May morning, made up of students, traders, and shopkeepers, all expressing sympathy with the lawyers. The crowd was swelled by a large number of railway workers and employees of the city's arsenal who by coincidence were on strike that day. Many of those attending were apparently angered when, during truncated court proceedings, an inquiry into what had passed on 21 April was halted, apparently at the behest of the Punjab Government. It's likely that the size of the crowd and the alleged flawed legal case against the lawyers were determining factors. In spite of this, disturbances followed for much of the rest of the day, during which houses and gardens adjacent to the court belonging to British officials were attacked.[30] Lala Lajpat Rai was asked to address another public meeting that evening to calm the mob of people still thronging the courthouse compound. According to Hardit, the organising committee, including the three lawyers, reconvened at the police headquarters. As one of the city's notables, Mohan Singh was summoned to attend. He took twelve-year-old Hardit with him, perhaps for his son to observe the playing out of historical events, possibly also to witness the courage of the lawyers in their renewed battle with Agnew, who forbade that the evening public meeting take place. Hardit recalled what happened next:

> A furious Agnew told them that if they persisted in holding the public meeting, he would order the police to break it up. The lawyers insisted that they would consider the matter. In those early days the British rulers were very much held in awe and this open defiance of the District Magistrate made a deep impression on me. In my eyes the lawyers were great heroes, even though, in the end, the meeting didn't take place.[31]

A week later Lala Lajpat Rai was arrested in Rawalpindi and subsequently deported to Mandalay in Burma without trial later that month, it having been decided by the British authorities that he had been the main catalyst behind the Punjab unrest. In November that year, however, he was allowed

---

30. Mittal, S.C., *'Freedom movement in Punjab, 1905-29'* (Concept Publishing: Delhi, 1977), p. 48
31. Malik, H.S., *'A Little Work, A Little Play'*, pp. 23-24

to return when the Viceroy of India, Lord Minto, decided that there was insufficient evidence to hold him for subversion.

The early years of Hardit's life, before leaving for Britain in 1909, were a pivotal time which laid the foundation for highly successful and distinguished careers in both the military and diplomatic services. He had received excellent tuition, well suited to the later rigours of a public school and University of Oxford education; developed proficiencies in sport and learned the value of personal independence, hard work and discipline. Hardit came from a supportive family, enjoying a happy childhood and being shown great love by his parents, something he viewed with gratitude to the end of his life. Growing up in the expanding military city of Rawalpindi played an instrumental part in his understanding of the British and the ways in which they exercised power over Indians, the injustices of which began to forge in him sympathy for the activities of those aiming for Indian independence. On occasions, he was privileged to witness his father's exchanges with the British judicial, political and military establishment, beginning to be conscious of their customs and culture, and the nature and extent of their power. His character, talents and values as a whole would enable him to succeed in Britain where many young Indian men who had trodden that path before him had failed. Hardit would draw on these qualities when walking alone as a young teenager on the beach at Eastbourne, or in the air over Flanders in 1917.

Chapter 2

Eastbourne
1909–1912

'I was anxious to go overseas to see the people of England
who, living 5000 miles away, were able to rule us for so long.'

Vallabhbhai Patel

The P&O Royal Mail Ship *Morea* was anchored a little out to sea off the
harbour at Bombay, which in those days had no major dock for the great
ocean-going vessels which visited in their thousands. A motor launch
was beginning to load passengers once more from the Apollo Bunder
pier, ready to ferry another assortment of nationalities out to the *Morea*
for the three-week journey to Marseille. Its pilot caught sight of a small
family group on the quayside above him. He wondered at what point
they would say their final goodbyes, noticing that the parting between
them appeared to take just a little longer than normal. He had witnessed
this valedictory scene many times before, though the group's prolonged,
seeming hesitation, held his gaze, curious as to which of the four people
would take their final leave down the flights of steps from the quay onto
the rapidly filling launch.

Apollo Bunder then, was the most important pier for embarkation and
disembarkation of passengers and goods in the city of Bombay. It was here
that the King-Emperor George V and Queen-Empress Mary, the first British
monarch and his consort to visit India, would disembark on their way to the
Delhi Durbar in December 1911. Yet, in the spring of 1909, there was no
such majestic alighting, the pier a maze of wharves and docks where brisk
trading took place. During the months of April and May, it was particularly
busy, with thousands of baskets of cotton being stacked ready for loading
onto ships. Close to the pier, there was frantic activity at the Cotton Green

railway station, at the Customs House and at the hydraulic presses where the raw staple was baled for export, stacked up as far as the eye could see.

The family on the quayside was oblivious to the labour going on around them and to the fact that the launch pilot's gaze had lifted from them, his attention directed elsewhere. He saw neither a young man prostrate himself at his parents' feet, that age-old Indian tradition of respect, nor his embrace of a younger brother, nor did he see him make his way down the steps to the launch, without a backward glance.

At the end of 1908, Hardit had persuaded his father that he should go to Britain to complete his education, following in the footsteps of his brother Teja, who was eight years his senior. It was not uncommon in the decade before the First World War for Indian men (women were a very rare exception) to cross continents to complete their education at a British university at the age of eighteen and sometimes older. It was rather less common for a fourteen-year-old to contemplate travelling alone to complete his schooling at a preparatory and then a public school. Hardit's mother and friends of the family agreed that the boy was too young to go alone, that the temptations and challenges of a foreign culture would be risks too far. Yet the appeal of going to _vilayat,_ partly inspired by Teja's presence and vivid letters from London no doubt, proved irresistible. He was perhaps influenced also by the allure of Ponsonby's English tales and the journeys with his father and Sant Attar Singh across the Punjab, which had given the young man a taste for travel and excitement. His tuition, fluent English and occasional encounters with the British had persuaded him that he would be able to live amongst them without too many challenges. A career in the ICS had also begun to cross his mind, the examinations for which before the First World War were held in London each August. In the end, it was his father's undoubted ambition, as well as faith in his son's character and personality which changed the course of Hardit Singh's life. As Mohan explained to his wife:

> Babuji, my son has been well brought up. He has my blood in his veins. I know that he will never do anything that is unworthy or dishonourable. If he does, he will no longer be my son. I will forget that he ever was.[32]

32. Malik, H.S., _'A Little Work, A Little Play'_, p. 26

Hardit would never disregard these words.

The one condition laid down for his son going to Britain was typical of Mohan Singh's approach to parenting: Hardit would take the journey on the condition that he organised all the arrangements himself, including booking train tickets for his parents and younger brother Iqbal from Rawalpindi to Bombay. Mohan needed to be sure, in the light of his wife's concerns, that the boy could look after himself. No passport was needed in the days before the Great War, so a steamer ticket from Bombay to Marseille was purchased, and information sought about tickets for the remainder of the journey ending at Charing Cross Station in London, where Hardit would be met on the platform by Teja, who was studying Civil Engineering at University College London.

So it was, that the Malik family went to Bombay in April 1909 and said their long farewells, Hardit seeing the ocean for the first time on the quay at Apollo Bunder. Holding his emotions in check, as his father would have wanted, the teenager was ferried out to sea aboard the motor launch to the RMS *Morea*. His loved ones didn't know it yet, but they would not see their son and brother for ten years.

On board ship, the exhilaration of what Hardit was undertaking quelled any nerves or regrets that he may have felt, basking in the sunshine above the sparkling waters of the Arabian Sea, only a few hours after encountering the ocean for the first time. It's clear from his later reflections that the ticket he had purchased in Rawalpindi was rather more first class than steerage, as was befitting his father's wealth and status. Nevertheless, once aboard, the British and Indian passengers kept to themselves, there being little intermingling, apart from the odd game of deck cricket in which Hardit was invited to take part. Another highlight he remembered during the early part of the voyage through the Gulf of Aden and up into the Red Sea, was a fancy dress ball. Indians in Rawalpindi were not permitted in venues where dancing took place, and restaurants frequented by his family had no dance floors. The spectacle was particularly memorable therefore:

> I found my first fancy dress ball quite fascinating! Everything was exciting, the music, mostly waltzes in those days, or two steps and, of course "the Lancers" – couples swaying to the music, the women in beautiful dresses. I can still remember

a lovely girl that evening in a tight-fitting white satin dress which showed her figure to full advantage.[33]

After navigating the Suez Canal, the customary stop-off at Port Said enabled Hardit to get ashore, taking his place in a passengers' cricketing eleven against the local club. Sport would frequently be the means by which the teenager became used to mingling with the British.

Several days later, the *Morea* docked at Marseille, giving Hardit his first sighting of Europe. Since the opening of the Suez Canal in 1869, Marseille had become a prosperous city, stimulated by increased maritime trade, the largest port in the Mediterranean. It serviced the increasing demands of the French Empire, taking on the role of the port from which Europeans began their voyages to the subcontinent. Its wide boulevards reminded Hardit of the Civil Lines at home, yet the demeanour of the people strolling in the sunshine was rather different, there was something more casual, somewhat more cheerful about their disposition he thought. Having hailed a hansom cab to take him to the Gare de Marseille-Saint-Charles, which was perched on the top of a small hill overlooking the city, Hardit was persuaded by the driver, a little against his better judgement at first, to abandon the cab and his precious luggage at the bottom of a small path and climb to the station above. It turned out to be a good recommendation. During the ascent, the station's architecture and position vaguely reminded Hardit of the drawings of antiquity from Ponsonby's tutorials back home. However, it was the wonderful views of the Old Port from the hillside in dazzling sunshine that stayed in the memory, with vessels of all types moored around the harbour wall. Hardit was beginning to enjoy himself.

That evening, a De Luxe Express with its magnificent sleeping compartments slipped quietly out of Marseille bound for Calais. The train was replete with wealthy Parisians returning from Easter vacations at the coast; those whom Hardit assumed to be members of the ICS and military types of the Indian Army heading into retirement. He revelled in the luxury of it all, ordering meals for the first time in his life in the restaurant car, making polite conversation with the wife of a trainee Indian lawyer, and a keen student cricketer from Calcutta off to prepare for his Civil Service entrance exam. Hardit also noticed that while British and Indians rarely

---

33. Ibid., p. 28

spoke together, French travellers would interact with all, one family in particular showering him with questions about the Punjab and his turban!

As the Express hurried further north, so the weather worsened, until heavy rain greeted the passengers at the port of Calais. Here, Hardit boarded a ferry bound for Dover, another familiar name of Empire. The voyage across La Manche was rather rough, one of those which reduced the passengers to silence, leaving them only able to concentrate on calming their nausea against the rise and fall of the waves and with half smiles to each other in reassurance. Hardit spent a miserable couple of hours nursing his seasickness, thankful that the voyage across the Mediterranean had been rather more tranquil and it was with some relief that he went ashore at Dover.

Several hours later, the teenager stepped onto the platform at Charing Cross Station in London, a prospect that he had been savouring for the last few months. He had grown up hearing about the might and majesty of the city, the seat of Empire and throne of King-Emperor Edward VII. At the station entrance, he caught sight of the familiar smiling face of his brother, the two hadn't seen each other for a year, and in spite of Hardit's growing self-assurance, it was with a measure of relief that he embraced Teja in the Strand. The two took a hansom cab to his brother's boarding house at Upper Addison Road in West Kensington run by a Mrs French. There were seven boarders altogether, three others of whom were Indian students.

Hardit spent a couple of weeks exploring the capital and acclimatising to British weather and culture. Touring London was a joy for the boy from Rawalpindi, who, sometimes travelling with Teja, sometimes with fellow Indians from the boarding house and occasionally alone, explored much of what London had promised and rather more. Horse-drawn motor buses were making their first appearances and along with the London Underground were the main ways that he toured a city full of interest, surprises and excitement at every turn. There was something about the capital that was paradoxically both familiar and strange at the same time, yet he didn't give the sensation much thought, rejoicing in the sights and sounds of the metropolis.

Hardit expected to feel somewhat more conspicuous than he did, and although he attracted a number of furtive sideways glances, he realised that many inhabitants had become used to seeing those from the far flung reaches of the Empire, including students, trainee lawyers and of course soldiers. From Queen Victoria's Diamond Jubilee, to the coronation of the current monarch in 1902, beturbaned Indian troops, such as Bombay and Bengal Lancers, had been on ceremonial service, enjoying occasional short periods off duty around the capital.

Hardit began to feel at home, delighting particularly in London's green spaces, coming into their best in the spring and which, to his eyes, were lush and green, so carefully protected and well looked after; the trees, the plants and the flowers, all a joy to see in this new world.

Before starting at his preparatory school at the end of May, there was just some time for the brothers to undertake a sightseeing tour of a bitterly cold Scotland, taking in Glasgow and the lakes in particular. Yet, Mohan Singh had ensured that his son's education was not to be interrupted for too long after arriving in Britain and Hardit and Teja returned to London therefore, for them both to resume their studies.

During his first year in Britain, Hardit attended Linton House Preparatory School in Notting Hill Gate run by its headmaster, a Mr Hardie, a strict disciplinarian, yet who he found to be kind and understanding. Hardie was the type of educator with whom Hardit was entirely familiar and was grateful to have found in his first year, particularly in light of the fact that Linton House would be his first formal schooling of any kind. The fees were paid for by his father, something that the boy must have been conscious of during his time in British schools and later at university.

After an uneventful year at Linton House, Hardit passed the preliminary entrance exam for admission to Clifton College, a public school in Bristol for the spring term in April 1910. It quickly became apparent however, that chapel attendance was compulsory and that those of all religions and none were compelled to join in the Christian religious services. A person of lesser integrity and courage of that age might well have acquiesced with the judgement, but not the independently minded fifteen-year-old, who promptly packed his suitcase and boarded a train for London, much to Teja's dismay. However, after a feverish, but thankfully brief period of submitting applications to a number of institutions, Hardit joined Eastbourne College on the south coast of England during May 1910. He recorded his address as 'c/o Malik Mohan Singh, Rawal Pindi (Punjab), India', though the impossibility of immediate communication with his father would have prohibited any ongoing discussions about the choice of school, advice and guidance coming particularly from Teja Singh and Headmaster Hardie at

Linton House.[34] In normal circumstances, Teja's address in London would have been recorded, but the eldest sibling would be leaving for India again after graduation from University College London that summer. Fortunately, Hardit was admitted to Blackwater House at Eastbourne College under the watchful eye of the Reverend F. Atkinson, who became his de facto guardian. During the holidays that followed, he lived with Atkinson, his wife and two daughters who created a welcoming and comfortable atmosphere. It's not clear how this came about, perhaps Atkinson liaised with Mohan Singh back in Rawalpindi via Teja and some sort of arrangement was agreed upon. It might be that the family took pity on the boy for whom it was impossible to return home during the long vacations.

What is clear, is that for the period of his time in Britain, Hardit's demeanour and ability to maintain good relationships with teachers, tutors and others in authority meant that he was often assured of hospitality beyond what he might have expected. For many people, living with a school master and his family would not have been an easy undertaking, but for the young Hardit, used to one-to-one tuition at home with academic, English educated lecturers, the time passed pleasantly in the charming atmosphere of the Atkinson household.

However, the induction to life at Eastbourne didn't get off to the best start, his only described experience of harassment taking place on the first evening as he later recalled:

> After supper in the House, a group of five or six boys [...] surrounded me and asked me to take off my turban as they wanted to see what was underneath it! I told them that I was a Sikh and would not take off my turban. They advanced towards me saying that they would like to take it off for me. I was furious but I said very calmly that while I was outnumbered, I wouldn't be able to stop them but the first one who touched my turban I would kill, sometime, somehow. Word had gone round that Sikhs carried knives, _kirpans_, and the boys realised that while they were just teasing, it was something that I would take seriously, so they backed off, unsure of what this native might do next. I was left in peace.[35]

---

34. '*Leaving Boys' Book*', Eastbourne College Archive
35. Malik, H.S., '*A Little Work, A Little Play*', p. 34

This wasn't to be the last time that Hardit's turban would bring him into conflict, though in reality, he was to find that while the British more often discriminated racially in their colonies, at home they were rather more hospitable and thus he began to forge friendships at Eastbourne, some of which would last a lifetime.

He seemed to have taken pleasure in life on the south coast from the beginning, riding bicycles along the seafront whilst teasing girls, once being fined ten shillings and sixpence for riding a bike 'to the danger of the public'. As Hardit was later to recount: 'some of us had whizzed past a policeman and in those days, it wasn't hard to track down a turban in Eastbourne'.[36]

During his two years of schooling at Eastbourne College, he found that the excellent tuition he had received in Rawalpindi, enabled him to make sound academic progress in all of his subjects, including Greek and Latin, which he was learning for the first time. He took an enthusiastic part in the Officer Training Corps, finding pleasure in the drill, training and shooting that he had seen no doubt on the parade grounds of his home city. He began to attend the college's chapel services too, coming to enjoy the communal singing of hymns and feeling more able to take part, for the very fact that attendance wasn't compulsory and in so doing, learning that persuasion is preferable to coercion, a principle which influenced his professional thinking later in life.

Yet it was at sport that he was to excel, taking up hockey in the winter, cricket in the summer and would like to have taken part in Rugby matches, though his turban precluded serious involvement in the days before sporting headgear for Sikhs was available. He escaped fagging too, joining up almost immediately with the Eastbourne College cricket First XI instead. He would go on to earn cricket colours for each of the three seasons he attended Eastbourne, from 1910 to 1912, scoring centuries for the college in the latter two years and topping the batting averages in 1912 at an average of over thirty runs per innings. An occasional bowler, he once took ten of the sixteen opposition wickets to fall in one match, though it was as a batsman that he was to flourish - *The Eastbournian* of 1910 however, gave its habitually censorious insight into Hardit Singh the cricketer:

---

36. Fishlock, T., 'When a child of the Raj could find an ever-open door', *The Times* (London), 16 October 1982

A promising bat who, but for his flourish, would get a good many runs. At present this does for him on a fast wicket. He has a good action as a bowler, but no length. Neat but slow in the field.[37]

Following his final season of 1912, he earned a somewhat less critical review:

A stylish bat who can get runs when he once gets set, but he is always apt to play a careless stroke and throw his wicket away. He is a good field in the slips, and a useful though uncertain change bowler.[38]

One of the regular opponents for the First XI were the Sussex Martlets, whose team often included guest players. The famous music hall comedian George Robey was one, another was the author of the fictional detective Sherlock Holmes, Sir Arthur Conan Doyle, who played against Eastbourne College on 1 June 1912. Hardit's innings of nineteen out of a total of eighty-five was ended that day being stumped off Sir Arthur's wily off spin. Occasionally opening the batting alongside him for Eastbourne was Dalpat Singh who later rose to become a major in the Jodhpur Lancers during the First World War, taking part in the India Corps' campaigns in France and then Palestine. After being awarded the Military Cross, he died of wounds inflicted during the Battle of Haifa, on 23 September 1918.[39]

Hardit passed the long vacations playing tennis with the Reverend Atkinson's daughters, watching cricket just down the road at the County Ground in Hove and cycling around the town and into the countryside. However, he would also pass the holidays in London, spending time with his brother's student friends at their boarding houses. One of them in Grover Street was run by the Spriggs family including their apparently beautiful daughter Cicely, who was much admired by Hardit and some of the other resident students. His feelings for 'Cissie' developed into something of a crush, so much so that he carried around the girl's photograph with him, as

---

37. 'The Eastbournian 1910', Eastbourne College Archive, p. 122
38. 'The Eastbournian 1912', Eastbourne College Archive, p. 89
39. Bowden, W. and Partridge, M., 'Major Thakur Dalpat Singh' (Old Eastbournian, 2012), pp. 18-19

he later remembered. However, when returning to the Atkinsons' home, he showed the portrait to his guardian, which is telling of the trust which had developed over the years between them. Nevertheless, the clergyman and his wife gently explained that nothing should ever come of the attachment to Cissie, as in the words of Hardit: '(they told me that) I could easily make a fool of myself. So that was the end of my first romance'.[40]

The time in the capital was spent with other Indian students going for walks, with the occasional visit to the theatre or music hall in the evening. As with all young men of his age, it was important for Hardit to keep in touch with those from home and to keep abreast of gossip and news from India. There was much to discuss in the years immediately after 1909, many in the student community regularly discussing or actively involved in organisations related to the campaign for Indian self-rule in London.

There were a number of reasons why increasing numbers of Indians were coming to Britain before the First World War. Travelling to the heart of the Empire was especially attractive to middle class students who, like Hardit, were often familiar with British ideals, officials and educators in India.[41] The opportunities for entry into higher governmental services and levels of law, along with the added prestige associated with them, made the long sea voyage a tempting prospect.[42]

Yet, many of those arriving to further their education were already advocates of, or would be drawn into, supporting the various campaigns for Indian independence. Owing to concerns about the radical and political tendencies of some of these students, the British government authorised the Lee-Warner Committee to investigate some of their motives in 1907. Its findings gave insights into the world in which Hardit Singh arrived eighteen months later. The committee found that at that time there were approximately 700 Indian students in Britain, of whom almost 400 were living in London.[43] Many of these were attracted by the cosmopolitan nature of the capital and the opportunities it provided; whilst for those wishing to

---

40. Malik, H.S., 'A Little Work, A Little Play', p. 38
41. Mukherjee, S., 'Nationalism, Education and Migrant Identities', (Routledge: Abingdon, 2010), p. 17
42. Ibid., p. 30
43. Mukherjee, S., 'Nationalism, Education and Migrant Identities', (Routledge: Abingdon, 2010), p. 17

be called to the Bar, London was the only place to gain admission to an Inn.[44] As Hardit was aware, London was also the place where the ICS exams took place each year. In addition, there were a number of institutions in the capital where those new from the subcontinent could gain support at a time when they needed it most, the National Indian Society and the Northbrook Society, chief among them. A more formal institution was the Bureau of Information for Indian students (Indian Students' Department from 1913), though as a governmental institution it was looked upon with suspicion by the student population. Nonetheless, the Bureau was established in 1909, under the auspices of the India Office, at 21 Cromwell Road, on the recommendation of the Lee-Warner Committee. Here students could be housed on their arrival in London and advised as to permanent quarters.[45]

As Hardit recalled, the seeds of a campaign for Indian nationalism in London were being sown in the years up to his arrival in the city. Whilst there is no evidence to support his active involvement in any of the nascent movements, it is evident that he tacitly supported their advocates.[46]

In March of 1909, the limited constitutional concessions written into the Morley-Minto[47] Reforms increased Indian political representation in both central and provincial legislatures in the subcontinent.[48] However, British officials retained a majority on all the legislative councils and refused to surrender their monopoly on Indian politics.[49] The repercussions from these very limited reforms were felt in London, adding to the sense of increasing injustice felt by the Indian student community in particular. In essence, the reforms were seen by radical voices as a sop to moderate Indian nationalist campaigners in India following the de facto ending of the Swadeshi movement. In London, advocates of more fundamental change rallied around the Indian Home Rule Society, that was formed in 1905, to promote the cause of self-determination. Its headquarters was at India House, a large Victorian mansion at 65 Cromwell Avenue in

---

44. Ibid.
45. Seton, M.C.C., 'The India Office' (Putnam & Sons: London, 1926), p. 272
46. Malik, H.S., 'A Little Work, A Little Play', pp. 38-39
47. Named after the then Viceroy of India, Lord Minto and John Morley, the Secretary of State for India.
48. Calcutta (now Kolkata) was the capital of India during the British Raj, until December 1911
49. Ranasinha, R., (Ed.) 'South Asians and the Shaping of Britain, 1870-1950' (Manchester University Press: Manchester, 2012), p. 12

Highgate.[50] It provided accommodation for up to thirty students and in addition to being a hostel, the mansion also served as the headquarters for several nationalist organisations, becoming a centre for meetings and the dissemination of revolutionary ideas.

Living in London at various times during the college holidays, as part of the relatively close-knit student community, Hardit was aware of the personalities involved and the ideas being advocated, if not actively involved himself, as he later remembered:

> In those years, the "All India Home Rule" movement[51] was gathering momentum among Indian students in London. Bipin Chandra Pal and Surendranath Banarjee were amongst the nationalist leaders to visit Britain from time to time, addressing meetings in Caxton Hall and other places under the auspices of the Labour and Socialist Parties, both comparatively small and unimportant political groups, but supportive of home rule. Among the students one of the most active was Veer Savarkar,[52] who later became the famous Hindu Mahasabha leader.[53]

Vinayak Savarkar was an Indian independence activist and politician who formulated the Hindu nationalist philosophy of Hindutva. The organisation of India House came under his leadership from 1907, Savarkar having arrived in London the previous year to study Law. Chandra Pal was a nationalist, the 'Pal' in the 'Lal Bal Pal' of the Swadeshi triumvirate, who studied comparative theology at the University of Oxford. He became a member of the Indian National Congress and opposed the partition of Bengal in 1905. Two years later, he returned to Britain, becoming associated with India House. Surendranath Banarjee was one of the senior leaders of the nationalist movement, though a moderate who favoured accommodation and dialogue with the British.

---

50. Not to be confused with the home of the 'Bureau of Information for Indian Students' established later at 21 Cromwell Road in 1909. The Bureau itself was renamed the 'Indian Students' Department' in 1913.
51. Here Hardit Singh is confusing the 'Indian Home Rule Society' formed in London in 1905 with the two home rule groups founded in India itself in 1916.
52. Actually, Vinayak Damodar Savarkar.
53. Malik, H.S., 'A Little Work, A Little Play', pp. 38-39

Caxton Hall in Westminster was one of the most commonly used venues for Indian self-rule meetings which were held to generate a sense of excitement and bring together Indian students from across Britain.[54] Lala Lajpat Rai, who Hardit and his father had encountered in Rawalpindi, was one of the speakers in December 1909. The hall was usually decorated with flags, and audiences of over 300 attended, patriotic songs being sung and stirring speeches made, some of them by India House radicals such as Bipin Chandra Pal, were described as 'objectionable' in the press.[55]

Hardit's arrival in London came at a time of heightened tension, not only because of the passing of the Morley-Minto Reforms in March 1909, but also because of an assassination which took place the following July:

> The greatest stir was created by the assassination of Sir Curzon Wyllie at the hands of a quiet young student, Madan Lal Dhingra, an Indian freedom fighter, political activist and a revolutionary studying in England. The assassination was hailed as one of the first acts of the revolution in the Indian independence movement. Political assassinations were a rare occurrence in England, so this was truly sensational.[56]

At India House, Dhingra had come into contact with Savarkar, who had been impressed by the former's perseverance and intense patriotism. Savarkar believed in revolution by any means and was the inspiration behind Dhingra's assassination attempt. Several weeks before murdering Wyllie, Dhingra had tried to kill Sir George Curzon, the former Viceroy of India, in a botched attempt, before turning his sights elsewhere. Sir Curzon Wylie had joined the British Army in 1866 and in 1901 he was selected to be Political Aide-de-Camp to the Secretary of State for India. He was also the head of the Secret Police and had been trying to obtain information about Savarkar and the revolutionaries at India House and was therefore a

---

54. In 1940, it was the place where the assassination would take place of Sir Michael O'Dwyer by Udham Singh, former Lieutenant Governor of the Punjab, as an act of revenge for the 1919 Jallianwala Bagh Massacre.

55. Visram, R., *'Asians in Britain: 400 Years of History'* (Pluto Press: London, 2002), p. 154

56. Malik, H.S., *'A Little Work, A Little Play'*, pp. 38-39

natural target. Later in life, Hardit made clear his feelings as a newly arrived fourteen-year-old in London about what happened next:

> Most of Dhingra's friends among Indian students promptly disowned him. Veer Savarkar was the one honourable exception and openly acclaimed Dhingra as a hero and a martyr to the cause of Indian Independence. Savarkar was promptly arrested, and I well remember how excited and thrilled we were on hearing that he had escaped while being taken to India under police custody. When his ship touched Marseille, he slipped through the porthole of the cabin in which he was locked up. How furious and indignant we were when the news came that the French had captured him and turned him over, illegally, to the British![57]

Immediately after the assassination, Dhingra attempted suicide, but was overpowered before he could do so, tried at the Old Bailey and hung at Pentonville Prison on 17 August 1909. Savarkar was arrested, sentenced to life imprisonment, though released in 1937, after which he continued his anti-Muslim, anti-British politics and became the ideological alternative to Gandhi's non-violence. After Savarkar's departure, India House was closed down in 1910.

Hardit finished schooling at Eastbourne College in July 1912, having passed the entrance examination and gained a place at Balliol College, Oxford. He would begin the Michaelmas Term, the following autumn, almost two months before turning eighteen. With time on his hands before going up to Oxford, he was invited by a friend to the Royal Eastbourne Golf Club that summer. It would be another life changing moment, as he recalled in an interview in the 1980s:

> I had never hit a golf ball – cricket and football were my games in India, but he insisted that I have a game. I was very impressed by the way the golfers dressed in plus-fours and jackets – no playing in just shirts in those days. I became fascinated with

---

57. Ibid.

golf. I took it up at Oxford, bought Harry Vardon's book *How to Play Golf* [58], taught myself to play without lessons, and in one year got down to scratch and earned my Oxford blue.[59]

Later in 1914, he met Vardon, who told him that the newly developed golf swing was identical to his own! Throughout Hardit's life, golf was an ever-present passion and joy, something which would lead him to play against such golfing greats as Ben Hogan and Bobby Jones. During his time in the diplomatic service, he would play with or against the Duke of Windsor and King Leopold of Belgium, just two of many such people of status. It was a sport which opened doors, enabling him to socialise and network in influential circles. In doing so, he would become one of the best of the Indian golfers, the first of any prominence who went abroad and projected Indian golf outside his own country.[60] He would later be awarded his blue for golf by the University of Oxford for a second time in 1921 when returning to the 'dreaming spires'.

58. Henry William 'Harry' Vardon, (1870 – 1937) was a professional golfer from the Bailiwick of Jersey. Vardon won the British Open Championship a record six times, and also won the 1900 US Open.
59. Severino, R., '*H.S. Malik, India's Grand Old Gentleman of Golf*', *Asian Golf Digest,* March 1980
60. Ibid.

Chapter 3

Oxford
1912–1915

'That sweet city with her dreaming spires
She needs not June for beauty's heightening.'
Matthew Arnold, poet and former student
at Balliol College, *Thyrsis*

Hardit's turban nodded along Parks Road in Oxford at a rapid pace. He'd been told a few times by friend Con Benson that the choice of Cambridge's pale blue headgear 'wouldn't wash' with the stiffer element in college, never mind the 'hearties' of the Bullingdon. At this very moment in time, Hardit didn't really care about the turban's colour. Something else was on his mind. He was late. Late for tea with the Master of Balliol. He'd been having a cricket net at the Parks, an obsessive refining of the quality of his cover drive had banished any notion of the hour, and so here he was, adjusting his collar and tie, sweating a little as he turned into Broad Street, with the sole intention of heading for the main gate.

Freshmen like Hardit, in that Michaelmas Term of 1912, were invited to the Master's lodgings in batches. What should have been a perfunctory occasion, one of the many that students had to undergo in their first term, was viewed by this newcomer with some trepidation - he hated cats. Con had already undergone the ordeal of tea with the Master, Strachan-Davidson, a couple of days earlier, and had discovered that the head of college's own feline was centre stage in easing any initial awkwardness of polite conversation. Having discovered Hardit's antipathy towards the creatures, Con played on it mercilessly, telling his friend, with barely concealed glee, that Strachan-Davidson judged undergraduates by the way they behaved with his beloved Persian, which was not untrue.

He sped through the main gate of Alfred Waterhouse's Broad Street frontage, round the front quadrangle and into the Master's lodgings via the Library Passage. A huddle of undergraduates stood sheepishly at the study door, eyes floorward after an initial nod of recognition, waiting to be admitted.

James Leigh Strachan-Davidson was one of the mainstays of the Balliol Senior Common Room in the late nineteenth and early twentieth century - indeed there were few positions of authority that he had not held at one time or another, culminating in the Mastership in 1907. Almost his entire life had been devoted to his college and the university.[61] He was particularly active on the various committees which debated the affairs of the ICS candidates and students, with a reputation for holding liberal views on foreign affairs, regularly advocating that 'international morality demanded that England relinquish India'.[62] Scholarly and introverted, the sixty-nine-year-old Strachan-Davidson was also found by Hardit to be a kind, simple man, a type not unusual among Oxford dons, possessing an almost naïve, childlike humour which put others at their ease, though not all.

With the introductory formalities and introductions over, Hardit noticed that the Master's cat had brushed his leg and taken refuge under the chair. Inaudibly, it leapt into his lap and settled there, eyeing provocatively the rather alarmed expression looking down. Hardit overcame the immediate impulse to throw the feline off, managing even to fondle the back of its neck, whilst concurrently nodding sagely at the overprepared indulgences of the callow Etonian making conversation next to him. Strachan-Davidson noticed his predicament with a barely concealed smile, or so Hardit thought. To his great relief, the Persian slipped away, and he hoped that he had passed the test.

He was about to leave the Master's lodgings, the last of the undergraduates, when Strachan-Davidson called him back, saying courteously that he had never seen an undergraduate with a beard or turban before and wondering if it wouldn't be easier for him to fit in with the other students if he looked like them. Maintaining his composure, Hardit replied that the beard and turban weren't mere eccentricities but were required by his religion. Slightly

---

61. MacKail, J.W., *'James Leigh Strachan-Davidson - A Memoir'* (Clarendon Press: Oxford, 1925), pp. ii-iii
62. Ibid.

embarrassed and tugging nervously at his own white whiskers, the Master asked for forgiveness, saying that he understood and then walked back to his rooms and closed the door without a backward glance. He would die suddenly in March 1916 from a brain haemorrhage, perhaps overcome with the seemingly endless task of writing the great number of letters of condolence to the families of Balliol men who had been killed.

Hardit was fortunate to take rooms in college at Balliol for his first two years at university, which included a bedroom and sitting room and the services of a 'scout' called Bliss who looked after the cleaning and chores for a number of undergraduates. Having had a servant back in Rawalpindi, Hardit was able to strike the right note of formality with Bliss, who had been unimpressed when acting as Lord Curzon's scout in the late 1870s.

Curzon, the Viceroy of India between 1899 and 1905, was one of three consecutive Balliol graduates in that role, being preceded by the Marquis of Lansdowne and the Earl of Elgin. It wasn't by chance that the Balliol-India connection had been created. Benjamin Jowett was the celebrated Master of the College from 1870 to 1893 and during his term, of forty-nine Indians at Oxford, twenty-two of those were at Balliol. He was particularly concerned with university reform and was consulted on the remodelling of the ICS, for many young men undertook their probationary training at Balliol. As Vice-Chancellor, Jowett opened the Indian Institute in Oxford in 1884, an establishment attended by Hardit Singh in the academic year 1920-21. Yet, it may not have been merely by chance that Hardit had been admitted to Balliol that autumn of 1912, for Strachan-Davidson was a keen advocate of continuing the legacy of the Balliol-Indian connection begun by Jowett. However, with growing numbers of Indians applying to the university during Hardit's time, the association was not appreciated by all.

The tutorial system at Oxford in those days comprised a small group of students meeting in their tutor's rooms to discuss papers on a subject given by him to be read out by each of the undergraduates, and only punctuated by the arrival of refreshments. The tutor guided the proceedings, recommending reading lists and future lectures to be attended appropriate for each. The lack of compulsion in these arrangements was considered ideal by Hardit, who seemed to have thrived, and later in life considered that he had gained an excellent liberal education. His own tutor was Francis F. Urquhart, better known as 'Sligger', a history don and a very well-known figure within the university. He later became Dean of Balliol, but was the Domestic Bursar when Hardit first met him in 1912. Urquhart was to play an important part in the life of the then seventeen-year-old, that Michaelmas Term, enabling him to adapt to university life and offering sage guidance. Hardit had been formally educated in Greek and Latin at Eastbourne and these were his preferred subjects. On arriving at Balliol, therefore, he decided to study the classics course, better known as the 'Greats'. The charming Urquhart had other ideas, and persuaded Hardit to take up Modern European History instead, perhaps believing that it would better serve the new undergraduate's ICS ambitions in the future.

Urquhart was the first Roman Catholic to act as a tutorial fellow at the University of Oxford since the sixteenth century and was somewhat an outsider in the academic fraternity, which may have bound him to the young Sikh, who considered his tutor to be not only a 'marvellous teacher, but also a true guide, philosopher and friend'.[63] In some ways, the don took on the role left vacant in Hardit's life by Sant Attar Singh. Urquhart's biographer summarised the quality of the friendships which his subject forged with many undergraduates:

> The start of friendship was with Sligger instinctive; many among those he met, especially among the young, had a natural liking for him; he liked them and felt that he must get to know them. But it was not always realised that after the first instinctive movement followed much thought and much effort. He wished to understand the mind and character of each one, so as to know how he might help him to be his best. If he had a genius for friendship, certainly a part of that genius was an infinite capacity for taking pains. This was the reason why each of his near friends came to feel that he was a special friend, and why in spite of the difference of years, he could maintain his friendships on equal terms.[64]

Consequently, Urquhart spent much time entertaining students, particularly aesthetes, who he would take on reading parties to Chamonix during the

---

63. Malik, H.S., *'A Little Work, A Little Play'*, p. 47
64. Bailey, C., *'Francis Fortescue Urquhart: A Memoir'* (Macmillan: London, 1936), pp. 119-20

long vacations. Undergraduates who were part of this circle included Harold Macmillan, Evelyn Waugh, Cyril Connolly, Anthony Powell, Harold Nicolson and Quintin Hogg. He is often taken as having influenced the fictional characters of Mr Samgrass in Waugh's *Brideshead Revisited* and, more closely, Sillery in Powell's *A Dance to the Music of Time.*

Among the fifty or so freshers who arrived with Hardit at Balliol that autumn term was the future British Prime Minister Harold Macmillan, who would serve in the Grenadier Guards during the First World War. He was wounded three times, most severely in September 1916 during the Battle of the Somme. He spent the rest of the war in a military hospital unable to walk and suffered pain and partial immobility for the rest of his life. Yet, Hardit was rather unimpressed at their first meeting, as he remembered:

> I happened to be sitting next to him at dinner, which we had every day in the College Hall. Macmillan was from Eton and a typical snob, coming as he did from one of the aristocratic British families. He was related to the Duke of Devonshire. We exchanged the usual pleasantries. Then he asked me which school I came from and when I told him, he raised his eyebrows in surprise, and said with a superior air, 'Eastbourne… Eastbourne? Where is that?' Irritated, I asked him from which school he came knowing very well he was an Etonian. When he said he was from Eton, I pretended that I had never heard of the place. No close relationship followed![65]

Nonetheless, he did form many good relationships at Balliol, a number of which were maintained throughout his life, several having Indian connections of their own. Some of these friendships were made inevitably through the Balliol cricket team, such as the future lawyer and politician Walter Monckton, the First XI wicketkeeper, who later became advisor and friend to King Edward VIII at the time of his abdication. During and immediately after the Partition of India, Monckton advised the Nizam of Hyderabad during the latter's doomed attempt to maintain a degree of independence for his state in 1948. As India's ambassador to France just before his retirement in 1956, Hardit would write to Monckton, the then

---

65. Malik, H.S., *'A Little Work, A Little Play'*, p. 42

Minister of Defence in the Eden government, to support his application for a post with the Dunlop Rubber Company.[66]

Another close friend was 'Brocas' Burrows who was a useful fast bowler for the college. His father, Sir Stephen Montagu Burrows, was 'Local Advisor' to Indian students at Oxford from January 1913, and later held the post of secretary to the Oxford University Delegacy for Oriental Students. These positions were intended to look after the interests and welfare of Indian, Chinese, and Burmese students during their time at Oxford. However, many undergraduates from the subcontinent viewed them with distrust, as increasing numbers of scholars came under scrutiny and suspicion by the authorities in the decade before the First World War. Maintaining a relationship with Brocas required a degree of tact and diplomacy therefore, attributes that Hardit was to demonstrate in abundance in a variety of relationships with British friends. In consequence, he gave Sir Montagu Burrows the benefit of the doubt about any motives relating to his Oxford role, when many Indians did not.

As Hardit began his studies at Oxford in 1912, the India Office and New Scotland Yard were becoming ever watchful of new forms of Indian nationalism, including those which advocated the use of violence. The Ghadar movement[67] was founded in 1913 by expatriate revolutionaries living in San Francisco, Seattle, and Vancouver. Many of these émigrés were Sikhs and the influence of the Ghadar, through its eponymous journal, had a particularly wide following in the Punjab.[68] At this time, the University of Oxford authorities became increasingly anxious about the activities of former students who were connected to both the Ghadar and other nationalist organisations, something of which Hardit would have been very aware.

One of the Oxford alumni who had been of interest to the authorities, was Lala Har Dayal, who earned a state scholarship to study in Britain. He joined St John's College in October 1905 to study Sanskrit. During his student days, Dayal visited India House in Highgate, later resigning his scholarship on ideological grounds. He returned to India in 1908, leaving again the following year for Paris. He eventually moved to the United States

---

66. Letters to and from Walter Monckton, 1956-60. Dep. Monckton 7R, fols. 19., Balliol College Archives & Manuscripts
67. 'Ghadar' being an Urdu word meaning treason or mutiny, as well as insurrection.
68. Bates, C., *'Subalterns and Raj'* (Routledge: New York, 2007), p. 116

in 1910 to take up a job as lecturer in Indian Philosophy and Sanskrit. By 1913, he had set up the weekly paper, *Ghadr*, in California and was one of the founding members of the Hindustan Ghadar Party. During his visits to India House, Dayal gained inspiration and corresponded regularly with its founder Shyamaji Krishnavarma who had first come to Britain in 1879 as a Sanskrit scholar and graduated from Oxford in 1883, before being called to the Bar the following year. Krishnavarma had studied at Balliol during Jowett's prolific period of office as Master, when the college had taken disproportionately large numbers of Indian students.

In February 1905, Krishnavarma founded the Indian Home Rule Society, establishing India House in Highgate as a hostel for students, which became a meeting place for revolutionaries in London, as we have seen. He fled to Paris in 1907 to avoid arrest and censure by the British Government in relation to his allegedly inflammatory published material, such as *The Indian Sociologist* journal, and his politically inspired activities at India House.

With alumni of the University of Oxford playing such central roles in establishing nationalist organisations in London and beyond, many Indian students believed that surveillance by the authorities in the city was increasing, becoming progressively suspicious of any formal government associations. This was the prevailing atmosphere during Hardit's time as a Balliol undergraduate and we know something of his thoughts and those of other Indian scholars at Oxford by their responses when submitting evidence to members of the Lytton Committee in the summer of 1921. Edwin Montagu, the Secretary of State for India, established the committee to look into the adequacy of arrangements and relations with Indian students in Britain. It was seen as a successor to the Lee-Warner Committee which had been convened in 1907 and was chaired by Lord Lytton, the son of the former Viceroy of India. Its modus operandi included interviewing representatives of both the academic staff and students of a number of British universities.

It is worth looking at the testimony at this point, for Hardit's responses to the committee related very much to his three years of study at Balliol between 1912 and 1915 and enabled a unique understanding of his perspectives at that time (Hardit's replies to the Lytton Committee can be seen in their entirety in Appendix A). [69]

---

69. Corrected summaries of the oral evidence taken at Oxford, 31 May to 03 June 1921, IOR/Q/10/4/2, Hardit Singh Malik testimony, 3 June 1921, pp. 1-3

At Balliol, the Lytton Committee interviewed the Master, Arthur Lionel Smith, a Professor Macdonell, Mr Pickard-Cambridge and the Reverend H. Gibbon (the responses of these witnesses are collectively summarised below as the 'Balliol group').[70] The committee also questioned five representatives of the University of Oxford Indian Majlis Society – Dr K.N. Bahl, Mr Tara Chand,[71] Mr Sapru, Mr M.C. Chagla[72] and Mr M. Habib[73] (the responses of these witnesses are collectively summarised below as the 'Majlis group').[74] The society had been formed in 1896 and followed the same format as the Oxford Union and the Cambridge University Majlis which had been created five years earlier. It would often take up debates of a political nature relating to Empire and India's relationship with Britain. The majority of Indian students at Oxford felt compelled to be part of the society and its political deliberations, which tended to be anti-imperialist, even if they were intending to take up positions sympathetic to the British in India such as in the ICS.

The testimonies from the Balliol group; the Majlis group and Hardit Singh gave an indication of the nature of the atmosphere in Oxford before and during the First World War. The summarised responses from the interviewees are described in relation to several themes for clarity.

The members of both groups and Hardit Singh all expressed beliefs that it was best for Indian undergraduates to be lodged in college in Oxford, rather than in hostels or boarding houses, the better to socialise with British students. Hardit judged that being in college was beneficial for each as an individual, there often being criticism about Indian 'aloofness' connected to broader accusations of failure to participate in the corporate life of universities.[75] Shyness and insecurity explained sometimes why many

---

70. Ibid., Balliol College testimony, 1 June 1921, pp. 1-4
71. Dr Tara Chand would become an archaeologist and historian specialising in the Ancient History and Culture of India. He would later become the Indian Ambassador to Iran.
72. Mohammed Chagla would become an Indian jurist, diplomat, and cabinet minister. At Indian independence, he would be appointed Chief Justice of Bombay. In 1958, Nehru would appoint Chagla as Ambassador to the United States, and then High Commissioner in London in 1961. Chagla would go on to be an education minister and then Minister of External Affairs in India, 1963-7.
73. Mohammad Habib would become an historian, who later worked at the Aligarh Muslim University.
74. IOR/Q/10/4/2, Indian Majlis testimony, 2 June 1921, pp. 1-7
75. Lahiri, S., 'Indians in Britain, 1880-1930', p. 119

young Indians enjoyed the company of their fellow countrymen, yet some did not merely gravitate towards each other, but actively avoided friendships with the British.[76] Hardit believed that 'Indians in the non-collegiate body[77] were inclined to congregate together and to nurse their grievances, until these grievances, real or supposed, became exaggerated'.[78]

According to the Balliol group, hostels were preferable to boarding houses because it was easier to manage the students in one venue, rather than a multitude of widely dispersed lodging houses. Conversely, the Majlis group members believed that hostels 'would deprive Indian students of the advantages of corporate life in the colleges'.[79]

The Balliol group's testimony may have indicated an ulterior motive for wanting Indians to be lodged in college: 'the number of Indian students at one University should not be too great or increase too rapidly [...] the best is for the men to get into colleges, those that cannot would be better in hostels, we think, than scattered in lodgings'.[80] As space was limited in colleges, it was possible for the Balliol group to argue for the social benefits for Indians of living in, on the one hand, whilst using it as a pretext for restricting overall numbers of Indians being offered university places, on the other.

A desire to restrict the numbers of Indians was widely held in many British universities at the time, following the tensions created by the Wyllie assassination and Morley-Minto Reforms in 1909, and for the reason that some scholars were involved in subversive activities and organisations, as we have seen.[81] Racial prejudice also played a part in the attempts to limit Indian numbers to universities such as Oxford. In 1907, for example, British undergraduates approached an influential tutor at St. John's and stated categorically that they disliked Indians and had too many in their college.[82]

Hardit accentuated the importance to be placed on students taking part in sports, the better to facilitate social interactions with British undergraduates:

---

76. Mukherjee, S., '*Nationalism, Education and Migrant Identities*', p. 85
77. Off campus accommodation
78. IOR/Q/10/4/2, Hardit Singh Malik testimony, 3 June 1921, pp. 1-3
79. IOR/Q/10/4/2, Indian Majlis testimony, 2 June 1921, p. 3
80. IOR/Q/10/4/2, Balliol College testimony, 1 June 1921, p. 2
81. Mukherjee, S., '*Nationalism, Education and Migrant Identities*', p. 19
82. Lahiri, S., '*Indians in Britain, 1880-1930*', p. 136

He felt convinced that if an Indian showed skill in a game he would have a perfectly good chance of getting into a team, either college or University. Indians were potentially very good athletes but many of them were too lazy to take the trouble to become good at games: their reluctance to take part was less due to physical activity than to a constitutional laziness. He had made some effort to organise clubs and games for the Indians, but he had not met with much response.[83]

From the time that his father had provided tuition back in Rawalpindi, Hardit was to excel at sports throughout his life, particularly in tennis, cricket and golf. Hardit's description of his fellow Indians as 'constitutionally lazy' were the words of someone who had undergone a very different education and upbringing by comparison to his Indian peers and one with an emphasis on sports at its heart. His critical attitude may reflect two things: frustration at his inability to recreate sporting teams and fixtures at Oxford, as he had done in Rawalpindi and secondly, that after passing through the British public school and university system, he had adopted something of the 'masculine' and sporting qualities so revered in British men at the time. A misleading stereotype held by many British people often attached to Indian students, was the complaint that they were reluctant to take part in sports. Indeed, this stereotype played to another: many believing that nature had not equipped Indians as a race for athletic pursuits.[84]

The Majlis group made no reference to the importance of sports in their testimony, while the Balliol group were in accord with Hardit Singh's judgements:

The types of persons (Indians) who had done best (at Balliol) were:
a) Men of superior intelligence, with really good minds.
b) Men of a manly type of character developed through games.[85]

Hardit's evidence about the Majlis Society itself gave the impression of an intention to provide an even-handed account, offering points both for

---

83. Ibid.
84. Lahiri, S., 'Indians in Britain, 1880-1930', p. 197
85. IOR/Q/10/4/2, Hardit Singh Malik testimony, 3 June 1921, p. 4

and against its activities. This perceived need for balanced judgement may have indicated an understanding of the sensitivity of the issues involved and the potential audiences for the final Lytton Committee report. It offered perhaps a glimpse of Hardit Singh, the prospective diplomat and embryonic member of the ICS:

> He (Hardit Singh) was a member of the Medjlis (sic), and considered it to be a valuable body, provided that its present tendency to become a political society did not increase. He did not think that complaints should be levelled against it on account of political utterances which emanated from it, as similar complaints might with justice be alleged against any society with definite views, such as the Socialist/Labour Societies. He would be in favour of admitting Englishmen to the Medjlis. He did not want to break up the Indian social traditions, but he thought that any form of Indian clique at Oxford was inadvisable.[86]

Hardit appeared somewhat uncomfortable with the political undercurrents at the Majlis, believing that such politicisation served only to alienate Indian students. Although a member, there is no evidence of his active participation in the agendas of the Majlis, one of many students no doubt, happy to observe proceedings.

When describing the University of Oxford Officer Training Corps, Hardit's witness statement displayed a comparable desire to be even handed as it was for the Majlis Society:

> He had been in his school O.T.C. and the English boys had shown no objection to his presence there. He did not think that the reason that the University O.T.C. was closed to Indians was a social reason, he thought that it was political. He considered the restrictions unfair, and that Indians greatly resented it. He did not think that there was, partly at least, any feeling amongst ex-service men that Indians should not be admitted to the corps.[87]

---

86. Ibid.
87. Ibid., p. 3

Hardit's testimony distinguished between the 'social' and 'political' reasons for Indians' exclusion from the Officer Training Corps, highlighting the belief that some Indians held that it was governmental and administrative structures which were institutionally prejudiced, not Society itself. In other words, it was not British people in general who were discriminatory, but the State which was to blame. Majlis group members maintained that there was a general desire amongst Indians to be permitted to join the university's Officer Training Corps. In 1915, the London Advisory Committee had been set up by the then Secretary of State for India, Austen Chamberlain to inquire into the grievances of Indian students, many of whom had tried unsuccessfully to enlist in the armed forces at the outbreak of war. 'The Committee brought up the quotas at Oxbridge (restricting the number of Indian students per college) as a proof of 'prejudice' and stated that exclusion from the Officer Training Corps had made Indians feel 'a slur upon their loyalty' and 'a humiliating differentiation from other British Subjects'.[88]

Hardit's statement underlined the benefits for Indian students of a British public school education:

He thought that (one) of the two types of Indian men who got most out of university were [...] those who had been to an English public school.

He thought that the record, both at Oxford and subsequently in India, of the men who had received a public school education had been a good one [...] Speaking of the difference in temperament between the Indian and English students he thought that the Indian was on the whole, more serious, both in his games, possibly his work and in his general outlook on life than the average English boy. It was because of this difference that the Indian, without the public school preparation, finds himself in a totally strange atmosphere when he comes to this country.[89]

88. 'Report of a Sub-Committee of the London Advisory Committee for Indian Students on Difficulties experienced by Indian Students in the United Kingdom' (Eyre & Spottiswood: London, 1915). Quoted in Mukherjee, S., 'Nationalism, Education and Migrant Identities', p. 63
89. IOR/Q/10/4/2, Hardit Singh Malik testimony, 3 June 1921, p. 1

Interesting here, is Hardit's implication that it was Indian boys' 'seriousness' which alienated them at university, and that a public school education enabled them better to acclimatise beforehand.

The Balliol group provided some statistical support for such benefits in their evidence:

> From the records of 40 students which were mentioned, 10 or 11 were stated to have been at English public school and all these had done well both at Balliol and afterwards. Of the others not more than 7 had done badly and the rest had done well or moderately.[90]

From the perspective of 1921, Hardit's opinions about arriving in Britain to begin a public school education were interesting:

> He thought that a man, if he had come over here to school and intended to go to university, should go home at least once during that time. He thought that it was essential for the Indian boy who came here to school to be placed in the care of a family in England, otherwise he was opposed to their coming at this early age.[91]

This testimony demonstrated something of the value Hardit placed on the pastoral support he received as a teenager from the Atkinsons at Eastbourne, from landladies such as Mrs French in Kensington[92] and Mr Hardie at Linton House Preparatory School. With the benefit of hindsight and experience, Hardit was contradicting his younger self and agreeing with his mother, who in the spring of 1909 was opposed to her fourteen-year-old son travelling alone to Britain. It may have said something too about some of the challenges that the teenager faced; loneliness and homesickness amongst them perhaps.

In reality, few Indian students, save the sons of the rulers of Princely states, had the resources to attend a British public school. Hardit's

---

90. Ibid., Balliol College testimony, 1 June 1921, p. 3
91. Ibid., Hardit Singh Malik testimony, 3 June 1921, p. 1
92. Malik, H.S., *'A Little Work, A Little Play'*, p. 31

upbringing and education were rather unique in this respect, in addition to the fact that Teja acted as a surrogate parent for his younger brother during the first all-important year in Britain. Many newly arrived Indians, of even university age, had little or no such support, as Mr Chagla described in his Majlis group evidence:

> [...] the young (Indian) student is removed, for the not inconsiderable period of three or four years, from family and surroundings and family associations. We are emphatically of the opinion that in this critical period of his life, it is highly dangerous to leave him without any moorings in a foreign country. The importance of this is, perhaps, not much realised in term time when intellectual and social activities demand all his time; but it is during vacations, when his fellow English undergraduates have returned to their respective homes, that his loneliness and the strangeness of his position is brought home to him in all their vividness. One aspect of his character, and a very important one, the emotional, is dwarfed, with, in many cases, calamitous results.[93]

The most significant difference in the respective testimonies between Hardit Singh and those in the Majlis group was in connection with the Oxford University Delegacy for Oriental Students. Its formation in 1916, was intended to sever the link between the Indian Students' Department, directed by the India Office in London, with the work of Local Advisors at universities. The change was intended to give greater responsibilities to universities at a local level and therefore enable greater trust between the students and those of the Delegacy earmarked to support them. It's safe to say however, that these new arrangements were still looked upon cynically by many from the subcontinent.[94] Nevertheless, when giving evidence to the Lytton Committee, it was clear Hardit had formed opinions about the matter from his recent experience of the Delegacy during 1920-21 and the role played by Sir Stephen Montagu Burrows

---

93. IOR/Q/10/4/2, Indian Majlis testimony, 2 June 1921, p. 5
94. 'Work of the Indian Students' Department Report', 1915-16, File 4459, IOR/L/PJ/6/1758, p. 9

during his earlier three years of study at Balliol. It will be remembered that Burrows held the role of Local Advisor and guardian to Hardit and other Indian students at Oxford, before being promoted as secretary to the Delegacy at its inauguration in 1916 and was still in post during 1920-21:

> (Hardit Singh) thought that the Delegacy for Oriental students worked very well, and apart from the inherent distaste for guardianship, that the Indians at Oxford respected it. His own relations with Mr Burrows had been very happy.[95] [96]

The appointment of a guardian or Local Advisor had been a prerequisite for each Indian studying at Oxford since the release of the Lee-Warner Report findings in 1907. Such close associations with those in authority were familiar to Hardit, who had benefitted from, and de facto required, the support of a series of informal guardians during his school years in Britain, including Headmaster Hardie at Linton House and the Reverend Atkinson at Eastbourne College, to whom he may well have felt indebted. For that reason, he was able to enter into the formal guardianship arrangement at Oxford with a greater level of trust and mutual understanding of British people in authority and their families, as well as the management of the interpersonal and familial challenges such relationships presented. Many Indians coming to Britain, at an even older age, would not have profited in these ways and their subsequent views of both guardianship and the Delegacy were more distrustful and indeed often hostile.

Consequently, Majlis group members had a rather different view of the Delegacy than Hardit Singh, their main complaint against it being the allegation that it supported the Oxford colleges in keeping down the number of Indian students, and was discredited in their eyes as a result. Mr Sapru's own statement of evidence indicated that the Delegacy rejected his own application to join the university made from India, yet he was able to enrol at Lincoln College by travelling to Britain alone, making his own local application without recourse to the Delegacy at all.[97] In essence, the

---

95. IOR/Q/10/4/2, Hardit Singh Malik testimony, 3 June 1921, p. 1
96. Stephen Montagu Burrows was knighted in the New Year's Honours List of 1923.
97. IOR/Q/10/4/2, Indian Majlis testimony, 2 June 1921, p. 6

members believed that the Advisory Committee[98] (In India), the Delegacy (in Oxford) and the Indian Students' Department (in London) were political institutions instigated and manipulated by the India Office and the University of Oxford to control the numbers of students coming to the city and to monitor and restrict their political activities once matriculation had taken place.[99] The Majlis group witness statements were clear about the remedies:

> As far as the system is concerned, we recommend that the Local Advisor at Oxford should be appointed by the Government of India for a period of five years, and should preferably, be an Indian. Further, he should be assisted by an advisory board of three members to be elected by the Indian students at Oxford. The Advisory Committee in India should be done away with, and their work should be made over to the universities.[100]

The testimony from the Majlis group made clear just how difficult it could be for some Indian students to come to Britain to study. Hardit had trodden a different path to most of his peers, something reflected in his witness statements. Yet, for him not to have joined the Oxford Majlis when all Indian students did so, would have been interpreted as unpatriotic at best and somewhat sinister at worst. No one wanted to stand apart, particularly those who did not distrust the British.[101]

As Hardit completed his second year at Balliol, during the golden summer of 1914, the world was about to change.

---

98. 'Provisional Advisory Committees' in India guided students about travelling to, being educated and living in Britain.
99. IOR/Q/10/4/2, Indian Majlis testimony, 2 June 1921, pp. 2-6
100. Ibid., p. 3
101. Kirpanali, S.K., *'Fifty Years with the British'* (Sangam: London, 1993), p. 53

Chapter 4

Cognac
August 1914–October 1916

'The people here (in France) show us more affection if
possible than our own mothers. When we are transferred, they
weep and embrace us repeatedly.'

Sikh Lance Dafadar Chandan Singh,
writing home, 18 April 1916

The heavy clouds over the St Lawrence cricket ground in Canterbury
threatened to halt play for the rest of the day. The players of the home side
Kent and their opponents Sussex had already left the field prematurely
twice during the morning owing to rain and the three-day game looked to
be heading for a draw.[102] The match was the centrepiece of 'Canterbury
Week', the oldest cricket festival In England, usually celebrated in row upon
row of hospitality tents, a society gathering to rival Henley and Wimbledon.
This year was different, with many of the festival's delights being shorn
away. Yet, it wasn't the drizzle, the state of play or the few surviving festival
events that held the attention of the players. War clouds were gathering.
It was 4 August 1914.

Hardit had earlier scored five runs for Sussex before the rain break
had come just after lunch to halt play once more. Escaping the confines of
the dressing room, he had wandered round the edge of the ground, to the
famous lime tree inside the boundary with teammate Kenneth Woodroffe.
Their discussion centred on the 'sticky' nature of the wicket owing to the
earlier downpours, when in theory Woodroffe's fast bowling should have

---

102. Pardon, S., (Ed.) *'Wisden Almanac, 1915'* (John Wisden & Co: London, 1915), Sussex
County Cricket Club Archive and Museum, Hove, p. 53

benefitted from the uneven bounce. Regrettably, he had taken no wickets in Kent's first innings, which rather exacerbated his gloomy mood. As the two strode in a leisurely way back to the pavilion, the sun's re-emerging rays signalling the session's imminent resumption, their conversation turned inevitably to the threat of war looming over the match. Two years older than Hardit, and an alumnus of Pembroke College, Cambridge, Woodroffe made clear that he would join up immediately should war be declared and he asked his teammate what he would do. Hardit merely shrugged his shoulders in reply and smiled wryly as he headed up the pavilion steps and strapped on his pads again. Kenneth Woodroffe would be gazetted to 6 Rifle Brigade, ten days after the match, to be killed in action in May 1915 near Neuve Chapelle, a couple of months after the India Corps had been blooded there.[103]

When play resumed, Hardit went to the crease in the Sussex middle order for the second time that day, his usual 'middle and leg' guard confirmed with a nod by the bespectacled umpire Blake at the other end. Whilst playing for Sussex, he had abandoned his more aggressive leg stump stance on the advice of his Eastbourne mentor Reverend Atkinson. Waiting to bowl to him was English cricket icon Colin Blythe. Blythe's orthodox slow left arm bowling was feared around the county circuit and Hardit was rather in awe of the man who had taken fifteen South African wickets in the Headingley Test Match of 1907. Having negotiated Blythe's over with a succession of meticulous forward defensive strokes and a single off the last ball, Hardit faced the first ball of the next over from another Kent and England legend Frank Woolley. [104] At this stage of his career, Woolley was bowling left arm medium cutters around the wicket, which were proving to be rather unplayable for the majority of the Sussex batting line up on this rain effected square. On the last ball of Woolley's over, Hardit was caught at silly point for six by the eponymous Arthur Fielder and the Sussex second innings folded soon after.

That Tuesday evening, one of the remaining social events of the diminished Canterbury Week calendar took place at the Cathedral. The Dean

---

103. His brother Sydney would earn a posthumous Victoria Cross aged nineteen at Hooge, close to Ypres, later that year. A third sibling Leslie would lose his life in action in 1916.
104. Colin Blythe was killed in action during the Second Battle of Passchendaele in November 1917. He enlisted in at the outbreak of war despite suffering from epilepsy.

entertained both teams and during the end of dinner speeches announced that Britain had indeed declared war on Germany. The following day, Kent would be bowled out cheaply to lose by thirty-four runs.

Hardit had come to the attention of the Sussex County Cricket Club whilst topping the batting averages playing for Eastbourne College in the summer of 1912. Having gone up to Balliol, he attracted attention too in the Freshmen's match in 1913 and in the Seniors' match the following year, going on to captain his college, though he was never to play for the full University of Oxford side before the First World War. Throughout the summer of 1913, having lived in Eastbourne, he qualified for the Sussex Martlets club where he again caught the eye of the county side. Hardit was to play five first class matches for Sussex in the County Championship during 1914, averaging a modest nineteen runs per innings with a top score of seventy-one. Another reason for his inclusion in the Sussex team, resulted from his skills being noticed at Eastbourne by a doctor, a friend of the great cricketer Ranjitsinhji, and who subsequently brought the teenager to the notice of the then Sussex captain Herbert Chaplin.[105]

Kumar Shri Ranjitsinhji was a cricketer for Sussex and England and a Prince of Nawanagar state in India. He was better known as 'Ranji' to his cricketing fans throughout the world. In 1888, aged sixteen, he went to Britain, joining Trinity College, Cambridge, and was the first Indian to win a cricket blue. In 1895, Ranji moved to Brighton, a town with many Indian associations and oriental influences, and began to play regularly for Sussex County Cricket Club.[106] Having faced opposition to his inclusion into the university side, a growing public debate developed as to whether Ranji should be allowed to play for the England national team. However, his skill level was such that he made his debut for England against the Australians at Old Trafford in 1896.

It is difficult to overstate the impact that Ranji had on the game, but between 1895 and 1904 he became a living legend of Victorian and Edwardian cricket. His influence went further still:

105. Fishlock, T., 'When a child of the Raj could find an ever-open door', *The Times* (London), 16 October 1982
106. Visram, R., '*Asians in Britain: 400 Years of History*', p. 154

[...] arguably his greatest achievement was to challenge the accepted stereotype of India and the Indians. By becoming the first Asian to play for England, and that at the height of imperialism also, he demonstrated that a coloured man could not only be the equal of an Englishman, but in his case, was indisputably superior. The "native" is, after all, not the poor spiritless fellow that John Bull thinks him to be, and [...] is capable of holding his own with the Englishman, even on the playground.[107]

By challenging such stereotypes, Ranji laid down the ground for other Indians to play competitive cricket for clubs, universities and school teams throughout the country, and thereby played a part in enabling access for Hardit to the Sussex side in 1914. For without Ranji leading the way, it would not have happened. Many other Indian players benefitted thereafter including Ranji's nephew Duleepsinjhi, who performed for Sussex and England in the 1930s.

The benefits of sporting inclusion went far further than merely what passed on the field of play though. Of arguably greater significance for Hardit, was that cricket gave him access to social intercourse, networking and the development of friendships which would empower him in the future. These gateways for creating social capital through sport were not open to Indians of a solely academic or legal background, even at Oxford.

When war broke out in 1914, Ranji helped the imperial effort, by converting his house in Staines into a hospital for wounded soldiers, donating troops from Nawanagar and going to the Western Front himself. In August 1915, he lost his right eye in a shooting accident in Yorkshire and played his last game for Sussex in 1920. As an Indian Prince, Ranjitsinhji took up many political responsibilities: he represented India twice at the League of Nations and was a delegate to the Round Table Conference sessions in 1930. He died in 1933 in one of his palaces in Jamnagar.[108]

---

107. Satthianadhan, S., 'Holiday Trip to Europe and America' (Varadachari & Co: Madras, 1897), p. 65

108. 'Kumar Shri Ranjitsinhji', - as of 26 May 2020 - www.open.ac.uk - 'Making Britain - Discover how South Asians shaped the nation, 1870-1950'

The end of the 1914 cricket season signalled the beginning of Hardit's final academic year at Oxford, one which would see him completing an honours degree in Modern History the following summer. The declaration of war ended a period of tension across the country, which to some came almost as a relief. This was reflected in an almost lighthearted air amongst some of the students at Balliol, many of whom joined up almost immediately, leaving the college with two discrete groups of residents: some of the older Fellows and a much-reduced student body. All attempted to carry on a version of the ordinary academic life of the college, but that wasn't easy, for Balliol's premises, like many of those in the university, were largely given over to war work. A recruiting office was opened on 19 August and a month later no fewer than 833 recruits had been enlisted at the college.[109] During the years that followed, the Broad Street site hosted thousands of British and Empire officer cadets on short training courses, mainly members of 6 Officer Cadet Battalion. These men were not members of Balliol or the University of Oxford; rather, the Army was in effect renting the property for the duration of the war.[110]

That August of 1914, with the queue stretching outside the front gate in Broad Street to Balliol's recruitment office, Hardit began to make enquiries about taking a <u>commission</u> in Britain's armed forces. It became apparent very quickly however that this was no easy matter for an Indian. Following more than one refusal, his frustration began to grow, as did his sense of increasing isolation in the absence of opportunities for either sports or socialising. He found it difficult to study, the vitality of his academic work diluted by the teeming reality around him and the resulting sense of impotence which followed. Nevertheless, urged on by the friends who remained, he continued to attempt to join the colours, to no avail, his last attempt at the India Office, the final straw, as he later recalled:

> The official British attitude towards Indian students was not helpful. It was as if most of us were looked upon as potential revolutionaries and terrorists not to be trusted in the fighting services. I was told that I had no hope of getting a commission.

---

109. Graham, M., '*Oxford in the Great War*' (Pen and Sword Military: Barnsley, 2014), p. 27
110. '*Balliol during the First World War*', - as of 26 May 2020 - archives.balliol.ox.ac.uk

In fact, it was suggested to me in all seriousness that the only way that I could fulfil my wish to take part in the war was to accept the job of an orderly in the hospital at Brighton where some of the early casualties among the Indian troops who had been fighting in Flanders were being looked after. That was hardly my idea of war service.[111]

His attempts to enlist were made despite any apparent political or patriotic reservations that he may have felt – it was after all only four years earlier that he had been delighted at the news of the escape of the Indian nationalist Savarkar from British detention. In what was framed as a 'war for freedom' against tyranny, many from the subcontinent, who were resident in Britain, agonised about joining the war effort of a country which denied their own its autonomy. Nonetheless, Hardit was clear in his own mind about the right thing to do:

The outbreak of war in 1914 shook me out of this normal course (of studying). I felt at once that this was one of those world-shaking events in which every young man must become involved. But how? I was convinced of the justice of the Allied cause and that German aggressiveness was a threat to human liberty and freedom. With all my heart therefore, I wanted to join in the fight.[112]

The Indian lawyer Mohandas Gandhi arrived in London from South Africa on 6 August and after wrestling with his conscience, he too came to a personal decision relating to the war, believing that every Indian should 'do their bit'. He went further, actively organising a Voluntary Field Ambulance, similar to the one that he had been a part of during the Boer War in South Africa. The rationale of his unconditional support for the war effort at this stage can be traced in his autobiography:

I knew the difference of status between an Indian and an Englishman, but I did not believe that we had been reduced

---

111. Malik, H.S., *'A Little Work, A Little Play'*, p. 56
112. Sapru, S., *'Sky Hawks'*, p. 221

to slavery. I felt then that it was more the fault of individual British officials than of the British system, and that we could convert them by love. If we would improve our status through the help and cooperation of the British, it was our duty to win their help by standing by them in their hour of need.[113]

By 1918, Gandhi continued to support the war effort conducting a personal recruiting campaign on behalf of the GOI, justifying his actions on the grounds that Indians who wanted freedom in their own country must assist in a war fought for freedom's sake.[114] Gandhi's support for the Raj on this basis would end once and for all on 13 April 1919, the day that Hardit was married.

Yet not all Indians supported the allied war aims from the outset. For many it signalled an opportunity for revolution in India, taking advantage of British distraction and the prospect of undermining their endeavours at a crucial time.

More than sixty Ghadar supporters in the United States aimed to set up revolutionary cells in north-west India and the Punjab and from there to commence a nationwide revolution.[115] They recruited hundreds more to travel to the US, many of whom were to be arrested before they ever reached India, though some slipped through, making their way to the Punjab where numerous incidents took place, most notably attacks on army arsenals.[116] The colonial authorities cracked down effectively on these revolutionaries, bolstered by the passing of the Defence of India Act of 1915. This piece of legislation enabled people to be held for indefinite periods of time and to be tried without resort to a jury.[117] The resulting execution of forty-six insurgents, with the further passing of sixty-four life sentences, put paid to the Ghadar movement, though the absorption of many of the principles of the Defence of India Act of 1915 into the Rowlatt Acts of 1919 would have far greater consequences, as we shall see.

---

113. Gandhi, M.K., 'An Autobiography – The Story of My Experiments with Truth' (Penguin Books: London, 2001), p. 557
114. Brown, J.M., 'Gandhi's Rise to Power: Indian Politics 1915-1922' (Cambridge University Press: London, 1972), p. 147
115. Bates, C., 'Subalterns and Raj', p. 118
116. Ibid.
117. Ibid.

The majority of University of Oxford undergraduates seeking enlistment did so with the sole intention of taking a commission to be an officer. Hardit was no different, yet why was it problematic for an Indian to enlist into Britain's armed forces, especially above the rank of non-commissioned officer, during the First World War? That was a question put to the War Office in August 1914 by the first Indian to be elected to Parliament in Britain. The former Liberal MP for Lambeth North and founding figure of the Indian National Congress, Dadabhai Naoroji had returned to India in 1907, but continued to fight for the rights of Indians in Britain until his death. In response, the War Office was forced to admit that 'the intention of the military authorities is to exclude all candidates [...] who are not of pure European descent, as a British private soldier will never follow a half caste or native officer'.[118] Since 1896, Naoroji had been challenging such exclusions from the commissioned ranks of the army, often quoting at length from Queen Victoria's Proclamations of 1858 and 1887 to support his case. These asserted that 'subjects of whatever race or creed, be freely and impartially admitted to Offices in our Service, the duties of which they may be qualified by their education, ability and integrity duly to discharge'.[119] Despite such declarations, the War Office's stipulation to the contrary was an example of the way in which the law frequently positioned South Asians beneath their white British counterparts, denying them full access to Britain and to the Britishness that was formally bestowed upon them.[120]

Since 1858, when the British Crown had assumed direct sovereignty over the territories previously under the control of the East India Company, all the inhabitants of British India, including Hardit, undoubtedly became 'British subjects' by virtue of the operation of common law principles.[121] In spite of this official position, British military law treated Indians as de facto 'aliens', almost without exception. The War Office, in its responses to Naoroji at the outset of the war, was making reference to the *Manual of Military Law, 1914*. The relevant section relating to a 'person of colour' or

118. Visram, R., *'Asians in Britain: 400 Years of History'*, p. 172
119. Ranasinha, R., (Ed.) *'South Asians and the Shaping of Britain, 1870-1950'* (Manchester University Press: Manchester, 2012), p. 22
120. Ibid., p. 23
121. Jones, M.J., *'British Nationality Law and Practice'* (Oxford University Press: Oxford, 1947), pp. 28-73

an 'alien' was Section 95, 'Special provisions as to Persons to be Enlisted' which stated:

> (1.) Any person who is for the time being an alien may, if His Majesty think (sic) to signify his consent through a Secretary of State, be enlisted in His Majesty's regular forces, however, the number of aliens serving together at any one time in any corps of the regular forces shall not exceed the proportion of one alien to every fifty British subjects, and that an alien so enlisted, shall not be capable of holding any higher rank in his majesty's regular forces than that of [...] a non-commissioned officer.[122]

Hardit Singh was in reality not a British subject at all, but an 'alien' in the eyes of military law. The 'provisions' continued, underlining this point, whilst at the same time, paradoxically attempting to emphasise the benefits of British subjecthood:

> (2.) Provided that, notwithstanding the above provisions of this section, any inhabitant of any British protectorate and any negro or person of colour, *although an alien* (author's emphasis), may voluntarily enlist in pursuance of this Part of this Act, and when so enlisted, shall, while serving in His Majesty's regular forces, be deemed to be entitled to all the privileges of a natural-born British subject.[123]

As a 'person of colour' therefore, Hardit was not able to hold a commission and would only be able to enlist at all when numbers permitted. In actual fact, the latter condition was hardly ever met, recruiting sergeants turning away 'people of colour' from their offices as a matter of course. Only a tiny number of Indians living in Britain found their way into the armed forces as 'other ranks' during the great period of recruitment into the armed forces between August 1914 and March 1915, including Naoroji's own grandson. Naoroji himself supported Britain's war effort in spite of any reservations

---

122. War Office, *'Manual of Military Law, 1914'* (HMSO: London, 1914), p. 471
123. Ibid.

that he may have had personally, dying at Bombay in June of 1917, having refused a knighthood twenty years earlier.

In the autumn and winter of 1914-15, having only just left his teens, Hardit was left in relative isolation, pacing the empty quads of Balliol. During the first autumn of the war, the India Corps had arrived on the Western Front in sufficient time to support the overextended British Expeditionary Forces, during the First Battle of Ypres at the end of October and much of November. News of their efforts filtered back in large numbers of square column inches in the newspapers and periodicals which emphasised that the British Empire was playing its part in the war. Also trickling back were the Indian wounded, the majority of whom were treated in the hospitals around Brighton. Envious though he was of his countrymen, Hardit was clear that he would not join the medical services on the south coast, nor did he want to fight for the Indian Army in Flanders. He wanted to join Britain's own armed forces, he had after all, been in the country for five years and was in his own mind no different to the other Balliol students who had been recently attested. He explained to his tutor Urquhart about his frustrations of being one of a mere handful of undergraduates left in college, either unfit for service or as yet too young to enlist, yet part of neither group. Even the younger dons had left, some of the seniors too, employed in government offices in London. Urquhart was also agonising about what part he should play in the war, in spite of being almost overage at forty-six to join the colours, so many of his university friends having left to do so. More than once during the vacations he would travel to Paris to act as an orderly in the American hospital at Neuilly. Later on, he would give invaluable help to the Foreign Office, both roles profiting from his fluency in the French language.

By 1915, Hardit had also developed a degree of articulacy in French, the result of spending his Oxford vacations back at Eastbourne. When not playing cricket the previous summers, he was a paying guest and pupil of Mademoiselle Specht, a middle-aged woman from Alsace, from an old Huguenot family who had settled in Eastbourne as a young woman and who ran a language school. Other members of the university, mainly French students, stayed with the spinster during the long summer holidays to develop fluency in English. It was there that Hardit met Clairette Preiss, another Alsatian and the two formed a strong friendship, though it was never more than that. (In fact, he later acknowledged to being in love with Clairette, but had decided not to 'marry outside my own country').[124] Her father Jacques Preiss was a lawyer and distinguished leader in Alsace, who was indignant at the injustices heaped on Alsace-Lorraine after its surrender to Germany following the defeat of France in the Franco-Prussian War of 1870-71. As a member of the Reichstag working for the freedom of Alsace, he was arrested at the end of 1914 and imprisoned. Although technically a German national, and therefore at risk of internment by the British authorities, Clairette was given special permission to travel to Alsace via neutral Holland early in 1915. Inspired by her father's nationalist credentials and frustrated by his failure to enlist, Hardit didn't need to be asked twice, volunteering to accompany Clairette to meet her mother at Flushing in Belgium, having acquired his first passport. Just before travelling, he hesitated, the reckless giving way to the more conventional side of his personality, and he wrote to the Master of Balliol, Arthur Lionel Smith, seeking his approval for the journey. Old and wise enough to know that the Master wouldn't or couldn't consent to such a trip, not least knowing that a male person of colour travelling with a European woman would have been impossible to sanction, he then regained his nerve and took off across the Channel for the first time in almost six years. Having accomplished the task, he returned home alone with a heavy heart to be met by the inevitable reply from the Master awaiting him back at college. Predictably, it had forbade 'any foolhardy escapade', but he heard no more.

The city of Oxford itself during 1915 was one of intense activity. Many of the university buildings were turned over to create one of the largest hospitals in the south of England, the Third Southern General, whilst others were taken over by battalions of the Oxfordshire and Buckinghamshire Light Infantry, prior to their being sent on divisional manoeuvres. A number of Belgian soldiers and a much larger group of evacuees from that country were also billeted in the city at this time, with a number of very well supported 'Flag Days' being held to raise funds for Belgian Relief, as Hardit later recalled:

> One morning as I came out of my college, I was accosted by a
> very attractive Belgian girl to buy a flag. I agreed readily, but
> when I dipped into my pocket for a shilling or a half-crown,

---

124. Malik, H.S., *'A Little Work, A Little Play'*, pp. 52, 56 & 111

I found that I had no change. I pulled out a one pound note from my wallet and asked her if she had any change. She put the note into her box, stepped up and pinned a flag on my lapel, saying with a smile, "Sorry, no change!" I immediately put my arms around her and kissed her soundly, saying, "I have my change!" She took it very sportingly but my friends could hardly believe their eyes at such boldness from quiet Malik![125]

The entirety of Hardit's life during the period throughout 1915 and the spring of 1916 is not well documented, nor comprehensively described in his autobiography. Nonetheless, it's possible to piece together something of what took place during that time. With less than a couple of terms at Oxford remaining in 1915, the immediate future looked relatively bleak. The range of options in front of him was limited: applications could only be made to the ICS at age twenty-three; he wasn't able to enlist in the armed forces, meaningful sporting activity had ceased and friends were few and far between. Although his father continued to finance his education, he was conscious that that time was coming to an end and the prospect of having little or no income in the summer added to his woes. With a degree of desperation, and having spoken to Burrows, Urquhart and other Indian undergraduates, he made the decision to take up Law and on 23 January 1915 enrolled as a trainee 'magistrate', at the Inner Temple in London.[126]

Today, the Honourable Society of the Inner Temple remains one of the four Inns of Court in London, professional associations for barristers and judges. Here Hardit was to receive a useful training for his future career either at the Bar or in the ICS, developing skills in advocacy and an understanding of legal matters. It was also possible for him to finish his degree, attend the lectures and dinners at the Inner Court and then take his final exams at Balliol. Joining an Inn of Court also provided a membership for life, which would be useful in terms of contacts and gave access to the facilities of the library and the hall.

---

125. Malik, H.S., *'A Little Work, A Little Play'*, pp. 53-54
126. The Inner Temple Admissions Database - as of 4 June 2020 - www.innertemplearchives. org.uk

So it was that Hardit's life settled into a more demanding routine conducted at a brisker pace. He divided his time between revising for his Modern History finals and commuting into London to attend the Inner Temple lectures. Then, having taken his degree that summer, he was free to concentrate on his embryonic studies at the Inner Temple during the autumn. With his short-term future settled, he began to forget about the war, now entering its second year, and immersed himself once more in a life of study, Urquhart having generously found him lodgings at Balliol in which he was to reside until April of 1916. In old age, he was confident of the benefits that his time studying at Oxford had accrued:

> I owe much to both (Balliol and Oxford). Apart from the education, the experience and knowledge I gained from daily contact and frequent discussions with my tutor, with other dons, with fellow undergraduates, has enriched my life, and equipped me for the many years of work and service which lay ahead of me. In the truest sense of the word, it was a liberal education. The knowledge I gained also inculcated in me tolerance – an ability to appreciate points of view different to my own. To me this is one of the most important things in life – to realise that other people have their beliefs which they value as much as I value mine. I believe this to be the very basis of civilised living.[127]

Urquhart himself had begun to spend the long vacations in support of the French war effort and had cultivated significant contacts whilst working at Neuilly in the American hospital there. Sensitive of Hardit's difficulties with enlistment and conscious too that the undergraduate was about to complete his degree, he used what influence he had to enable his former charge's active participation in the war. It wouldn't be the last time.

Consequently, in the early summer of 1915, Hardit received an offer to enrol in the Croix Rouge Française from the wife of the French Military Attaché in London, Madame de la Panouse. She was the President of the British branch, as well as being in some way related to Urquhart. Having declined an orderly's post at Brighton at the onset of the war, he now had

---

127. Malik, H.S., *'A Little Work, A Little Play'*, pp. 111-112

the chance to get to France and closer to the frontline. Believing that it was better to do something rather than nothing, he accepted the offer without a second thought, yet it would be some time before he received his posting.

Having been informed that his service with the Croix Rouge Française would be as an officer ambulance driver, he devoted his time to studying at the Inner Temple, learning how to drive, rudimentary first aid and to improve his French. Hardit's patience was pushed to the limit however, for in spite of making a constant stream of enquiries of Urquhart and the de la Panouses, it would not be until the summer of 1916 that his services were required, following the German assault at Verdun in February. He was then called to the headquarters of the British branch in London to take possession of an ambulance – actually the chassis of an old Wolseley on which was fixed the body of an ambulance. Having resigned from the Inner Temple, never to return, Hardit set off for Southampton bound for Le Havre in June 1916.[128] Understandably, after so much delay, he was somewhat nervous driving the ambulance to the south coast of England, particularly aware also of the limits of his technical knowledge needed to maintain the vehicle.

Having survived the Channel crossing to the port of Le Havre, Hardit headed south-west, bound for the town of Cognac where he was to serve Hôpital Auxiliare 5 of the Croix Rouge Française. The journey of three hundred and fifty miles, which would take him almost to the Atlantic coast, passed slowly initially, but as his confidence in the ambulance's efficiency grew, so exponentially did his appreciation of the French countryside. At a steady thirty miles an hour, he travelled through the chateau country of the Loire and into the rolling landscape of the Charente Départment, the novelty of the scenery an antidote to any residual nerves. He spent one night at a small inn, relishing the opportunity to practise his language skills and drawing a warm response in return. Hardit had visited Paris with friends whilst at Balliol, but this memorable journey would be the start of a love affair with France and the French which would last a lifetime. Little did the twenty-one-year-old know he would become India's first ambassador to France after Partition.

The young man's arrival at the hospital during the evening caused something of a stir, the beard and turban almost immediately heralding the long-lasting assumption that an Indian prince had arrived, which his

---

128. No actual date is recorded for his leaving the Inner Temple.

protestations to the contrary did little to dispel among the bemused staff. That he was an Oxford graduate with a sophisticated English accent and assured French only added to the seeming mystique for some.

The German offensive on the Meuse however, meant there was little time for pleasantries and during the days that followed, Hardit was introduced to the roles that he would play in the eight months ahead. The Croix Rouge Française expected a high standard of its ambulance drivers who were trained to have a professional attitude in spite of their volunteer credentials. Though the ambulances were mainly used for base work, drivers were sometimes placed in the line of fire when transporting wounded men from the front – Hardit spent some time therefore supporting the evacuation of casualties at Verdun in the autumn of 1916.

Yet most of the time at Hôpital Auxiliare 5 was spent ferrying the *infirmières,* the volunteer nurses, from their billets to the hospital and back throughout the day. They were women of all ages and backgrounds, though the majority were from middle class families (the equivalent of Voluntary Aid Detachments in Britain). It was a job Hardit enjoyed, offering constant opportunities for brief conversations, gossip and a little flirtation. These informal exchanges were an ideal way to hone spoken French too, breaking down barriers and any initial shyness. The administrative staff, doctors, nurses, and patients in the hospital came from all over France and the colonial French Empire, and Hardit found the diversity of his new colleagues' origins rather different to what he had experienced in Bournemouth and Oxford. Having the rank of 'Officer' meant also that he was able to eat in the officers' mess, along with the soldiers who were convalescing. It was here that he gained a sense of the horror, but also of the comradeship which war brings. The potential for any monotony was occasionally relieved by the influx of large numbers of casualties from the front on trains arriving at Cognac station, Hardit's Wolseley joining the long convoys of ambulances conveying the wounded men to the hospital. It was in the course of his time in Cognac that he began to crave a greater role in the war, in particular he became inspired by the dream of flying:

> I had always been of a romantic nature, my favourite reading as
> a boy, apart from poetry, being tales of chivalry and romance.
> In France at that time the great hero was Guynemer,[129] the

---

129. Georges Guynemer was the second highest-scoring French fighter ace with 54 victories during the First World War and a French national hero at the time of his death.

famous fighting pilot whose exploits were told and retold in households, a veritable knight in shining armour. It was he who fired my imagination and inspired my first thoughts about being a fighter pilot. This thought had never even occurred to me before.[130]

As he was to do throughout life, Hardit developed friendships easily during his time in Cognac, an undoubted charm and relaxed conversation putting others at their ease, and as a result he began to be invited into their homes for dinner. Not least of those befriended, were both the chairman of the hospital committee, Castillon du Perron and its Director Monsieur Pataa. Both were associated with the great French brandy companies: the former was head of Hennessy and the latter of Martell, and initially against his better judgement, Hardit made an acquaintance with fine brandy, an association which would last rather longer than he anticipated. As a devout Sikh, alcohol was forbidden, but du Perron in particular was insistent, and the ever polite Hardit balked at offending his generous hosts. In the end, the hospitality shown to him by the family in their chateau home a few miles outside Cognac proved irresistible.[131]

The wounded came to the hospital from all over France, as well as the French Colonies in Africa, and in the mess, there were officers from Algeria, Morocco and Libya. There was little that wasn't talked about, typical of young men throughout time and thrown together in extremis. The theme of what was then called 'racialism', was a regular subject of conversation returned to repeatedly. When travelling to Paris on leave with a group of these officers during that time, Hardit recalled an incident involving an Algerian Major, that he believed illustrated the difference between British and French colonial racial attitudes:

He and I were walking down one of the famous boulevards. A young white French lieutenant passed us without saluting my Algerian friend who was a Major. He immediately pulled up the young officer saying. *"Monsieur, vous faites partie de l'armee Française?"* The young officer immediately realised

130. Sapru, S., '*Sky Hawks*', p. 222
131. Malik, H.S., '*A Little Work, A Little Play*', p. 62

that he was in the wrong, saluted the African Major and went on his way.

I noticed a great contrast between the French attitude and that of the British soldiers in India towards the Indian commissioned officers when I came home (to India in 1919) whilst still serving in the Royal Air Force. I deliberately avoided wearing my uniform during this visit because I didn't want to put myself in a position where I'd be insulted by the British soldiers neglecting to salute me simply because I was an Indian. I would have been able to do nothing about this because it was the accepted British practice.[132]

Hardit may never have been aware of it, but as an officer in the RAF during the latter half of the war, his own case would be deliberated upon at the highest levels of government, part of a debate about the 'Indianisation' of the Empire's armed forces, which focused on the possibility of granting Indians equal status with British officers.

---

132. Ibid.

Chapter 5

Aldershot
November 1916–April 1917

'He who has no faith in himself can never have faith in God.'
Guru Nanak, *Sri Guru Granth Sahib*

A bleary eyed Hardit peered from between the flaps of the tent he shared with other RFC cadets. It was with some relief that reveille had sounded, bringing to an end another disturbed night with precious little sleep. The unseasonably cold weather for early April 1917 was making already difficult conditions almost intolerable. Snow covered the ground, and as Hardit's eyes adjusted to the light, there was little to be seen except the sleet blowing almost horizontally across the nearby parade ground. So far, the two days of basic training at Aldershot were proving to be a thoroughly miserable experience in a very badly equipped camp. His uniform was constantly wet, the bedding inadequate and the arrangements for washing and other essential facilities primitive. The only taps available were outside the main barracks. After living in Britain for eight years, Hardit believed that he had become inured to the joys of British cooking, but he wasn't prepared for the three indigestible meals served up so far. He had tried in vain not to hark back to the culinary delights served up by the *cuisinère* in the officers' mess in now far away Cognac. The deplorable conditions were so bad that on the previous night one of the cadets had been evacuated with a high temperature, coughing up blood-streaked mucus, sure signs of pneumonia. He never returned.

Hardit wasn't about to be thwarted, however, having invested much of his own time and the kindness of others in joining the emergent RFC. He struggled into a damp uniform, tied the khaki turban, having detected the previous day that the dye he had applied was beginning to seep into his scalp. A couple of curious cadets had quizzed him about his headgear and the *kara* given to him by Attar Singh, the newly designated Air Mechanic 3rd Class responding with his usual studied politeness. He was equally well versed in ignoring the odd aside and stare. Besides, everyone had too much on their minds surviving in the conditions. Shivering, he made his way from the tent to join the other trainees on the frozen parade ground for the first time. An archetypal British sergeant major greeted the dozen cadets with an equally icy stare. He was 'a strongly built man with a red face and big moustache, a commanding voice and a bull like neck'.[133] Having bided his time without saying a word, he walked slowly to the end of the line and back again. Becoming increasingly florid, the sergeant major looked 'pop-eyed' at the khaki turban as Hardit recollected:

> "Why aren't you in uniform?" he bellowed. I replied that I was, and that I didn't understand what he meant. He pointed to my turban, "Where is your 'at?" I tried to explain that as a Sikh I must wear a turban which had to be accepted as part of my uniform. But he would have none of it, and might even have tried to force me to put on a hat.[134]

Hardit's career in flying might have ended there and then, before it had even begun, if not for the intervention of the Adjutant who had been nearby. He calmed the situation, explained that the cadet could wear the turban for the time being and that the matter would be brought before the local base commander. In the days that followed, nothing further was said about the incident owing to the tact and understanding of the commanding officers at Aldershot, who referred the matter to the War Office. In due course, special dispensation was granted authorising the turban be worn as part of the uniform.[135]

Back in September 1916, Hardit had returned from Cognac to Oxford once more to accept the hospitality of Urquhart. For the several days of his furlough from the Croix Rouge Française, space was found for him in the upper reaches of Balliol and the two of them exchanged recollections

---

133. Malik, H.S., *'A Little Work, A Little Play'*, p. 67
134. Ibid.
135. Ibid.

of their times in France. Although grateful for the opportunity to be at the front, Hardit was nevertheless frustrated at being an ambulance driver. He told his former tutor that through some of the convalescent officers and influential contacts in Cognac, he had begun to make enquiries about enlistment into the French air force – the Aéronautique Militaire. Although Urquhart listened attentively to Hardit during this visit, he was furious that his former charge had been denied the opportunity to serve in the British armed forces for over two years.

Having returned to Cognac, a member of the Aéronautique Militaire actually gave a suggestion to Hardit that he would be able to enlist as a cadet and how to go about it. In one of his regular letters back to Balliol, Hardit explained the situation to Urquhart. During December, developments began to move at a rapid pace according to his version of what happened next:

> (Sligger) replied without delay that on receipt of my letter, he had gone to see General Henderson, then Head of the RFC, and told him how scandalous it was that although I was a British subject, the British armed forces had no use for me, while the French were willing to enlist me. This outspoken protest had immediate effect. Soon I received communication from the War Office telling me that on my next leave in London I was to call on the General.[136]

As we shall see, this version of events was not quite accurate, though what was beyond doubt was that Urquhart's connections and social capital beyond Oxford were playing an important role in advancing Hardit's military aspirations. Having received special dispensation from the hospital committee in Cognac, he arranged a short leave in London and not long after secured an appointment with General Henderson. At the end of an 'agreeable interview', Henderson told Hardit that he would be admitted to the RFC subject to passing a medical examination. Thrilled, he ran out of the War Office in Whitehall to the French Embassy in Knightsbridge to secure his resignation from the Croix Rouge Française from General de la Panouse. He was in. After returning to Cognac, he bade a sentimental

---

136. Malik, H.S., *'A Little Work, A Little Play'*, p. 65

farewell to his many friends. Throughout his life, he looked back with great fondness on the time spent in the beautiful town of Cognac during 1916.

Hardit intended to be an officer. Everyone who knew him believed him to be officer material. The majority of his peers at university had enlisted as officers. Yet, as we have seen, it was not permissible for an 'alien', a 'person of colour' to become an officer in the British armed forces. Urquhart's letter to General Henderson had been perfectly timed however.

The Battle of the Somme had ended that November of 1916 leaving 420,000 British casualties. France and Russia's forces were at the point of exhaustion, America was in isolation and the so-called allied 'sideshows' in Mesopotamia, Gallipoli and Salonika had all come to nought whilst absorbing large numbers of allied formations. The planning by the British High Command for 1917 was well advanced and it was perceived that further large-scale offensives would be needed if the German Army was to be defeated on the Western Front. Britain would be the main protagonist opposing Germany in the west, a role demanding ever greater numbers of reinforcements. One potential major source of recruits was from India. *Sepoys* had already been playing a major role in Flanders, East Africa, Palestine and most notably in Mesopotamia, yet it was evident to many in Whitehall that ever greater numbers could be drafted from the subcontinent in the future.[137] If such recruitment campaigns in India were to come fully to fruition, then some argued it would be beneficial if the British Government was to offer some concessions to Indian nationalist opinion.

At the beginning of the war, the Princely States, the Indian National Congress and the All India Muslim League had backed British war aims and it is undeniable that this loyalty was maintained throughout the war. Yet the conflict also 'infused a new enthusiasm in the mind of the (Indian) people and created new aspirations for political progress'.[138] Such patriotism and a growing self-respect were grounded upon the major roles being played by Indian troops – almost 1.5 million *sepoys* would have been recruited by its end - and its financial, industrial and manufacturing contribution to the war. As has been seen, it had not gone unnoticed in India that the war was ostensibly

---

137. A small Indian contingent had also been present at Gallipoli.
138. Pati, B., *'India and the First World War'* (Atlantic Publishers: New Delhi, 1996), p. 173

being fought for 'Freedom'. The rise in the number of those Indians seeking to take violent action in pursuit of home rule had grown in previous years, culminating in the abortive Ghadar campaign in the Punjab and the resulting Defence of India Act in 1915. Nonetheless, there were many more moderate voices in India who wished to use the war as an opportunity to pressure Britain to make political changes by peaceful means, whilst at the same time supporting Britain's war aims. 1916 witnessed the creation of the 'Home Rule Leagues', the only major and serious political action taken by those in favour of Indian self-rule during the First World War. The designation was given to both of two short lived organisations of the same name established that April and September, respectively, by Indian nationalist Bal Gangadhar Tilak and British social reformer and Indian independence leader Annie Besant. The term was inspired by a similar movement in Ireland and aimed to galvanise the efforts of Indian nationalists through education, debate and by peaceful means. Tilak's group, founded at Poona, concentrated its efforts mostly in western India, and that of Besant, set up at Madras, had more of an all-India influence. Both however, worked toward the same objective of mobilising Indian public opinion in favour of self-government, and from the start each worked closely with the other.

There were other pressures on the GOI also. The aspiration for political progress driven by the war had begun to sweep away petty differences between moderate and extreme nationalists within the Indian National Congress and to an extent between Hindus and Muslims, which opened up new paths of co-operation and created a degree of nationalistic unity. This countered the possibility of the GOI manipulating the former divisions between them or, exploiting opportunities to resort to the longstanding ploy of 'divide and rule'. In addition, the disastrous military campaign in Mesopotamia the previous year, had weakened the GOI's reputation and damaged British prestige in the region.

Even before the war, the object of Viceroy of India Lord Hardinge's whole tenure had been to appease the clamour of moderate Indian opinion with progressive measures. He hoped thereby to strengthen Britain's hold on India by doing so. [139] By the spring of 1916, that commotion was growing

---

139. Martin, G., 'The Influence of Racial Attitudes on British Policy Towards India during the First World War', in *The Journal of Imperial and Commonwealth History*, Volume 14, issue 2 (May 198), pp. 91–113

ever louder, not least in Britain where the very favourable response to reports of the overwhelming demonstrations of Indian loyalty to the Empire would help to revive the question of not if, but how concessions might be made. The outgoing Hardinge demonstrated that he well understood the changing spirit of the time on the subcontinent in a memorandum of 1916, notwithstanding his choice of grandiose language:

> Affairs in India have now reached a stage where concession to Indian sentiment is necessary to maintain the faith of the people in British justice, the cornerstone of British rule in India. It is essential, therefore, for the future good relations between India and the British Empire, that full scope should be given to the general impulses of the English people and that nothing should be refused to which India can fairly justify her claim. Through England's generosity yet another link may be welded in the golden chain binding India to Great Britain and the British Empire.[140]

As a result of a debate which ensued at the heart of government in both Britain and India, particularly from August 1917 onwards, one of the concessions being considered to influence Indian political and public opinion related to an old question.

The rank of 'King's Commissioned Officer' in the Indian Army (from 2nd lieutenant to general) was the exclusive preserve of the governing race, the British. It was widely believed by its military establishment that non-commissioned officers and private soldiers would never be led by a 'native' when on service. In 1858, a category called the 'Viceroy's Commissioned Officer' was created by promotion from amongst the Indian Army rank-and-file to act as communicators between the British officer and the *sepoys*.[141] The possibility that Indians could aspire to the rank of King's Commissioned Officer had been much sought after in the subcontinent before the First World War and one always denied, not least, through the

---

140. Hardinge Papers, (microfilm), Roll 15 Sl., 116, p. 1 quoted in Pati, B., *'India and the First World War'*, p. 183
141. Gupta, P.S., & Deshpande, A., *'The British Raj and its Indian Armed Forces 1857-1939'* (Oxford University Press: Oxford, 2002), p. 229

opposition of the British officer corps.[142] Nationalists, conversely, thought that, by not allowing such commissions, the British were not honouring the promise in the Queen's Proclamation of 1858 to open employment to Indians in all branches of British-India's government and military.[143] Such demands for throwing open the commissioned ranks to educated Indians (by analogy of the opportunities given to them in imperial services like the ICS) had always been resisted. As we shall see, some concessions would be included in the 'Montagu-Chelmsford Report' of July 1918,[144] but almost two years earlier, the issue was beginning to be considered seriously by the GOI and the India Office for the first time, now that politically it couldn't be disregarded or rejected out of hand.

The Incoming Viceroy of India, Lord Chelmsford, picked up where his predecessor Hardinge had left off and in a despatch of 24 November 1916, the position of the GOI was made clear to the Imperial War Cabinet back in London:

> [...] one of the most important questions that will call for early settlement is whether the time has not come for opening to Indians, British Commissions in His Majesty's Army...This has all been changed from the day that the Indian Regiments valiantly passed through their baptism of fire on European battlefields. They have seen how quickly their small band of British officers can be swept away; they have seen or heard that in the French or Russian Armies men of the African and Asiatic regiments may rise to full commissioned rank. They have seen Turkish officers bravely leading their troops in the most modern warfare, and they must ask themselves why to Indians alone this privilege should be denied.[145]

---

142. Martin, G., 'The Influence of Racial Attitudes on British Policy Towards India during the First World War', pp. 91–113
143. C.S. Sundaram, 'Reviving a 'Dead Letter': Military Indianization and the Ideology of Anglo-India, 1885-1891', in P.S. Gupta and A. Deshpande, eds., 'The British Raj and its Indian Armed Forces, 1857-1939', pp. 45-97
144. See Chapter Six
145. Indian Reforms. Grant of Commissions to Indians, Imperial War Cabinet papers, quoted in despatch of 24 November 1916, TNA, CAB-24-20-80

The despatch made it clear that there would be many obstacles to reform and that a cautious incremental approach would be required. Nevertheless, it laid out the rationale for granting King's Commissions for Indians and the principles were discussed at the highest level of government. It was during the following month, that Urquhart's appeal on behalf of Hardit Singh was made to General Henderson. It couldn't have been better timed.

The debate about granting King's Commissions to Indians was also contributed to by another class of recruits never foreseen by any governmental departments. In spite of the legal and racial impediments before them, a small number of Indians living in Britain, had been recruited into British Army units during the first eighteen months of the war and were now being recommended by their commanders in the field for promotion to the rank of officer.[146] From the perspective of the War Office, this presented an even thornier problem. It was one thing to consider granting a King's Commission to an Indian as part of say a Sikh battalion, commanding *sepoys* on the North-West Frontier, but quite another to have one leading 'Tommies' in a British battalion on the Somme. The War Office had consistently been opposed to any compromise on the issue, but more liberal voices were to be heard, reflecting the ever-changing political landscape.

Yet, it wasn't only into the British Army that Indians were looking to enlist. The RFC had been formed in 1912, and its recruitment practices were also governed by the *Manual of Military Law, 1914,* and therefore accepted only those recruits with European parentage into its ranks. Yet, prior to, and during the Somme battle of 1916, an increasing shortage of trained pilots added to the wider political pressures on the War Office and the Air Board to relax the enrolment criteria into the RFC. General Hugh Trenchard,[147] who had succeeded David Henderson as head of the RFC, was clear about the challenges facing his command that September, as historian Jill Bush makes clear:

---

146. Two such cases, those of Naoroji (the former MP's grandson) and Rudra were recorded alongside Hardit Singh's own by the India Office in: 'Commissions for Indians: cases of Cadets Naoroji, and Rudra and 2nd Lieutenant Hardit Singh Malik of Royal Air Force', Collection 430/9, IOR/L/MIL/7/19015: 1917-1920.

147. Hugh Montague Trenchard. He has been described as the 'Father of the RAF'. Trenchard, Henderson and Brancker were instrumental in the early development of the RFC.

In France, watching the day by day depletion of squadrons and aircraft, he was deeply mindful of the sacrifice his men continued to make. Replacements were out of control and his anxiety showed through his blunt questioning of commitment to the fight at home: 'It is not a question of difficulty of supplying pilots, it is a question as to whether it can be done or whether it can't be done…if we cannot do it then we are beaten.'[148]

As a result of the changing political and military landscape, 'a small number of Indian military pilots did take part in the air war, as officers of the RFC and later the RAF'.[149] They began to enlist in the autumn of 1916. The first to do so was Jeejeebhoy Piroshaw Bowmanjee Jeejeebhoy, who was commissioned with the rank of temporary Honorary 2nd Lieutenant on 6 November 1916. However, his career was cut short by ill-health whilst studying at 2 School of Military Aeronautics at Oxford and he was found unfit for further service in May the following year, apparently with impetigo.[150] [151] An 'Honorary' rank was usually granted on retirement, or in certain special cases awarded to a deserving civilian. Generally, it was treated as if it were substantive, but usually did not grant a corresponding wage or pension. Equally importantly, the bearer did not exercise any real power.[152]

A second Indian applicant, Shri Krishna Chunda Welinkar, applied for a temporary commission in the RFC on 22 November 1916. At the time of his application, Welinkar was a student at Jesus College, Cambridge. According to a handwritten note made on his application on 6 February 1917, Welinkar had been 'recommended by a Brigadier-General Brancker

---

148. Letter to Brancker, MFC 76/1, RAF Museum, 21 September 1916, quoted in Bush, J., *'Lionel Morris and the Red Baron: Air War on the Somme'* (Pen & Sword: Barnsley, 2019), p. 163

149. Richards, C., 'The Origins of Military Aviation in India and the Creation of the Indian Air Force, 1910-1932', part two of the *Royal Air Force: Air Power Review*, 11.1 (2008), pp. 20-50

150. 2 School of Instruction was based at Christ Church, Oxford.

151. Gorasia, J., 'Indian Pilots in the RFC', unpublished thesis - 2015, Eastbourne College Archive

152. Indeed, the German Kaiser Wilhelm II held an honorary rank in the Royal Navy during the First World War!

and approved for Officers' Cadet Wing, RFC'.[153] Unlike Jeejeebhoy, Welinkar did not receive an honorary commission, but was enlisted initially into the Oxfordshire and Buckinghamshire Light Infantry on 13 February, before being posted to 6 Officer Cadet Battalion, RFC as a cadet on the same day. Eventually, he was appointed a temporary 2nd Lieutenant on 24 May.[154]

Exactly a month earlier, Erroll Suvo Chunder Sen was awarded a commission as a temporary Honorary 2nd Lieutenant and reported to 1 School of Military Aeronautics at Reading on the same day.[155] One of the common factors behind these enlistments, and that of Indra 'Laddie' Roy[156], who was to begin Officer Cadet training on 26 March 1917, was that each had received a recommendation to enlist, as was to be the case when Urquhart had advanced Hardit's case the previous December. It seemed to have made a difference if an Indian was nominated to the War or India Offices by influential sponsors.

The reason for this group of enlistments was the presence of a number of sympathetic voices in Whitehall who were willing to speak up on behalf of Indians looking to enlist into the RFC. The aforementioned General Brancker had served in India before taking on senior roles during the First World War:

> Brancker served as the RFC's senior representative in Whitehall [...] holding the posts of Director of Air Organisation in the War Office between March 1916 and February 1917 and Deputy Director General of Military Aeronautics between February and October 1917. As such, one of the then Brigadier-General Brancker's responsibilities was the selection and commissioning of RFC officers; and in a paper presented to the Air Council in September 1918, he referred to 'four

---

153. Richards, C., 'The Origins of Military Aviation in India and the Creation of the Indian Air Force, 1910-1932, p. 28
154. Ibid.
155. Ibid.
156. Indra Lal Roy, DFC, was the sole Indian flying ace of the First World War. While serving in the RAF, he claimed ten aerial victories. He was killed-in-action over Carvin on 22 July 1918.

Indians whom I had trained about two years ago in the Royal Flying Corps.'[157]

Hardit mentioned in his autobiography that Brancker 'had served in India and took a special interest in me'.[158] It's not clear exactly what part Brancker played in Hardit's enlistment and training, but he would also play a role at the end.

As the third Christmas of the war approached, Hardit waited impatiently for his call up by the RFC. He spent the next few months with friends in Oxford, Eastbourne, and London, kicking his heels whilst waiting for news. Meanwhile, on 29 December, the Parliamentary Under-Secretary of State Lord Islington wrote to his boss, the Secretary of State for India, Austen Chamberlain, about the issue of granting King's Commissions to Indians:

> As you know, I consider that the delay in disposing of this important matter is deplorable and I venture to suggest that the formation of the new War Cabinet requires that it should be brought to the notice of the Prime Minister and his colleagues at a very early date.[159]

The creation of a new cabinet was necessary following the fall of Prime Minister Asquith's coalition government. David Lloyd George structured a new partnership dominated by the Conservatives on 7 December. Later in the memorandum to Chamberlain, Islington continued:

> I should like to take this opportunity of mentioning to you the case of Mr Malik, an Indian graduate of Oxford University and a golf blue, who recently applied to this Office to help him into the French Flying Corps where, it is understood, he would get a commission. The anomaly of our encouraging a

---

157. Richards, C., 'The Origins of Military Aviation in India and the Creation of the Indian Air Force, 1910-1932, p. 28
158. Malik, H.S., 'A Little Work, A Little Play', p. 98
159. Papers transferred from public and judicial department records regarding grant of Indian Army commissions to Indians, Collection 430/1, IOR/L/MIL/7/19006: 1911-1923, 29 December 1916, p. 162

British subject to enter the Army of one of our Allies when he was inadmissible for our own was so striking and would have led to so much misconception, that I have brought the case personally to the notice of Sir David Henderson who has arranged that the young man shall be given an Honorary Commission in the RFC. Even so, we are still faced with the difficulty that the Hon. Commission will carry no pay, and Mr. Malik, I understand, cannot afford to serve without pay. The question is still under consideration by the Students' Department,[160]and I am prepared to approach Sir David Henderson again if the difficulty cannot be otherwise solved. Sir David Henderson has also been instrumental in enabling a Parsee named Mr Jeejeebhoy to get an Hon. Commission in the RFC. The fact that these cases should be possible shows how absurd it is to maintain the rule against regular Commissions to Indians in the case of selected candidates.[161]

There are several points within this paragraph worth further scrutiny, the better to understand the process of an Indian being recruited by the RFC at this time. According to Islington, Hardit's application to enlist came directly to the India Office with a view to his joining the Aéronautique Militaire. Islington claimed that he himself then brought the matter before Henderson, who was acting as Director-General of Military Aeronautics for the RFC in Whitehall at that time. It will be remembered that Hardit claimed in his autobiography that Urquhart had actually 'gone to see General Henderson,' though this meeting may have happened after the initial approach to the India Office, as Islington described it. In these situations, it was usual practice for the India Office to name the British sponsor of an Indian looking to enlist, yet Urquhart's alleged involvement was not referred to in any of the documentary evidence amongst the India Office correspondence. This may merely represent a simple omission on Islington's part of course. Assuming that the Urquhart-Henderson meeting took place, it's conjectural, but of value asking if the Balliol man had emphasised the possibility of a Aéronautique Militaire enlistment for his former student, to use as leverage

---

160. Indian Students' Department was associated with the India Office. See Chapter 2
161. IOR/L/MIL/7/19006: 1911-1923, 29 December 1916, pp. 162-3

with the military authorities? As Islington suggested, it was not only potentially embarrassing for an Indian to be enlisted by Britain's closest ally the French, he may also have been aware that there was sensitivity in Whitehall to the fact that African officers were able in limited numbers to take up commissions in the colonial formations of the French Army.[162] [163]

On the cusp of 1917, these events were timely, in the light of the deliberations in government about granting King's Commissions to Indians, Urquhart, Henderson, Brancker and Islington all seemingly playing a part in the successful enlistment of Hardit Singh. Urquhart and Henderson may have known each other socially, having a common Red Cross connection, Urquhart with his hospital work at Neuilly and Henderson later taking on the role of the Director-General of the League of Red Cross Societies in Geneva after the First World War. It was Urquhart who had suggested the posting into the Croix Rouge Française in the first instance. Missing from the actual correspondence about Hardit's enlistment was the name of General Brancker, though the latter would later claim to have played a key role in the recruitment of the group of Indians into the RFC at the start of 1917.

On 28 March 1917, Hardit Singh Malik formally attested into the RFC as a cadet at South Farnborough in Hampshire at the rank of Air Mechanic 3rd Class.[164] He would have to wait a little to become an officer. He was recorded as being twenty-two years and four months old, five feet, eight inches in height and with a girth of thirty-four inches. His address was noted as 'Balliol College, Oxford', while his previous military service had been with the 'Eastbourne College Officer Training Corps' and he continued to record his 'trade or calling' as 'Student' in spite of his time in Cognac.[165]

Having survived the appalling weather and the attentions of the sergeant major during basic training at Aldershot, Hardit was posted to 1 School of Military Aeronautics at Reading on 5 April 1917. The school provided preliminary training for cadets and taught theoretical aspects of flight,

162. Forgarty, R.S., 'Race and War in France: Colonial Subjects in the French Army, 1914–1918' (JHU Press: Baltimore, 2008), pp. 96-133
163. Nevertheless, the numbers of black French officers were limited and their authority was restricted and often undermined.
164. Air Ministry: Air Member for Personnel and predecessors: Airmen's Records, Hardit Singh Malik, TNA, AIR 79/634/68661
165. Ibid.

including map-reading, gunnery and mechanics. On that same day, he was discharged as an Air Mechanic 3rd Class: 'His services no longer required having been selected for appointment to an Honorary temporary 2nd Lieutenancy'.[166]

As with Jeejeebhoy and Sen before him, so Hardit was promoted to the rank of temporary Honorary 2nd Lieutenant. The 'Honorary' prefix enabled Indians access to the RFC, whilst conversely enabling them neither to command the British rank-and-file nor to receive pay. There is no evidence for who was responsible for creating the honorary rank for Indian pilots, however, by this time, it had become fairly common practice to bestow token honorary prefixes to the titles of heads of Indian Princely States and their offspring, usually a reward for their contributions to the war effort. The continuation of such a practice created the perfect stratagem for enabling the RFC enlistments, after all, whilst in France with the Croix Rouge Française, Hardit was assumed, rather more often than he liked, to be the son of an Indian prince. At a time when there was much opposition to the granting of King's Commissions to Indians within the War Office and elsewhere, the granting of an Honorary rank was a useful cover for enlistments. It may just have been the work of General Sefton Brancker, who having consulted the *Manual of Military Law, 1914,* had found the loophole he had been looking for in a final footnote to Section 95, 'Special provisions as to Persons to be Enlisted':

> (the law) [...] forbids an alien to enjoy any office or place of trust, but does not prevent honorary rank in the British Army being conferred upon an alien, whether or not such honorary rank is accompanied by a formal commission. Such a distinction is a mere matter of honour and dignity, and does not fall within the Act so long as the possessor does not by virtue of his rank or commission exercise any actual command or power.[167]

Hardit was now an officer cadet, a testament to his perseverance and dogged determination. A tribute also to those of his friends who had enabled

---

166. Ibid.
167. War Office, '*Manual of Military Law, 1914*', p. 471

his participation in the war, for without his ability to form long-lasting friendships with the influential, his enlistment would have been rather more difficult or not have happened at all. Around the time of his deployment, he wrote to his brother Teja in Delhi, in order to explain his decision to join the RFC. He explained that he hoped his family would approve:

> For I do believe that a man is all the better for having been tested in the forge of modern warfare and having been brought face to face with the elemental problems is fitter to live like a man, when all this war and the talk of war is over. There is of course the risk, but then the risk is not magnified. There are millions of human beings running the same risks today and surely one is not fit to live if one is not ready to face death and smile. Besides, we Sikhs have a great fighting tradition and we should not make too much fuss about death. I am not so foolish as to think of nothing. Naturally, one takes precautions – all possible precautions – against death for the sake of those who are left behind, but you being a religious man, will I think, agree with me when I say that one should utterly despise death and scorn it.[168]

It is evident that Hardit was writing here with various audiences in mind: for his parents who had not seen him for eight years, there is reassurance. For his brother there is an uncompromising, spiritual reckoning with the possibility of his own mortality. There is a sense too of a young man rationalising to himself the decisions he has made, preparing to go off to war, wanting to test himself, aware of his heritage, a Sikh warrior, conscious of the risks, yet utterly committed to the path he has chosen.

---

168. Malik, H.S., *'A Little Work, A Little Play'*, p. 66

Chapter 6

Yatesbury
April–October 1917

'In the corner by the window
Lay a man in slumber deep.
When the train swept round the turning,
Curving on embankment steep,
Then the man stirred in his corner,
Mutt'ring in his troubled sleep,
"Bank and rudder together,
Together, you hun, you fool!"'

Anon. *The Instructor*[169]

With one week remaining of his six week training course at 1 School of
Military Aeronautics at Reading,[170] Hardit took the usual ten minute stroll
from the digs found for him by the RFC. He had been living with a family,
who after a little uncertainty and the shedding of inhibitions, had warmed
to their new tenant. Indeed, after a while, the landlady had introduced him
to the two next door terrace neighbours, proud of their much talked about
resident. Many of the other cadets at the school lodged in halls of residence,
but Hardit enjoyed the early morning and evening walks along pleasant
treelined avenues onto the campus on the eastern side of town.

---

169. RFC flying instructors nicknamed their students 'Huns' believing them as dangerous
as the enemy.
170. In December 1915, the RFC had commandeered buildings belonging to the University
of Reading, at first for the purpose of training flight instructors, but by the following
October, the school was expanded to include cadet pilot and observer training and
given its formal designation.

On arrival, Hardit headed into the refectory for breakfast as usual with friends Harold Boston and Arthur Stewart. Both listened in a desultory fashion to Hardit's excited account of his round of golf at the nearby Sonning Club the Sunday before, with the secretary and former winner of the British Open, Harold Hilton. Hardit had been playing a little too much golf after work than was good for him, but he hadn't been able to resist the temptation of a drink with Hilton, a scouser with a dry sense of humour and one of the most knowledgeable and reflective golfers of his day.

Having eaten, the three men headed onto the parade ground for inspection. Hardit had clarified the 'status' of his turban at the outset with the school's Adjutant, Captain Parker-Jervis, his copy of a confirmatory letter from the War Office saving any further confrontations. To demonstrate their cadet rank, candidates were required to wear a white band around their peaked caps, fitting it just above the brim. Hardit had wound his own band neatly around the turban to the satisfaction of the school's commanding officer, Colonel Bonham-Carter, the adjutant having brought Hardit's case to his attention.

When newly arrived from Aldershot early in April 1917, Hardit, Boston and Stewart had met during the first parade, having fallen in next to each other. They found much of the initiation rather amusing, including the senior instructor's eyeing of the newly dyed turban and their friendship was cemented as a result.[171] Through being part of the same 'squadron', they had become inseparable, studying and spending much of their leisure time together. The summer of 1917 came unusually early that year and it was tempting for the cadets to go out in the evening with their instruction books to swot up for the following day's lectures. The lure of the Thames at Pangbourne and its neighbouring reaches proved particularly irresistible, to the accompaniment of throngs of nightingales.[172]

After parade that morning, they passed the school's headquarters in Yeomanry House, and then Wantage Hall, where most of the lectures were

---

171. Harold Boston's son Robin maintains links with Hardit Singh Malik's descendants to this day. Hardit's family were regular visitors to the Boston family home, not least when Hardit was Indian Ambassador to France, as Robin remembered recently.

172. Boston, W.H., 'Some Memoirs of An Unknown Pilot in The Royal Flying Corps and Royal Air Force 1917-1918' (Barbara Boston: Shropshire, 1991), p. 5

delivered.[173] The impending class was a practical in Upper Redlands Road and on the way there they discussed the options given to them about the next stage of their training. The three had been given a choice of several venues across the country, but as Francophiles had decided to go together to Vendôme in the Loire Valley.

They joined the remainder of the cadets for a practical session involving naming the parts of a Lewis machine gun and being able to replace its broken bolt. Some of the cadets had found much of the training overzealous and pointless and this morning there was more eye-rolling and moaned asides than normal, particularly from those men who had transferred to the RFC from infantry battalions, having not long returned from the Western Front. The school presented, what for all intents and purposes was, a concentrated university course, compressed into the space of six weeks or so, but veterans of trench warfare had very little patience for theoretical abstractions and word soon went round that it was difficult enough to change a Lewis gun bolt on the ground, never mind in the air. They soon got out of the instructor too that British planes carried no spares either.

Hardit's struggle to enlist afforded him a little more patience than those joining the course straight from military duty in France and Flanders. Initially, he was relieved to be out of the frozen tents at Aldershot, but as time passed, he found joy in learning about a multiplicity of subjects, ranging from theories of flight to a knowledge of rigging.[174] He was particularly fascinated to learn about aerial observation and wireless telegraphy, even finding interest in a day's instruction about 'Mess Etiquette'. Yet, as the course approached its conclusion at the end of May, Hardit looked forward with relish to getting airborne alone.

After Reading, the three officer cadets were posted on 22 May to the town of Vendôme, which was at the heart of a triangle made by the cities of Le Mans, Tours and Orléans. The flying school at Vendôme was run by the Royal Naval Air Service (RNAS), in the time before it was merged with the RFC to form the RAF on 1 April 1918. Hardit remembered the month spent there as being:

---

173. Ashworth, C., '*Action Stations: Military airfields of the Central South and South-East*' (Patrick Stephens: Yeovil, 1985), p. 245

174. Malik, H.S., '*A Little Work, A Little Play*', p. 68 (Flight theory - the 'Smith-Barry' or 'Gosport' system was actually only formally instituted in the autumn of 1917).

[...] extremely pleasant at the heart of the picturesque chateau country. The flying school was commanded by a Naval Captain named Briggs whom we never saw unless we were in trouble [...] he maintained iron discipline, running his school as if it was a battleship of His Majesty's Navy! My flying instructor, Captain Carr, was a particularly pleasant person, and under his guidance, I learned to fly quickly and with confidence. We started with dual instruction on a French aircraft known as the Caudron, which was very heavy on the controls. [175]

Flying at this time without complex instruments, pilots had to use their judgement and instincts to stay airborne. Dual instruction often meant that a cadet rested his hands and feet lightly on the controls while the instructor flew the plane, the trainee attempting to absorb what the instructor was doing while observing the results of these actions on the machine. Dual flights were always of short duration, taking place at low altitudes within sight of the airfield. The reason for this was that only a limited number of cadets could be airborne at any one time, the remainder standing on the field to observe. In fact, many training flights were no more than a succession of landings and take-offs.[176] Usually, after as little as two to three hours dual control tuition, it would be time for the cadet to take his solo flight:

Under Carr's instruction, I made rapid progress and after only three hours "dual" when one flew with the instructor with dual controls, I was allowed to go up solo in a Curtiss, an American plane to which pilots graduated after grappling with the Caudron.[177]

The thrill and excitement of that first solo flight was never to be forgotten, though in his initial anxiety Hardit pushed the control wheel down a little too much on take-off, almost hitting the ground with the propeller. Having exuberantly circled the airfield a few times, he realised that he had to land the plane, at which his self-assurance momentarily disappeared – he had

175. Malik, H.S., 'A Little Work, A Little Play', p. 70
176. Skeet, M., 'RFC Pilot Training', - www.theaerodrome.com – accessed 1 July 2020
177. Malik, H.S., 'A Little Work, A Little Play', p. 70

already seen a number of fellow cadets damage their planes and themselves coming back to earth. Fortunately, these thoughts focused the mind and the touchdown was a success. Not all trainees were so lucky. Training to be a pilot was a dangerous occupation and exceedingly costly, in terms of both men and machines. The RFC had an attitude toward training accidents that seems outrageously casual from a twenty first century perspective. The typical training airfield and its surroundings were constantly littered with crashed aircraft in varying degrees of destruction. There could be upwards of two dozen smashes per day at each aerodrome when flying was going on at full pace; this led to a steady haemorrhage of cadets; on average, one trainee pilot died each day in Britain until a new training regime was put in place in the autumn of 1917.[178] It was during this time, that Hardit made a decision to have an adapted flying helmet created, one that would fit over the turban. He approached a hatter in Piccadilly who expanded the sides of the helmet and elongated the goggle straps, thereby fulfilling the regulations required by the RFC. Though there are a number of photographs of Hardit standing next to planes or indeed inside the cockpit during his flying career, only one features this headgear, which is a pity, though entirely understandable from the point of view of a proud Sikh. It's also the case that on some later flight operations he wore only the turban with flying goggles, as fellow member of 28 squadron Norman Macmillan remembered from their time together in Italy.[179]

Hardit was part of a congenial group of cadets who shared the same Nissen hut at Vendôme, going out on jaunts into the French countryside and dining at the *Hotel du Commerce*, where they enjoyed excellent cuisine and occasional flirting with the pretty waitresses. Harold Boston was another member of that party who remembered his time in the Loire fondly also:

> We were lucky, the French countryside was at its loveliest with weather to match. No signs of the war activities in which all England seemed to be absorbed – and our spare time, between lectures and flying, was spent in bathing in the local rivers and streams. I especially remember the luscious cherries which grew profusely in all the hedges as it was now summertime.

178. Skeet, M., *'RFC Pilot Training'*, - www.theaerodrome.com – accessed 1 July 2020
179. Macmillan, N., *'Offensive Patrol'* (Jarrolds Publishers: London, 1973), p. 62

A narrow-gauge roadside railway near our aerodrome took us to a neighbouring village. It was drawn by a jubilant little tank engine and ran so close to the trees that as it flew along, rocking from side to side, it was our pleasure to snatch at the ripe cherries which dangled from many trees, some of which were just within our reach and, my recollection tells me, were the most delicious ever grown since the world began.[180]

Under Captain Carr's tuition, Hardit seemingly passed with ease the basic flying tests during his month in the Loire, waiting with anticipation to be posted to the next phase of his development as a pilot: advanced flying training in Britain. Having graduated from the RNAS Flight Training School Vendôme, he was initially given permission to report to RFC Headquarters in Duke Street, London, after taking a few days leave in Paris.

There was one unexpected delay however, which remains unexplained. As Hardit was about to depart, he was called before the school commander Captain Briggs on a charge of having 'broken all the rules I have made for this aerodrome'. A nonplussed cadet asked for clarification, but was given none, Briggs insisting that he repeat many of the flight tests and doubling down on the trainee by cancelling his leave. A furious Hardit confronted Carr, who was outwardly equally bewildered by Briggs' behaviour and the two of them went through the flight trials once more. Having successfully completed the course, the still incensed Hardit recklessly took an extra couple of days leave in Paris, before blagging his way to another two weeks on returning to London.

His next posting came on 24 June, to Filton in Gloucestershire, north of the city of Bristol, to join 62 Squadron of the RFC. During the early part of his training, Hardit was earmarked by his flight instructor Captain Chadwick as a fighter pilot - he had good hands, excellent reflexes and a steady nerve. He was taught to fly a number of different aircraft including the Avro 504, the Sopwith Pup and the Bristol Scout chiefly among them, though given a choice, his preferred plane was the 'stable and dependable' B.E.2c.[181] Initially, Hardit flew with Chadwick on dual controls once more,

180. Boston, W.H., 'Some Memoirs of An Unknown Pilot in The Royal Flying Corps and Royal Air Force 1917-1918', p. 7
181. Malik, H.S., 'A Little Work, A Little Play', p. 74

which he found rather frustrating, but he kept his head down, forming a good working relationship with his instructor, who in actuality was not a good deal older than himself. After a couple more hours flying together, Hardit began the first of a regular series of often nerve-wracking solo flights, for in reality, the unspoken consensus of RFC instructors before autumn 1917, was that students had a better chance of becoming good pilots if they taught themselves. This amounted to a tacit admission that there was little that an instructor could teach beyond the rudiments of taking off, turning, simple manoeuvres and landing.[182] So it was, that Hardit went solo for the first of what would amount to twenty-four hours flying unaccompanied. Journalist Somnath Sapru, who interviewed Hardit in the 1970s and early 80s, described that first flight:

(Hardit) climbed in and for a moment a terrible sense of loneliness gripped him. With a roar the Gnome engine caught and he turned the machine 'till he was facing the patch that would give the Avro 504 enough distance to take off. Soon, his speed increased and when he judged it was the right moment, he eased the stick back and suddenly felt the loss of a sense of touch with the ground. He was airborne. But it was just a momentary aside in his thoughts – which were a jumble. He had to gain height. He levelled and banked and did one circuit over the airfield and then headed off in a westerly direction.

The altimeter read 2000 feet. The speed was only 60 mph. The machine was under his, and only his control. What an exhilarating feeling! He tried out the rudder bar, banked to the right and then left and finally gained a little more height. He wondered if he could dive a little and put the nose down. The scream of the Gnome and the oil spitting out. The speed reached 80 and then 85. The Avro 504 was by now vibrating a good deal and he decided that he'd had enough.

Gliding down with utter concentration, he held the stick tight and then heard the unmistakeable thud as he touched the ground. He steadied her roll and was soon taxiing towards

182. Skeet, M., *'RFC Pilot Training'*, - www.theaerodrome.com – accessed 1 July 2020

Captain Chadwick. He crawled the last bit and soon stopped. For a minute, all was quiet. He felt a sense of detachment and then suddenly panic. Had he done everything all right?[183]

On 13 July, Hardit Singh Malik was awarded his 'Wings' by the RFC after almost three months of training and the recommendation of Captain Chadwick. He was now a qualified Flying Officer and able to sew the revered cloth badge onto his uniform.[184]

Whilst at Filton with 62 Squadron, Hardit renewed acquaintance with an old friend that he had met whilst golfing during his time at Balliol. It was another reminder of the power of both sport and association with the University of Oxford to facilitate lifelong friendships. Randal, 8th Earl of Berkeley, who had been born in 1865, was a chemist, a Friend of the Royal Society and an enthusiastic golfer. In 1893, he bought a house at Foxcombe on Boar's Hill, just outside Oxford, where he established a small laboratory, the better to carry out his work. He laid out a golf course at Foxcombe, a replica of the greens at the family seat, Berkeley Castle in Gloucestershire, and it was to this historic house that Hardit flew the fifteen or so miles from nearby Filton to renew acquaintances shortly after receiving his wings.[185] Somnath Sapru later described the newly qualified flying officer's arrival at Berkeley Castle. The Earl, his family and indeed the whole village seemed to have turned out to welcome him:

> Malik at the controls of the B.E.2c selected a meadow near the castle, put down the plane into the wind and brought it down to a smooth landing. By this time, the entire population of the village including the Mayor, in his top hat, arrived to see the plane. Champagne was brought out and toasts were offered to Malik.

> (After this short initial visit) [...] he got ready to take off, someone turned the propeller and with a roar the engine caught

---

183. Sapru, S., '*Sky Hawks*', pp. 174-176
184. Occasionally, 'wings' were only permitted to be worn after flying-in-action during the First World War, or at the other extreme, merely after a solo flight. It seems to have been dependent on a squadron commander's discretion, amongst other factors.
185. Hartley, H., 'Randal Thomas Mowbray Rawdon Berkeley, Earl of Berkeley. 1865-1942' *Obituary Notices of Fellows of the Royal Society'*, vol. 4, no. 11, 1942, pp. 167–182, www.jstor.org - accessed 29 June 2020

and the last glimpse that Malik had on take-off was the look of surprise on the faces of the villagers at the strong wind raised by the slipstream of the propeller. The first casualty of this was the Mayor's top hat![186]

Having taken a good deal longer than the usual practice flight duration, Hardit hoped to escape the attentions of Captain Chadwick on his return, in spite of the fact they had already become good friends. It was rather typical of Hardit that he should have formed such a close bond with a senior officer, who, having 'pretended to be angry', was apparently mollified by the offer of tea with the Earl and rather impressed by Hardit's social connections.[187]

It's obvious that Hardit thought a great deal of Berkeley, who was something of a great raconteur as well as a polymath and amateur golfer. During his time at Filton, Hardit would spend much of his leave with the Earl, the two meeting at various times to play golf together. During a trip to North Berwick, on the Scottish east coast, however, a more unpleasant incident took place over dinner. One of the other invited guests was a man called Gardiner who held a position of authority locally in coastal defence. During the evening, Gardiner took the Earl of Berkeley aside and explained to him that although he was sorry, he was required to ask Hardit to leave North Berwick. Gardiner continued to say to an increasingly astounded Berkeley, that under the terms of the 'Defence of the Realm Act' directives, no 'foreigner' could stay within three miles of the coast. A scene ensued in which the indignant host demanded an apology from Gardiner, explaining that his guest held a commission and was a flying officer in the RFC and could in no way be described in such terms. The demanded apology was not forthcoming and the dinner party broke up abruptly in some acrimony.[188] The infuriated Earl took up Hardit's case again several days later with the area naval commander and received a belated apology. To Gardiner, Hardit, as a 'person of colour' was de facto an 'alien', as we have seen, and in spite of his honorary commission, his friendships with Captains and Earls and his recent flying qualification, he was not able to enjoy the status of fellow officers owing to the colour of his skin therefore. Indeed, in the eyes of

---

186. Sapru, S., 'Sky Hawks', p. 221
187. Malik, H.S., 'A Little Work, A Little Play', p. 75
188. Sapru, S., 'Sky Hawks', p. 173

zealous custodians of military law such as Gardiner, Hardit was viewed at best as a 'foreigner', or at worst a potential 'enemy alien'.

Following the award of his wings, it was to Yatesbury he went to join 28 Squadron, sometime soon after 23 July. That was the date of the unit's arrival at the Wiltshire aerodrome, some thirty-five miles east of Filton, close to the small town of Calne and the Neolithic stone circle at Avebury. This was a definite step towards war preparedness for the squadron and in doing so, it replaced 55 Training Squadron, which went in the opposite direction.[189]

28 Squadron was to be the formation with which Hardit would go to war and into combat with. It was designated a 'Higher Training Squadron', one in which cadets were encouraged to fly every day and to develop the advanced skills they would require in combat. Whereas at the elementary training squadron all flying had been basic in nature, involving little more than circuits of the airfield and landings, higher training broadened the scope considerably, instructors regularly sending cadets on distance trips cross-country. Some flights required the students to climb above 8,000 feet, while others were devoted to specific activities such as observation, aerial navigation, the interpretation of ground-based signals from the air, and even bombing practice.[190]

Yatesbury, on the Wiltshire Downs, was a relatively desolate spot, having only hangars, Nissen huts and a grass landing ground. Hardit trained on the Avro 504 and a number of other different scouts: the Nieuport, the Bristol Scout, the Sopwith Pup and the de Haviland DH.5. He was expected to become proficient in flying a number of different aircraft, able to hone his skills, prepared for any eventualities required of a fighter pilot. During that August of 1917, he practised 'looping the loop', spinning, rolling and what was known as the 'Immelmann turn'.[191] The training was intense, nerve wracking and occasionally dangerous, but it was during this period, through mastering these proficiencies, that his confidence grew steadily. Hardit knew that without these skills, his life over the Western Front would be a short one.

---

189. Royal Air Force Operations Record Book – Appendices, 28 Squadron, TNA, AIR-27-335_1, p. 2
190. Skeet, M., *'RFC Pilot Training'*, - www.theaerodrome.com – accessed 1 July 2020
191. The term 'Immelmann turn', was named after German First World War Eindecker fighter ace Leutnant Max Immelmann, and referred to a sharp rudder turn off a vertical zoom climb (almost to a full stall).

On 29 August, Hardit travelled to attend 2 (Auxiliary) School of Aerial Gunnery at Turnberry on the west coast of Scotland. Here trainee pilots were given first-hand experience of live air-to-air and air-to-ground gunnery, something not provided for hitherto in training. A number of the pilots from 28 Squadron stayed in the adjacent hotel and its famous golf courses. Inevitably, there were rounds to be played at Turnberry and a chance encounter with professional Tom Fernie, who had been invalided out of the war when wounded in 1915, ensured that Hardit's clubs rarely lay dormant during his free time from the school. In spite of his wounds, Fernie collected the Scottish Open Championship five times and finished a creditable fifth place in the British Open of 1923. Hardit found him to be a charming companion, revelling in the challenge of taking on one of the best competitors in Britain.

He arrived back at Yatesbury on 17 September to find that 28 Squadron was undergoing a significant change, with a good deal of excitement evident amongst the pilots who had been left behind.[192] The squadron had been the first in the RFC to be re-equipped with a new scout – the Sopwith Camel, a machine by reputation as difficult as any to fly. Nothing else in the air prepared the pilots for the demands it would place on them, each day during September heralding the arrival of one or two of the new planes. By the end of the war, the Camel was credited with having destroyed more enemy aircraft than any other in the hands of pilots of the RFC and RNAS.[193] It would be in this plane that Hardit would take on enemy aircraft during the 'Second Battle of Passchendaele', that coming October.

His first flight in a Camel took place on 19 September, a brief sortie of twenty minutes around the airfield, after the instructor had shown him around the cockpit.[194] The Camel was powered by a single rotary engine and was armed with twin synchronised Vickers machine guns which could not be moved around, and the plane had literally to be pointed at the target before opening fire. Though difficult to handle, it was highly manoeuvrable in the hands of an experienced pilot, a vital attribute in the relatively low-speed, low-altitude dogfights of the era. 28 Squadron records during the end

---

192. General Papers (Correspondence) Returns and Courts of Enquiries, 1916-17 in 28 Squadron, Officers' Confidential Reports, January 1917- January 1919, TNA, AIR 1/1854/204/213/12, 19 September 1917
193. Ralph, W.D., '*Barker VC*' (Grub Street: London, 1997), p. 79
194. AIR 1/1854/204/213/12, 20 September 1917

of September and early October, bear witness to Hardit's increasing time in the cockpit as he remembered:

> The Sopwith Camels were considered to be the best fighting machines in the RFC at the time, because of their high manoeuvrability. In the Camel's cockpit, the pilot, who wore only his flying helmet, was totally exposed with no protection from rain, hail, sleet, snow or bullets, only a small windshield protected him from headwind created by his plane's flight. He had no parachute or wireless telephone.[195] [196]

The 2 October brought a new arrival to the squadron, one who would have a significant impact on everyone, not least Hardit. Captain William Barker was a Canadian from Manitoba, an experienced observer and pilot who had fought in the Somme and Arras battles. During much of 1917, he was on reconnaissance and artillery spotting duties with 15 Squadron, gaining such a reputation for the effectiveness of his work and the courage with which it was executed, that he earned a bar to his Military Cross and was promoted to the rank of Captain commanding a 'Flight' of aircraft. RFC squadrons had three flights, consisting of four to six planes each, depending on overall strength and the number of available aircraft. Having a full strength squadron of eighteen planes was not unusual, emphasis being placed on maintaining a full complement of pilots. The commander was generally a Major, flight commanders were generally Captains. Captain Barker was given command of both C Flight and the only Sikh pilot in the RFC, who from the outset Barker referred to warmly, though predictably, as the 'Indian Prince or Rajah'.[197]

Normally, a newly arriving pilot, even at the rank of Captain, like Barker, would not have been expected to have been promoted to flight commander immediately, but as Hardit remembered 'a most outstanding youngster called White [...] crashed and died before we left for France'.[198]

---

195. Malik, H.S., *'A Little Work, A Little Play'*, p. 77
196. Pilots in the Royal Flying Corps, however, were not issued with parachutes. Initially the design of cockpits meant there was barely room for the pilot and no room for a bulky parachute. The extra weight of the parachute was also said to have had a negative effect on the plane's fuel efficiency and handling. Unofficially however, parachutes were seen as being an easy escape route for pilots if their plane ran into difficulty.
197. Ralph, W.D., *'Barker VC'*, p. 3
198. Malik, H.S., *'A Little Work, A Little Play'*, p. 78

This 'youngster' was actually twenty-year-old Captain L.S. White, who was killed on 28 September, when he lost control of the aircraft, crashing into the ground near Wantage when delivering a new Camel to the squadron. White had been the commander of C Flight and Barker was immediately promoted into his place, his reputation in the RFC securing the advancement.[199] However, Barker's instant elevation had consequences for increasingly poor relationships within the squadron. Personality conflict was not unknown between aggressive pilots and the promotion infuriated the well-liked and experienced officer, Lieutenant James 'Mitch' Mitchell, who had previously been earmarked for command of C Flight. Mitchell continued to hold a grudge against Barker, in spite of being promoted to command of his own flight a little later. Barker's forceful personality also created a tense relationship with 28 Squadron commander Major Glanville before the unit arrived in France.[200] There was tension between the two at the first meeting and Barker usually worked around, rather than through Glanville for operational planning, something which would have consequences for Hardit later in October.[201] Barker's arrival also exacerbated existing animosity between the British pilots and those from the Dominions, quite a number of whom were Barker's fellow countrymen. Hardit made no mention of these personality clashes and no doubt tried to maintain a studied neutrality, but although it can be described as an effective unit in the air during his time with it, 28 Squadron was not a harmonious unit on the ground.

Meanwhile, as Hardit's training was progressing during the summer of 1917, the issue of granting King's Commissions to Indians reached the highest level of government. Two days after his enlistment at South Farnborough at the end of March, the relatively new Prime Minister Lloyd George assembled his new cabinet. The recruitment of Indians to fight on behalf of the Empire was on the agenda:

> The Cabinet further considered a telegram, dated the 28th March, 1917, which the Secretary of State for India had sent to the Indian Government, urging the latter to raise another

199. Ralph, W.D., 'Barker VC', p. 75
200. Ibid.
201. Ibid.

100,000 men, to be ready at any rate by the spring of 1918, and, with this object in view, to tap fresh sources of recruiting and to improve its recruitment methods.[202]

In this telegram, the then Secretary of State for India Austen Chamberlain, explained that additional recruitment of *sepoys* was to be primarily directed to relieve British troops in India, Mesopotamia, or Egypt. It was also brought to the attention of the cabinet that such an increase in the numbers would create an additional difficulty: securing sufficient officers of the highest standard to meet the demand. Chamberlain explained that the solution was being discussed with the GOI, with definite proposals expected to be laid before the cabinet before long.[203] In the light of the large casualties sustained by the Empire at the Somme, the matter was becoming urgent:

> You will understand the necessity for exerting the maximum strength of the Empire is so great that every means that can be devised should be employed, and that all possible sources of recruitment thoroughly examined afresh.[204]

However, Chamberlain's time as Secretary of State at the India Office was coming to an end. Following the investigation into the acute failings of the Mesopotamian campaign (undertaken by the Indian Army) in 1915-16, including the loss of the British garrison following the end of the Siege of Kut, Chamberlain resigned his post on 17 July, as the minister ultimately responsible. He was widely acclaimed for such a principled act, but before leaving his position, he wrote to the War Office on 1 June explaining the progress that had been made jointly in relation to granting King's Commissions to Indians by his own department and the GOI. The War Office had long opposed such commissions and Chamberlain knew that ongoing communication with the Army Council would need to be particularly persuasive:

> In view of the difficulty of supplying sufficient officers of pure European descent to the Indian Army, of the effect on

---

202. Imperial War Cabinet, Agenda and Minutes, TNA, CAB-23-40-6, 30 March 1917
203. Ibid.
204. Ibid., Chamberlain to Cabinet, 28 March 1917

recruiting of the racial bar, of the Government of India's strong recommendations, of the widespread demand in India for higher military employment for Indians, and of India's services to the Empire during the war, Mr Chamberlain is convinced that the time has arrived when the principle of the granting of King's Commissions to Indians must be admitted.[205]

The response from the War Office dated 5 July was uncompromising:

> [...] I am commanded by the <u>Army Council</u> to inform you that after the most careful consideration, they have come to the conclusion that to grant commissions to natives of India would entail great risk from a military point of view, in that it involves placing native Indian officers in a position where they would be entitled to command European officers. For this reason, the Council are not prepared to take the responsibility of advising such a step.
>
> The Council further suggest that the question might be deferred for consideration at the close of the war, together with many other Imperial matters affecting the Army as a whole, all of which will then be brought forward for review.[206]

It's difficult to escape the conclusion that the Army Council was only interested in obstruction and delay, particularly when after the war, the subject of commissions would not be urgent. For both Chamberlain, and his successor Edwin Montagu, who took over as Secretary of State for India on 17 July, the issue was one of principle, and the matter *was* an urgent one. Three days after taking up his post, Montagu circulated a memorandum to the cabinet, determined to pick up the baton where his predecessor had left off. This briefing paper had been compiled by Chamberlain, and Montagu made it clear that he was in accord with his predecessor on the matter. The granting of King's Commissions to Indians would need to be pushed through cabinet in spite of any reservations the Army Council might have.

---

205. Indian Reforms, Grant of Commissions to Indians, TNA, CAB-24-20-80, Chamberlain to War Office, 1 June 1917
206. Ibid., War Office to India Office, 5 July 1917

Without change at the highest level, potential officer recruits such as Hardit Singh would never have the right to equal status with British officers. The memorandum laid before cabinet members on 3 August, set out a series of proposals issued by the GOI, which outlined ways in which Indians might access King's Commissioned Officer status:

    (i)   by qualifying as a cadet through the Military College, Sandhurst, or under the regulation prescribed for British University candidates through a University which has established a suitable course of military instruction and has been approved by the Army Council;

    (ii)   by the selection of especially capable and deserving Indian officers or non-commissioned officers of Indian regiments, who have either been promoted from the ranks or joined their regiments on direct appointment as Jemadars, and who have gone through a course of instruction at a military school in India;

    (iii)   by the bestowal of honorary British commissions on Indian officers who have rendered distinguished service, but whose age and lack of education preclude their being considered for King's commissions under (ii).[207]

Indeed, the GOI had already begun the process, nine Viceroy's Commissioned Officers had been recommended for King's Commissioned Officer status, in recognition of their service during the war. Edwin Montagu added his own reasons for supporting the GOI's proposals in an accompanying cabinet paper:

> I maintain that it is absolutely impossible to tell an Indian that he may control the destinies of Englishmen if he becomes a judge or an Indian Civilian, that to the talking people and to the politicians all avenues are open, but that if he fights for the

---

207. War Cabinet and Cabinet Memoranda, Commissions for Indians, Correspondence between India Office and Indian Government, TNA, CAB-24-49-28, despatch from the Government of India, 3 August 1917

Empire, he can never expect to hold a position of authority. I ask the Cabinet to sanction an announcement that the Cabinet has decided to accept in principle the appointment of Indians to Commissioned rank in His Majesty's Army.[208]

Montagu was under no illusion however, that the process would be a difficult one in the face of opposition from the Army Council, influential members of the cabinet and officers in the British and Indian Armies. He was also mindful that the proposals were an unhappy compromise, offering neither authentic command of British 'Tommies' by Indian officers and therefore distasteful to even moderate Indian opinion, whilst at the same time galvanising the support of those opposed to any further expansion of the project. He therefore felt compelled to offer reassurances to the cabinet about the GOI's proposals:

> In case the objection is urged that these men, if granted commissions, may be placed in a position in which they might have to issue commands to Australian troops (or even British troops for the present) I may say that I do not think that this is a contingency that need be apprehended. We are all anxious to make the scheme a success, and I should propose to give the Government of India a hint to prevent any risk of the kind that might jeopardise the prospects of the new departure.[209] [210]

Upon taking office, Edwin Montagu was aware that in India the home rule movements' activities were gaining ground, resulting in increasingly repressive reprisals from the GOI, which only served to harden the attitudes of the agitators and strengthen their resolve to resist. Annie Besant was arrested in June and later the next month, Bal Gangadhar Tilak and Mohandas Gandhi began to compile a petition aimed at collecting a million

---

208. Grant of Commission to Indians – Montagu E.S., TNA, CAB-24-21-87, 1 August 1917
209. The aim of the scheme was to enable Indian King's Commissioned Officers to serve alongside their British peers commanding the Indian rank-and-file in Indian regiments in the first instance. Montagu knew that the concept of 'natives' commanding British troops was the main sticking point for the Army Council, though British officers in Indian regiments were hardly enthusiastic about any such schemes.
210. CAB-24-21-87, 1 August 1917

signatures in favour of home rule. Montagu had long known he would have to act, and on 20 August he signalled a change in policy, by adopting a more conciliatory tone.[211]

The 'Montagu Declaration' would set out the underlying vision for India's political future, leading ultimately to the Montagu-Chelmsford Report of 8 July 1918. Included in this report would be the proposals put forward by the Secretaries of State for India, Chamberlain and Montagu, to the cabinet about granting King's Commissions to Indians. In turn, this report became the basis for the Government of India Act 1919.[212] At its core, the importance of the Montagu Declaration, was that from now on, the demand for home rule or self-government could no longer be treated as seditious:

> The policy of His Majesty's Government [...] is that of the increasing association of Indians in every branch of the administration and the gradual development of self-governing institutions, with a view to the progressive realisation of responsible government in India as an integral part of the British Empire.[213]

The details of these political developments and the responses to them, both in Britain and India, go beyond the scope of this work. Yet, between the Montagu Declaration and the passing of the Government of India Act in December 1919, Hardit Singh's case as a serving Honorary commissioned officer in the RFC and RAF would both challenge and reflect the tensions on the path towards the possibility of granting King's Commissions to Indians.

As Edwin Montagu stood up in the House of Commons to deliver his Declaration, Hardit was about to leave for gunnery training at Turnberry. He would soon be going to war.

211. Chandra, B., 'India's Struggle for Independence', pp. 167-168
212. Frederic John Napier Thesiger, 1st Viscount Chelmsford was Viceroy of India from 1916 to 1921.
213. Chandra, B., *India's Struggle for Independence*, p. 168

Chapter 7

Droglandt
October–December 1917

'When God protects the true devotee, no magic or enemy can
cause any damage to him.'

Sant Attar Singh Ji, *Life Story*

Hardit was a frustrated man. The other pilots of 28 Squadron had departed
for France in their Sopwith Camels, leaving him alone, pacing up and down
outside the hangar at Lympne aerodrome in Kent, to the west of Folkestone.
In January 1917, its airfield had been designated as 8 Aircraft Acceptance
Park for delivery of aircraft to, and reception from, the Western Front.
The whole RFC seemingly passed through Lympne at one time or another
and this morning it was the turn of those flying in from Yatesbury. It was
8 October, a cold Monday morning, the first to see a severe temperature
drop that autumn.[214]

What should have been a perfunctory stopover to take on fuel and to
undergo final technical checks before the Channel crossing, was being
prolonged for Hardit's Camel alone. A piece of the wire rigging, which
braced the wings had come loose. In other circumstances, in another plane,
on a shorter flight, Hardit might have risked accompanying the squadron,
it had happened before. But he wasn't willing to gamble on this day of all
days, in a plane as notoriously difficult to fly. The other pilots led by Barker
had headed to St Omer in northern France an hour earlier and Hardit became
increasingly impatient as he waited for the engine fitter to complete his work.
Adding to his irritation was the fact that he was nervous, something which

---

214. According to the squadron logbook, this flight took place on 8 October. Barker's letters
home contradict this fact, stating 10 October as the date.

had come as a surprise that morning, to his usually phlegmatic self. There was excitement too, but the tension he was feeling had even angered him a little. He'd seen pilots killed, badly burnt and maimed during training and he thought he knew something of the dangers. Like many young men going off to war, he managed to make light of, or erase from immediate thought, any consideration of the risks. Yet, the training begun in freezing Aldershot back in April had led inevitably to this moment. He'd managed to send off letters to Eastbourne and London the previous day, able to disguise the fact of his imminent departure from the prying eyes of the military censor. He was reflecting that it was the valedictory tone of this correspondence, which had initiated his sense of unease, when suddenly the nod of approval was forthcoming from the engine fitter.

He forced his way into the tiny cockpit, behind the joystick on which were located various switches.[215] This shaft controlled the fore and aft, as well as lateral movement of the plane. Hardit had very little protection from the elements behind the tiny windscreen, though it did provide some relief from the continuous headwind created by the plane's flight.[216] To combat the cold, he pulled up the red scarf he wore under the collar of his 'Sidcot Suit' which had been developed only recently during the winter of 1916. This one-piece khaki twill outer with a rubberized cotton and fur lining, had a large buttoned chest flap, open pockets on the knees and buttons at the wrist and ankles. It had been issued to Hardit on his arrival at Yatesbury and was a significant improvement on the leather sheepskin-lined jerkin and trousers he'd worn at Filton. Cursing slightly under his breath, he promptly slipped on the oversize flying helmet and goggles and then pulled the heavy sheepskin gauntlets over his woollen mitts.[217] Hardit made eye contact with the engine fitter and nodded, the signal for the ignition procedure to begin, and which ended with the word 'contact', at which Hardit threw the ignition switch and the engine fitter pulled down hard on the propeller for the rotary engine to burst into life in a billow of white smoke.

Following an uneventful forty minute flight, Hardit approached Clairmarais aerodrome, east of St Omer. As he circled the airfield, he recognised the distinctive markings and livery of the olive drab fuselages

215. Sapru, S., 'Sky Hawks', pp. 178-179
216. Ibid.
217. Boston, W.H., 'Some Memoirs of An Unknown Pilot in The Royal Flying Corps and Royal Air Force 1917-1918', p. 2

of 28 Squadron's Camels parked in a neat row besides the hangar. On the right side of the upper wing and either side of the fuselage was a large white square, the distinctive squadron marking. Towards the tail on either side could be found the number of each plane, Hardit's own machine was numbered B3887, and it had a much larger number '5' on both sides, just behind the cockpit. The red, white and blue RFC roundels completed the iconic appearance of a British biplane during the First World War.

Clairmarais airfield was L-shaped and on a slope, with a ten foot hedge on one side and tall trees along another. Hardit swore to himself, aimed at the one responsible for designing such a landing ground, as he began to make the final approach. By now, this had become a routine operation and one he had made tens of time before, but perhaps owing to nerves, or the newness of the aerodrome, he came in too rapidly, having to open the throttle to overfly the grass strip and another large hedge beyond it. He circled once more determined to correct the basic error, and to his incredulity, was forced to stay airborne following a second aborted attempted landing. By now he had noticed that a larger crowd had assembled outside the hangar entrance, and that one of them was holding out a large handkerchief to highlight the fact that Hardit was landing the plane dangerously downwind. This was now embarrassing and at the third attempt he landed the aircraft.

The other pilots had lunched and were now waiting impatiently for the 'Prince' to catch them up, before the last leg of their flight to the front line. As Hardit taxied his machine towards them, he knew what was in store, and sure enough, Mitchell, Fenton and Shanks broke away, jeering as the Camel came to a halt. For a while, they teased him mercilessly, to which Hardit could only retort lamely, that it took a real pilot to land downwind. Aside from the frivolity, he noticed Barker's stony face emerge from a Nissen hut. The commander of C Flight had only been with the squadron just over a week and yet it was he, rather than Major Glanville, the squadron commander, who had led them across the Channel.[218]

After an overnight stay, accompanied by the usual inedible RFC meals, Hardit got back into the cockpit and followed Barker into the air. 28 Squadron was bound for French Flanders, to a *commune* adjacent to the Belgian border. Droglandt was a small aerodrome which would be their home base for the next three weeks. It lay fifteen miles west of the city of Ypres and its infamous salient,

---

218. Ralph, W.D., *'Barker VC'*, p. 76

with the well-known town of Poperinge lying halfway between. The pilots of 28 Squadron were not thrilled by what they found at Droglandt. The landing ground had been a small orchard which had been cleared, but during October, the strip had become a boggy marsh, in spite of the cinders which had been laid over it, and with the wind in one direction landing was always to be difficult.

Hardit shared one of the several Nissen huts with three other officers, the best billets having been secured by the members of 32 Squadron who were by now well embedded, having arrived in Flanders at the beginning of July. The facilities were basic to say the least and reminded Hardit of the conditions at Aldershot. This time was different however, they were at war, and the knowledge that the infantry was a short distance away suffering far worse conditions in the front line put the state of the Droglandt washing facilities into a different perspective. Hardit also noticed from the time of their arrival that the atmosphere in the officers' mess, which was positioned within a thatched enclosure, was noticeably quieter than at Yatesbury.

The Third Battle of Ypres was coming to an end. Inaccurately, but better known in Britain as the battle for Passchendaele, the assaults by British and allied forces to break out of the confines of the salient east of the Belgian city would last from 31 July to 2 December 1917. The offensive began with encouraging gains, but terrible late summer weather soon bogged the offensive down. By August, the assault was clearly failing in its objectives and had descended into attritional fighting. In spite of attempting to apply new techniques of waging war learned at the Somme, progress was agonisingly slow for the British, at enormous cost in casualties. Bad weather in October led to the battlefield becoming an impossible quagmire. 28 Squadron's arrival at Droglandt positioned it ready to support the final push for the Passchendaele ridge, what became known in the formal terminology, as the 'Second Battle for Passchendaele' beginning on 26 October. The weather for the first week or so of 28 Squadron's stay in the sector was appalling, making it impossible for anything other than test and practice flights. Although this delayed the long awaited going into action, adding to the nerves of some, it was a mixed blessing overall, enabling a settling in period with time to identify landmarks and the varied course of the trench lines around 'Wipers'.[219] This was of benefit, for the majority of the squadron's

219. AIR-27-335_1, p. 2

pilots were on active service for the first time. Nonetheless, the first loss came as a shock, when Lieutenant Winter failed to return from a practice flight on 11 October, it being presumed that he had been ambushed by a formation of <u>Albatros</u> scouts while preoccupied with the lie of the land and shot down.[220]

Although he only joined 28 Squadron on 2 October, Captain William Barker seems to have made a significant impression on Hardit:

> I soon got to know him quite well and came to admire him, though in many ways he was a tough nut. Our Squadron was commanded by Glanville, an old regular, quiet, colourless, and quite ineffective as a Squadron Leader. Barker soon established himself as the real leader, both with the pilots and with those up the hierarchy. He would take up two pilots at a time over the lines and initiate them into the intricacies of fighting in the air. He himself practised a great deal, flying whenever he could to acquaint himself with the whole area. This was of vital importance when many pilots were shot down before they had become accustomed to the light. The enemy often came out of the sun, or manoeuvred themselves into the blind spot under the enemy pilot's tail, therefore being difficult to spot.[221]

Barker's arrival and attitude to combat was to have a major influence on Hardit's RFC career. He made an immediate impression upon arrival at Droglandt, when the squadron's three flight commanders were met by high-ranking officers. In spite of having only been on the ground for an hour, permission was given for a sortie to view the allied lines, but not to cross no-man's land. It was Barker who disobeyed this order, crossing deeply into the German sector and then diving at twenty-two enemy Albatros planes, taking his fellow flight commanders with him. After a short but tense dog fight, all returned back safely to Droglandt, but Barker had laid down an aggressive marker, which was not only for the attention of the Germans. As a member of the Canadian's C Flight, Hardit had duly taken note. It was going to be a testing time.

---

220. Ibid.
221. Malik, H.S., 'A Little Work, A Little Play', p. 82

The weather continued to be poor during the first half of October, hampering the infantry assaults on the ground and the ability of pilots to get airborne. There was no wireless or radar communication and when visibility was bad, pilots used their compasses in conjunction with an increasing knowledge of landmarks in their sector. Between 10 and 12 October, Hardit was posted temporarily to 23 Squadron with some of the other rookie pilots. This squadron had been in theatre for some time and such temporary postings enabled the newcomers to learn the ropes and to talk to fellow pilots about the opposition, local conditions and landmarks. It was during this time, that the squadrons were given an update about progress, or lack thereof, being made by the infantry. Thereafter, 28 Squadron busied itself for the most part with mock battles, target practice and with enemy plane identification, adding only to the tension of those who had never seen combat.

Hardit's first flight over the German lines in action occurred on 18 October, when each of the three flight commanders took off accompanied by two other pilots. The aim of this combined sortie with 32 Squadron was to patrol the front lines, with the Camels protecting the slow and clumsy R.E.8 planes carrying out their primary role of spotting for the artillery on the ground, in preparation for the next major assault in the salient. Between 1000 and 1100 hours that morning, Hardit fired off several long-range bursts at enemy aircraft to no avail, knowing that the only way to make a kill was to get up close, yet coming into contact with the enemy for the first time relieved the tension somewhat.

The following day, 19 October, C Flight took to the air once more, a pair of aircraft at a time, the visibility once more truly appalling. Much time that day was spent preparing for the first big 'show' the following day, when 28 Squadron would go into action alongside 70 and 23 Squadrons. The aim of the operation was to make a combined attack against the important German aerodrome at Rumbeke, close to Roulers.[222] Rumbeke was the home of Jasta 2, the German squadron named after its now posthumous commander Oswald Boelcke.[223] The raid was an ambitious one for the relative newcomers, though taking part in a large formation of over seventy

---

222. Neale, D., 'Whatsoever you may do – 28 Squadron RFC and RAF', in the journal of the *Society of First World War Aviation Historians*, Vol. 31 2 2000, pp. 61-88

223. Jasta 2 (also known as Jasta Boelcke) was one of the best-known German Luftstreitkräfte squadrons in the First World War. Its first commanding officer was the great aerial tactician Oswald Boelcke.

aircraft offered some protection, yet once dogfights began there were few places to hide. The machines employed in the operation would be required in both fighter and ground attack roles, and while 70 Squadron was tasked with bombing the aerodrome, those of 23 Squadron were to patrol at high altitude and pick off enemy fighters. Hardit's task with 28 Squadron was to sweep around as far to the east as possible and surprise those Germans sent up to engage the bombers. That morning, he took up Camel B3887 alone at 1000 hours on a short test flight, perhaps uncertain about its performance. Reassured, he left Droglandt at 1110 hours, part of the entire squadron complement of eighteen machines, under the command of Captain Barker.

> It was a tremendous thrill to be part of such a large formation, over fifty planes, all looking for Germans. We soon ran into a small party of them, taking them by surprise. Shooting started and there was considerable confusion. Our planes and those of the Germans got hopelessly mixed up. There were bullets flying in all directions. We had been instructed that each pilot was to pick out one particular target, and I soon found myself diving on the tail of an enemy who, instead of turning back to attack me, kept on diving. He must have been as frightened as I was! I must have started shooting from too great a distance, for at first nothing seemed to happen. But suddenly I hit him and first his plane started to smoke, and then went down spinning in flames.[224]

Meanwhile, the raid on the Rumbeke aerodrome was going well. The bombing attack had gone in at a height of 400 feet, falling on the Albatros D.Vs lined up on the airfield, whilst other munitions burst in the hangars and sheds. This was followed by the Camels of 70 Squadron firing at the ground crews and into the hangars and buildings from low level.[225] As Hardit followed down his falling victim, he could see the black smoke issuing from the burning buildings in the distance, but he had other more pressing considerations to attend to. He had dropped too low and needed to climb quickly if he wasn't to share the same fate. There was nothing

224. Malik, H. S., 'A Little Work, A Little Play', p. 84
225. Guttman, J., 'Sopwith Camel' (Osprey Publishing: Oxford, 2012), p. 83

more vulnerable than a machine close to the ground from an attack from above and his Camel was also isolated. Fortunately, Barker had spotted his predicament and brought C Flight down to his aid. The six of them climbed back to a safer altitude and headed for Droglandt.

For Hardit however, the excitement of his first day of serious aerial combat wasn't over. On the way back, he encountered some desultory anti-aircraft fire from the German positions below. He thought nothing of this until he began his landing procedure at 1235 hours, an hour and twenty-five minutes after taking off:

> I found to my horror that when I tried to straighten out from the mild dive while approaching the airfield, there was no response when I pulled the joystick back to flatten out. So, I dived straight into the ground and my plane broke into three pieces. I found myself still strapped in my seat, with that section of the plane upside down, the petrol from the gravity tank pouring down my face! Fortunately, the plane did not catch fire and I was pulled out by our engine fitters who had rushed out to the crash. The gods were certainly with me because I did not even have a scratch. When we examined the wrecked plane, we found that one of the wires from the control stick to the elevator had been badly damaged. It had been hit either by a bullet or anti-aircraft fire, and the one strand that was holding it together must have snapped when I pulled out of the dive.[226]

An alternative version of events exists in relation to his plunging into the ground that day. The commander and fighter ace, Lieutenant Ludwig Hanstein of Jasta 35 was credited with bringing Malik down as part of the action of 20 October, following their dogfight south-west of Moorslede.[227]

Nevertheless, having recovered his composure, Hardit joined the others in the officers' mess, where there was an air of celebration. Everyone had returned from the mission unscathed and the wiser for the experience, and

---

226. Malik, H. S., 'A Little Work, A Little Play', p. 85
227. Guttman, J., 'Sopwith Camel', p. 83

the squadron's contribution was judged to be a great success by the high command:

> On the conclusion of the operation, congratulatory telegrams poured in on the Squadron from all sides. The General Officer Commanding Fifth Army wired, congratulating it on a 'splendid start', and General Trenchard telegraphed to the same effect. [228] Rarely had a newly arrived squadron made such a successful showing of its first serious operation.[229]

There was also disappointment for Hardit however. Whilst Barker, Mitchell and Mulholland of 28 Squadron were each awarded a 'decisive combat' in the squadron logbook, the term for an enemy plane being confirmed shot down, or a 'kill' or 'victory' as it was usually known, the only statement against Hardit's name was 'crashed on landing', which was of course accurate.[230] There were a number of reasons possible for the discrepancy between Hardit's claim of a kill and the lack of an official confirmation. Once combat reports were submitted, they were assessed by Wing headquarters to decide upon the merits of each. These were then passed up to Brigade headquarters. The final decision rested upon the degree of verification available vis-à-vis each claim. The way in which kills were defined may have made a difference also. By 1917, the sheer number of 'out of control', 'driven down' and 'forced to land' victories claimed by British pilots was overloading the system. As the volume of aerial combats soared to the point where fifty such claims might be submitted on any given day, the process became overwhelmed. During this time therefore, the procedures and definitions for claiming kills were beginning to undergo an overhaul. In short, the most likely reasons for the official denial of Hardit's claim of a victory on 20 October, were either that it could not be verified, or didn't fit the current interpretation of the criteria for one. To put into some context Hardit's claim, the majority of such victory declarations included in

---

228. General Sir Hubert Gough, General Officer Commanding Fifth Army, 1916-18.
229. AIR-27-335_1, p. 5
230. Particulars of Officers, in subseries within AIR 1 - 28 Squadron RFC, TNA, AIR-1-1855-204-213-24 & 25, 20 October 1917

RFC 'Combat Reports' often ended with the squadron commander's words: 'I consider the above combat to be indecisive'.

The following day, Sunday 21 October, saw various dawn and morning patrols carried out by the squadron, except for Hardit, who spent much of the morning awaiting the delivery of a new machine from 1 Aircraft Depot at St Omer. At 1110 hours, after satisfying his engine fitters and himself that all was well with new Camel B5406, he took to the air for a test flight lasting twenty-five minutes. Fortunately, the new aircraft handled as well as the previous one and the omens seemed good. Yet, although these first couple of weeks at Droglandt were found to be exciting by the young pilots, the potential for tragedy was never too far away. During that early afternoon, 2nd Lieutenant Shanks was wounded on patrol and committed to hospital, while 2nd Lieutenant Shelton was killed making a forced landing a short distance away. The following day, Mulholland's Camel lost most of its tail section, but he somehow managed to nurse it back to Droglandt, though Smith wasn't so lucky, being brought down and killed by anti-aircraft fire over Roulers.[231]

Hardit's own *sang froid* was shaken a little that week, by the accidental burning down of his Nissen hut whilst eating in the mess. Everything he owned, apart from the uniform he was wearing and his beloved *kara,* were destroyed. The three men who shared the hut with Hardit were equally devastated to have lost their souvenirs, photos, books, letters and kit, forced to beg and borrow provisions in the days ahead.[232]

Soon after arriving at Droglandt, one name was frequently heard on everyone's lips: Richthofen. Manfred Albrecht Freiherr von Richthofen, known in English as Baron von Richthofen, and most famously as the 'Red Baron', was considered the ace-of-aces of the First World War, being officially credited with eighty air combat victories. Richthofen flew the celebrated Fokker Dr. I triplane from late July 1917, the distinctive three-winged aircraft with which he is most commonly associated. Only nineteen of his eighty kills were actually made in this type of aircraft however, despite the popular link between Richthofen and the Fokker triplane. By October 1917, Richthofen was leader of Jasta 11 and also the larger fighter wing unit Jagdgeschwader 1, better known as 'The Flying Circus',

---

231. Neale, D., '*Whatsoever you may do – 28 Squadron RFC and RAF*', pp. 61-88
232. Malik, H.S., '*A Little Work, A Little Play*', p. 86

or 'Richthofen's Circus'. These names were reputedly given because of the bright colours of its aircraft, and perhaps also because of the way Jagdgeschwader 1 was transferred from one area of allied air activity to another – moving like a travelling circus, and frequently setting up in tents on improvised airfields. By this time, Richthofen was regarded as a national hero in Germany, and respected by his enemies.[233] His reputation was well known at Droglandt and it was very definitely on the mind of the ambitious and energetic Captain William Barker.

In the run up to the start of the Second Battle of Passchendaele on 26 October, the weather precluded any meaningful artillery observation from the air, thereby inhibiting the effectiveness of the preparatory bombardment by the artillery, always a prerequisite for any meaningful advance during a battle. Barker's frustration with the resulting inactivity may have resulted from his being one of the most effective RFC observers earlier in the war, knowing the crucial part played by airborne reconnaissance and 'spotting' in support of the artillery. It may also have resulted from his poor relationship with the squadron commander Glanville, Barker believing that his superior was too passive, too accepting of poor weather grounding operations. Hardit himself later said of Barker, that he was 'always looking for action'.[234]

Whatever the reasons, on 25 October, Barker appealed for volunteers for a ground attack on Richthofen's aerodrome at its base at Marckebeeke, about thirty miles due east of Droglandt, on the western side of the city of Courtrai. It's difficult to speculate about Hardit's motivation, but although he later described the decision to fly that day as a 'foolhardy plan', he was to take to the air alongside fellow C Flight officers, Fenton and Jones, to go and machine gun the Flying Circus on its home turf. No doubt the pressure not to be seen to be backing out played a part in his volunteering, in addition to the excitement of the moment and the reputation of the proposed adversary. The three volunteers had only known Barker for just over three weeks, but he was a man not used to being denied. Glanville was opposed to the undertaking but told Barker he would give his permission to approach a superior officer up the chain of command. Permission having

---

233. Grey, P.& Thetford, O., *'German Aircraft of the First World War'* (Putnam: London, 1970), p. 100
234. Malik, H.S., *'A Little Work, A Little Play'*, p. 86

been achieved; the planes were prepared for the following day. Hardit must have been aware that he had hardly flown his newly acquired Camel and certainly not into action before.

The following morning, the four machines of C Flight were rolled out of their canvas hangars and while the fitters prepared the engines, Barker briefed the three volunteers. They could just pick out the hedge at the end of what passed for the cinder track runway. Thick fog with a heavy drizzle pervaded the scene and the fliers felt chilled by the cold. Barker's confidence, enthusiasm and intensity helped to dispel some of their nerves, though not all. It may have crossed their minds with some regret that the remaining members of the squadron were enjoying a leisurely breakfast, but there was no going back.[235] At 1045 hours, the Camels trundled forward through the mud onto the cinders. After a tense take-off, the four planes joined formation at 500 feet, rather than the normal 1000, and taking a bearing of 110 degrees headed out across the Ypres Salient. With landmarks invisible below, flying by compass was the order of the day at a speed of approximately eighty miles per hour. Each pilot fixed his eyes upon the inclinometer, used to maintain wing level when flying blind.[236] The four planes flew in a loose echelon formation, staggered behind the commander's right wing. Hardit was next to Barker as number two, with Jones and Fenton behind, a position which enabled Hardit to keep Barker closely in sight in such poor visibility. They crossed the artillery scarred landscape on a flight of approximately twenty minutes, with no incoming anti-aircraft fire as they passed over the village of Hooge below. Still climbing, C Flight suddenly emerged into sunlight above the clouds, yet Hardit could no longer see either Fenton or Jones behind, though Barker to his left was still in sight, as he recalled:

> After about fifteen minutes, we flew into a gap in the clouds at about 4000 feet where the sky was quite clear. Some other Germans made for this clearing and soon we were surrounded by a dozen German fighters and a dogfight ensued.[237]

---

235. Ralph, W.D., 'Barker VC', p. 2
236. Ibid.
237. Malik, H.S., 'A Little Work, A Little Play', p. 87

The combat in which he was involved was to be a life changing one for the man from Rawalpindi, and one worth looking at in detail.[238] Inevitably, in the confused struggle which took place, there were significant discrepancies in the written narratives of Hardit, Barker and one of the Germans involved, Lieutenant Paul Strähle. Strähle was not part of Richthofen's squadron, but of Jasta 18, another famous German formation.[239] Jasta 18 Albatros livery incorporated a crimson front section, hence the nickname 'The Red Noses'. As a result, both Barker and Malik assumed, in their later accounts of the action of 26 October, that they were fighting against 'Richthofen's Circus'. This was not the case, another one of the occasions that airmen claimed in honest error to have been fighting Richthofen, when in fact they were engaged with other units.[240]

In short therefore, although Barker's intent was a ground attack on Richthofen's Jagdgeschwader 1, there is no evidence that what took place involved any planes from that unit.[241] What is clear, is that four pilots from Jasta 18 took off from Harlebeke to the north-east of Courtrai in their Albatros D.V aircraft, they were: Otto Schober, Arthur Rahn, Johannes Klein and Strähle himself. It is without doubt that these four came into combat with Barker and Hardit on 26 October. No other Jasta mentions the combat, and this is important for the two RFC men claim in various accounts that the Germans opposed to them that day numbered between twelve and twenty aircraft.[242] What is also in doubt in the British accounts, is the course taken by the members of C Flight on its outbound journey. Barker stated that the action took place west of Roulers and that it continued to the east of that city up to the town of Tielt to the north-east. There is no reason not to accept this as accurate, in which case Barker was leading his men off course to the north, on a bearing of approximately eighty degrees

238. Unfortunately, 'Combat Reports' associated with 28 Squadron were stolen from TNA in the 1990s.
239. Van Wyngarden, G., 'Jasta 18. The Red Noses' (Osprey: New York, 2011), pp. 46-49
240. Greg Van Wyngarden in internet discussion with the author, thread: 'Jasta 11 Richthofen on 26 October 1917' – as of 19 July 2020 – the aerodrome.com
241. Hardit Singh believed this to be the case in his 1981 interview with Trevor Fishlock: Fishlock, T., 'When a child of the Raj could find an ever-open door', The Times (London), 16 October 1982
242. See Malik, H.S., 'A Little Work, A Little Play', p. 87; Fishlock, T., 'When a child of the Raj could find an ever-open door', The Times (London), 16 October 1982 and Ralph, W.D., 'Barker VC', p. 4 & Van Wyngarden, G., 'Jasta 18. The Red Noses', p. 49

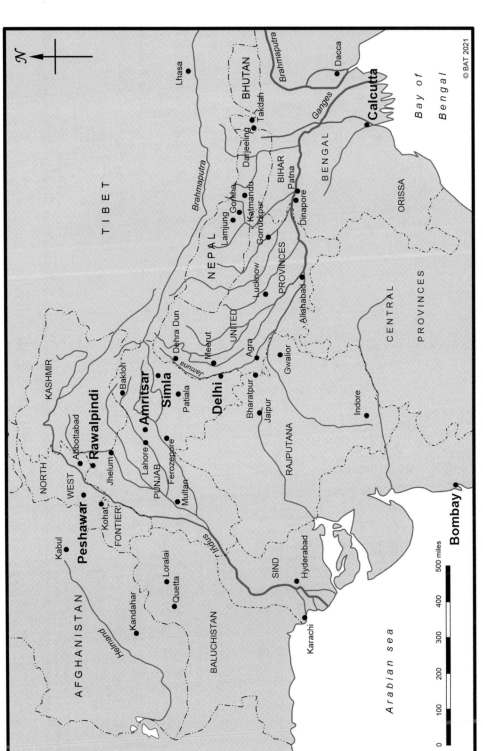

Key locations in India (pre-Partition)

© BAT 2021

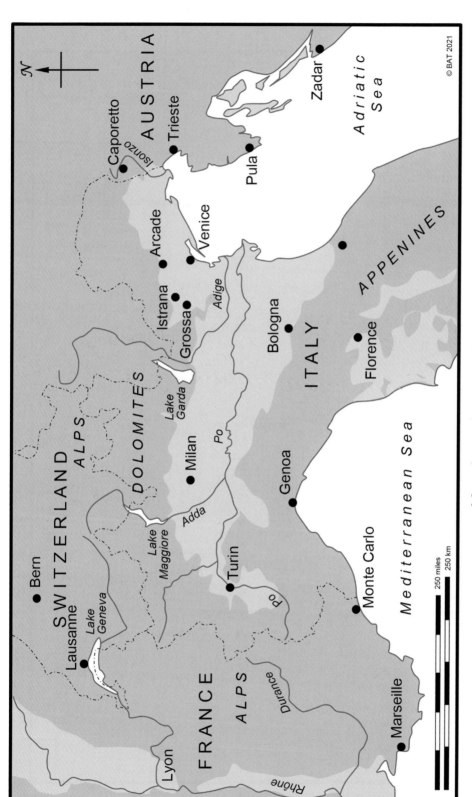

Key locations in Italy

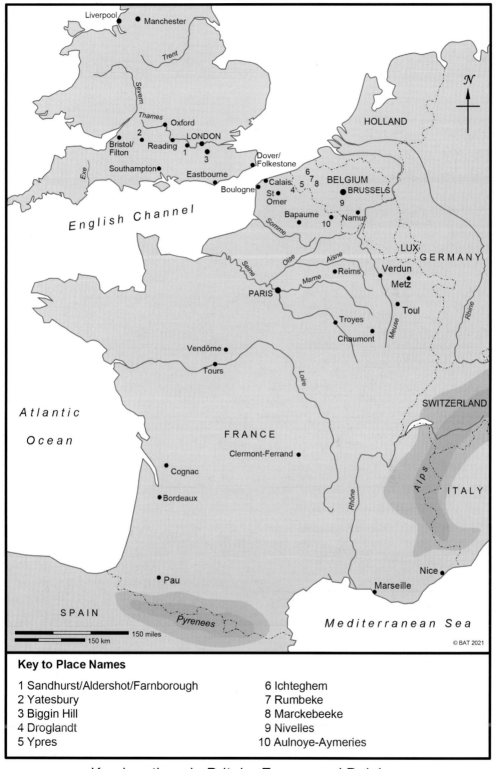

Key to Place Names

1 Sandhurst/Aldershot/Farnborough
2 Yatesbury
3 Biggin Hill
4 Droglandt
5 Ypres

6 Ichteghem
7 Rumbeke
8 Marckebeeke
9 Nivelles
10 Aulnoye-Aymeries

Key locations in Britain, France and Belgium

Hardit (left) as a boy in Rawalpindi with his parents and brothers. The cricket bat is already in hand. (Image courtesy of Santhya Malik)

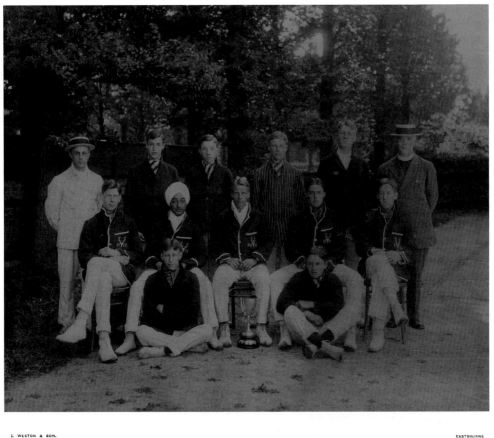

Blackwater  House XI.

Winners of the House Cup, 1911.

B. Tordoff, Esq.   E. L. Ridley.   G. H. Hopewell.   G. E. Goolden.   J. H. Goolden.   Rev. F. Atkinson.

O. G. Hake.   H. S. Malik.   H. A. V. Maynard.   A. D. Clark.   C. H. M. Dennys.
(CAPT.)

E. H. Shrager.   E. G. Passingham.

Eastbourne College Cricket House Cup winners, 1911. Hardit's guardian the Reverend Atkinson is on the right. (Image courtesy of Eastbourne College Archive)

Left: Playing for Sussex County Cricket Club in the summer 1914. The *kara* is firmly in place on the right arm. (Image courtesy of Sussex Cricket Museum)

Below: Sussex in the field against Leicestershire at Hove in August 1914. The white turban is unmistakeable at cover point. (Image courtesy of Sussex Cricket Museum)

Right: With tutor Francis 'Sligger' Urquhart at Balliol College, Oxford in 1916. (Reproduced by kind permission of the Master and Fellows of Balliol College)

Below: With the ambulance of the Croix Rouge Française, at Cognac in the summer of 1916. (Image courtesy of Santhya Malik)

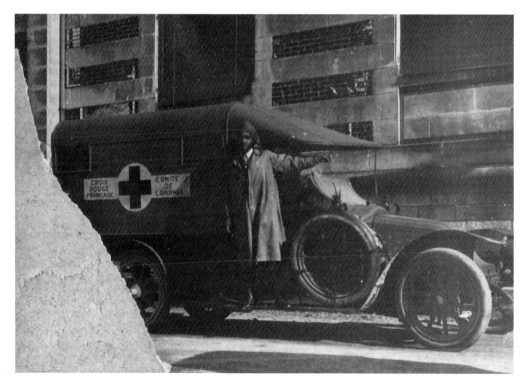

Left: A moment of joy! During training at Vendôme, June 1917. (Image courtesy of Robin Boston)

Below: Celebrating the award of his wings at Berkeley Castle in Gloucestershire with the Earl during July 1917. (Image courtesy of Santhya Malik)

Above: With a Sopwith Camel in 1917. Hardit's holding the oversized flying helmet to put over the turban when flying. (Image courtesy of Santhya Malik)

Right: William George "Billy" Barker, Hardit's Flight Commander in No. 28 Squadron. He remains the most decorated serviceman in the history of Canada to this day. (Public domain, via Wikimedia Commons)

Sopwith Camels of No. 28 Squadron being prepared for a patrol on the Italian Front early in 1918. (Durham J (photographs), Public domain, via Wikimedia Commons)

Posing with other pilots of No.141 Squadron at Biggin Hill and the advertising sign taken from a teashop in the nearby village of Westerham. (Image courtesy of Mark Haselden)

A cheerful Hardit aboard a Sopwith Camel at Manchester in March 1918. (Image courtesy of Santhya Malik)

Above left: Edwin Montagu, Secretary of State for India between 1917 and 1922. (Central News Agency – Creative License via Wikimedia Commons)

Above right: Air Vice-Marshal Sir William Sefton Brancker. (The *Flight* magazine archive from Flightglobal, Public domain, via Wikimedia Commons)

Above left: In RAF uniform at the end of the First World War. (Image courtesy of Santhya Malik)

Above right: Newly married at Bournemouth in the autumn of 1919. (Image courtesy of Santhya Malik)

With Harold Boston when on holiday with their wives Prakash and Lucy in Cornwall in September 1919. The two men had met when training at Reading in the spring of 1917. (Image courtesy of Santhya Malik)

Hardit and Prakash golfing with friends most probably during 1920. (Image courtesy of Santhya Malik)

With Mademoiselle Specht in Bournemouth in 1920 when visiting with Prakash who is behind the camera. Mademoiselle Specht had taught him French in 1915. (Image courtesy of Santhya Malik)

With Prakash on the golf course sometime during 1920. (Image courtesy of Santhya Malik)

Hardit on the golf course at sometime during 1920. (Image courtesy of Santhya Malik)

Right: Resplendent in a Balliol tie in 1921. As Hardit Singh would have appeared as a newly qualified member of the Indian Civil Service. (Image courtesy of Santhya Malik)

Below: Playing in 'The World v Scotland' golf tournament in the late 1920s. (Image courtesy of Santhya Malik)

Christmas card sent by the Malik family when Hardit Singh was Ambassador to France during the 1950s. The recipients were the Boston family who maintain contact with the Maliks to this day. (Image courtesy of Robin Boston)

and away from Richthofen's 'Flying Circus'. As we shall see later, this has implications for an understanding of the course that Hardit was to take later during the combat.

As the four members of Jasta 18 entered the clearing in the clouds, the two Camels of Barker and Hardit were silhouetted below them, offering a tempting target and the Germans dived steeply down to attack. In response, Barker threw his machine to the right, seemingly forgetting his wingman, who could not follow such a steep turn in time. Nevertheless, Hardit too dived quickly to escape, but was unable to shake Paul Strähle from his tail. The German later gave an account of his combat with Hardit:

> At about 1200 metres, we fired at two enemy single seaters, one (Hardit Singh) dived to fire at targets on the ground and I went after him. The other (Barker) was engaged by Klein and Schober. Rahn stayed with me. In a tough dogfight lasting more than a quarter-of an hour, sometimes only a few feet off the ground, I fought the enemy scout as far as Ichteghem, where unfortunately I had to break off because my guns had jammed. For me this flight was the hottest and most exciting that I had in my whole fighting career. Apart from the good pilot, his machine was faster and more manoeuvrable than mine, to which must be added the lower altitude, showers and rain. But for this I might have got him. Once I thought he would have to land, as he had a long trail of smoke, but it was not to be. I landed on the aerodrome at Ichteghem, where it was raining heavily. For the whole of the fight, I had used full throttle (airspeed 200km/hour, 1600 rpm). Three times we were down to ground level! His machine had a "5" next to the cockade on the left upper wing.[243] [244]

Hardit gave his own account of this action:

> A German dived on me and hit me almost immediately, but only in the right leg. He was obviously as scared as I was,

---

243. Ibid.
244. This assumes that the aircraft number '5' had been painted on Hardit's Camel B5406 after delivery on 21 October.

for instead of flying off, he continued past and below me, still diving, and I simply pulled the triggers of both my Vickers guns straight at his tail as he flew past, and had the satisfaction of seeing him burst into flames (it was this 'kill' which *was* later recorded in the squadron logbook). I saw Barker also in a struggle surrounded by German fighters, and with the odds, I felt that both of us were done for.[245]

Both Strähle and Rahn from Jasta 18 pursued Hardit's Camel and it is therefore unclear who the latter had shot down in this description, nor which fighters had 'surrounded' Barker, who later claimed two kills during the combat, one of which was Schober. However, Strähle gave his own view about who was responsible for Schober's demise:

Ltn Schober was attacked almost vertically from below and shot down by the other Englishman (Barker) who had spun away before. Schober himself was hit by several bullets and dived straight into the ground.[246]

Hardit was in trouble however, with at least two Germans, Strähle and Rahn in pursuit of him:

I had been hit in the right leg and immediately smelt petrol, so I feared that the plane would explode into flames! The bullet that had hit me pierced the main pressure petrol tank which, in the Camel was located beneath the pilot's seat. Fortunately for me, the bullet which must have been red hot, came through the lower part of the tank which was still full of petrol. Had it hit the tank a little higher where the petrol vapour was collected, the plane would have immediately exploded. It was a fantastic, almost miraculous bit of luck![247]

---

245. Malik, H.S., *'A Little Work, A Little Play'*, p. 87
246. Van Wyngarden, G., *'Jasta 18. The Red Noses'*, p. 49
247. Malik, H.S., *'A Little Work, A Little Play'*, p. 88

Hardit was pursued for some time, apparently heading north as far as Ichteghem (see Strähle above) which was in the direction of Ostend on the coast! If Barker was correct and the fight began west of Roulers, then this northern pursuit of Hardit's Camel went on for up to fifteen miles. During this chase, he stated that he was followed by four enemy planes at one point, though Strähle gave up the hunt and 'landed at Ichteghem aerodrome', as we have seen. It was something of a miracle that Hardit survived, bullets raining in constantly upon Camel B5406. He remembered them hitting the wooden part of the plane above his head and ricocheting through the rigging:

> I was almost like a winged partridge running along the ground unable to fly, with four guns blazing away. The strange thing was that in the first few moments I felt sure I would be killed, or at least shot down and captured. When that did not happen, I felt quite calm and confident, believing that I was under divine protection, and would escape. My pursuers just did not have the bullet with my name on.[248]

Having shaken the enemy planes, Hardit had no idea where he was. As the engine began to falter, he felt the urgent need to head due west back in the direction of the British lines. It is a fair supposition to accept that having reached the front lines approximately seven miles from the coast, he would then have turned south, keeping the only distinguishable landmark – the British trenches - in view to his left. Having reached the relatively familiar back areas of the Ypres Salient again, he caught sight of the triangular form of Zillebeke Lake, to the south-east of the city, but by now well behind the front line and crash landed into the mire below, upon which he passed out.

Meanwhile, what had become of Barker, Fenton and Jones? The Captain of C Flight had carried out a brilliant evasive manoeuvre which had saved him, but with the rest of his wingmen out of sight, the attack on Marckebeeke was no longer feasible. He began to hunt alone and eventually encountered fifteen enemy machines east of Roulers.[249] The two pilots downed allegedly

248. Ibid.
249. Ralph, W.D., 'Barker VC', p. 4

in the ensuing combat were Schober and Klein, both of Jasta 18.[250] The War Diary of Jagdgeschwader 1, the 'Flying Circus', is rather inconclusive for 26 October 1917: 'No special occurrences. Rain. Combat flights: 7. Enemy air activity low'.[251] Short of fuel and having become lost forty miles south of Droglandt, Barker was forced to land close to Arras. He had returned back to his base by 5pm. Fenton, having left the formation, attacked a German convoy on the Staden-Roulers road, and having set two wagons on fire, was wounded by ground fire and returned to Droglandt to be transported immediately to hospital. Jones flew around for an hour without contacting enemy aircraft and he too returned to base.

28 Squadron log recorded two 'decisive' combats for Barker and one for Hardit Singh on 26 October.[252] Barker agreed that the mission had been a 'balls up', promising in the future that he would take better care of his wingmen.[253] Both he and Hardit believed the other to have been killed, delighted to have been proved wrong and that all four men of C Flight had returned alive.

Hardit awoke to find himself on a stretcher at a Casualty Clearing Station with two bullets in his right leg. The surgeons left the bullets alone, believing that the petrol through which they had passed had sterilised the wounds. Events moved quickly and within thirty-six hours, Hardit found himself back in Britain at the Prince of Wales Hospital for Officers in what had been the Great Central Hotel in Marylebone Road in London.[254] He would remain in hospital for two months and then having been passed fit for further service by a medical board on 13 December, he prepared to re-join 28 Squadron.

Meanwhile, at the same time that Hardit had arrived at Droglandt, back in London, the cabinet had agreed to support the principle of granting King's Commissions to Indians. Although at this stage the agreement related only to soldiers in the Indian Army, the same principle would later be considered

---

250. Ibid.
251. Greg Van Wyngarden in discussion with the author, thread: *'Jasta 11 Richthofen on 26 October 1917'* – as of 19 July 2020 – the aerodrome.com
252. AIR-1-1855-204-213-24 & 25, 26.10.1917
253. Ralph, W.D., *'Barker VC'*, p. 4
254. Air Ministry, Officers' Service Records: Hardit Singh Malik, 1918-19, TNA, AIR 76/331

for those seeking officer status in the RFC and later the RAF. An undated note from the India Office confirmed the decision made by the cabinet:

The War Cabinet decided: -

> To sanction an announcement that they accepted in principle the appointment of Indians to commissioned rank in His Majesty's Army; that the general conditions in which such Commissions will be granted in future are being discussed by the Government of India, the India Office and the War Office, but that for War Service nine Commissions will at once be granted, 7 Captaincies and 2 Lieutenancies to Indians recommended by the Government of India.[255]

Change was in the air.

---

255. IOR/L/MIL/7/19006: 1911-1923, undated, p. 109

Chapter 8

Grossa
December 1917–October 1918

'The mountain remains unmoved at seeming defeat by the mist.'
Rabindranath Tagore, *Fireflies*

The blinds at the carriage window had long been pulled down making it impossible to judge the time of day. The four occupants of the carriage were sleeping deeply except one. Each was hidden under a khaki army blanket, great coat, or tunic, dozing or sleeping with varying intensities of exhalation amongst the detritus of three days consumption: brown paper bags, tins, biscuits and the uneaten remains of various items of anonymous Italian fare. Having contemplated quietly escaping the compartment's confines whilst he came to, Hardit felt for his *kara* to reassure himself that it was in place on his wrist, as was his custom, and then gingerly picked his way to the sliding door without disturbing the others' slumbers. Entering the narrow, empty corridor, he headed for the *urinoir,* his eyes beginning to adjust to the light. Swaying back into the passage, he lowered the window a little, refreshing himself with a blast of cold air, an antidote to the prevailing fug in the compartment. He'd believed he had become accustomed to the lures of mountain scenery, having had daily opportunities in childhood to survey the sumptuous views across Kashmir, yet the landscape that December morning held his attention. An immense red sun was glancing over the snow topped mountains, casting a warm glow over a village built entirely of white stone. The countryside between the village and the track was populated by mountain cattle that grazed indifferently. The beauty of the landscape reminded him fleetingly that he needed to finish a letter home, the previous days' attempts rendered futile by an interminably swaying engine over an uneven track. His companions

114

slept on as he craned his neck through the open corridor window, the train approaching Verona with the towers of the Duomo and Sant' Anastasia in the distance. The Shakespearean associations with the city weren't lost on him, and reinvigorated, he returned to the carriage to finish his correspondence. There was much to say.

The four RFC officers were making their way to postings in northern Italy, having met several days earlier whilst waiting to embark for a Channel crossing at Folkestone. The officer on the gangplank, who greeted Hardit warmly, had not long returned from the subcontinent after many years' service and jokingly suggested that the three Britons look after their Indian comrade. In the event, it was the Sikh who had just about managed to shepherd three bleary eyed Britons aboard the Marseille bound train from Gare de l'Est in Paris twenty-four hours later. It was just after breakfast on Christmas Eve 1917.

The night before, Hardit had decided to stay quietly in the 19th Arrondissement hotel, intending to draft Bournemouth and Punjab destined mail, having explored the delights of the city on previous leaves, but the others had no doubts about plunging into the Parisienne night life. So it was that all were reunited in the hotel lobby the next morning forced to make a dash from their dingy hotel to the nearby station. Once aboard, the partygoers recounted breathlessly the previous night's events, one involving a number of women in less than salubrious bars. The following morning had begun with the new girlfriends throwing pepper into the eyes of the callow officers and ended with their wallets being stolen for good measure. Mercifully, their official papers remained strewn across the floor.[256] In consequence, for much of the first day's travel to Marseille, Hardit was left with his own thoughts by the indolent airmen.

The four were bound for Milan initially, and then ultimately to aerodromes east of Verona. In peaceful times, the journey from Paris to northern Italy would have taken in Dijon and Geneva, but in time of war, the Swiss were defending their neutrality from both sides with equal vigour. As a result, a four-day journey was necessary along the French Riviera from Marseille, taking in Nice and Genoa on the way to Milan, where an overnight hotel stay was required before the final leg. The train halted at many small stations along the way, and though the novelty of seeing British reinforcements had

---

256. Malik, H.S., 'A Little Work, A Little Play', p. 90

subsided somewhat among the Italian populace since the heady days of early November, the newcomers still saw an occasional elderly couple standing in the doorway of a picturesque cottage, waving tattered and torn versions of 'il Tricolore'. Although the military bands had long since departed, union flags still remained to adorn the ends of now deserted platforms. During prolonged halts at major stations however, women, old men and children surrounded the train offering flowers, sweet treats and slaps on the back, though in time such pleasantries became tiresome and Hardit began to yearn for active service.[257] The overnight stay in the Metropole Hotel in Milan was some relief, though there was only time for a little sightseeing at the Duomo di Milano before the penultimate leg of the journey for the four men began. It ended in Verona, where each departed to different units, leaving Hardit to take a final train to Vincenza and then a lorry to 28 Squadron's relatively new base at Grossa. It would soon be the year's end.

The airfield of Grossa di Gazzo had been built in front of a Palladian villa, on a vast plot of roughly rectangular shape. It had been created in early 1917 and had been made available to the RAF in extremis from November that year. The squadron's pilots considered the airstrip no less of a challenge than the one left at Droglandt, owing to the dykes and trees which surrounded it. It was situated within the broad Venetian Plain with the Gulf of Venice to the east, an agricultural area broken up into fields bordered by willows and irrigated by criss-crossing drainage ditches. On the horizon to the north, were the snow-capped mountains of the Italian Dolomite Alps, some of the peaks of which rose up to five thousand feet in height at no great distance from the aerodrome. As he pulled the kit bag from the back of the truck, nodding his appreciation to the driver, Hardit looked to the mountains once more and this time was moved, much to his surprise. It had been a while.

Two months earlier, as Hardit had recuperated at the Prince of Wales Hospital for Officers in London, back at Droglandt, 28 Squadron received its orders to move on 29 October 1917. Initially, there was some mystery about their final destination, but the command to 'crate up' all nineteen Camels confirmed that it was not to be the Western Front. The first train leaving northern France departed on 9 November and arrived in Milan three days

---

257. Robson, R., 'Lt Eric Godwin Chance: A Gloucestershire Airman', in the journal of the *Society of First World War Aviation Historians,* Vol. 19 4 1988, pp. 182-185

later. The machines were then reassembled in rapid time, Captain Barker persuading the head of a local factory to permit use of local workshops for the purpose. Everyone in the squadron was heartily sick of travelling by then, eagerly volunteering night shifts to complete the task earlier than planned. They would then fly into the province of Verona and await the designation of a new aerodrome, which was finalised on 28 November.[258]

Following the 'October Revolution' in Russia, a top priority of the newly established Soviet government was to end the country's involvement in the war. On 8 November 1917, Vladimir Lenin signed the 'Decree on Peace', which called upon 'all the belligerent nations and their governments to start immediate negotiations for peace' and proposed an immediate withdrawal of Russia from the First World War. This departure enabled German divisions deployed on the Eastern Front to bolster the flagging formations of the Austro-Hungarian forces facing the Italians across the Isonzo River. The Battle of Caporetto, which began on 24 October, lasted for a month approximately, and was a disaster for Britain's Italian allies. It obliged the cabinet in London to despatch an all arms force to bolster Italy's forces and government, at a critical moment of the war. The Italians were forced back to the River Piave and made a stand to stem the tide of German and Austro-Hungarian divisions flooding across the Venetian Plain.[259] 28 and 34 Squadrons were to take up position in support of the Italian forces which had settled on the line Vidor, Mount Grappa, Asiago and Rovereto along the River Piave. As the Camel flew, it took twenty minutes to reach the river from the Grossa aerodrome.

Having reintroduced himself to the commanding officer, Glanville, in the office, a standard wood-planked hut with a tar paper roof nailed down with strips of wood, Hardit made his way to one of the ubiquitous metal clad Nissen huts to which he had been allocated. The nineteen Camels were housed as normal in their canvas hangar tents. He then headed to the officers' mess which was located in a large barn to see who was about. He soon renewed old acquaintances, noticing that the empty chairs of those killed during the last days at Droglandt had now been filled with his arrival. Amongst the newcomers who had joined the squadron at the end of the

258. Ralph, W.D., 'Barker VC', p. 85
259. Neate, D., 'Whatsoever you may do – 28 Squadron RFC and RAF', pp. 61-88

previous October was 2nd Lieutenant Clifford McEwan, a Canadian, who like Barker had been born in Manitoba and would end the war as an ace with twenty-seven kills. The two immediately struck up a friendship which would last until the Canadian's death in 1967. One of McEwan's abiding memories at Grossa, was of the pleasure he gained from listening to Hardit quote poetry, in particular the works of WB Yeats.[260]

Having been given the last of the available Camels, one which had been encased in France, Hardit was eager to put machine B6364 through its paces on the last day of 1917. He took it for a brief five-minute test flight at 0945 hours, coming back down for his engine fitter to make some mechanical adjustments.[261] Twenty minutes later, he took to the air again, this time one of five planes on an 'offensive patrol' which would later involve escorting the R.E.8 planes of 34 Squadron on a reconnaissance and photographic mission. The first part of the assignment involved flying to 34 Squadron's aerodrome at Istrana and awaiting Barker and the rest of the aircraft before the mission proper could begin. Unfortunately, Hardit was the only one not to arrive at Istrana, becoming lost in poor flying conditions over an unfamiliar landscape. As a result, a forced landing was necessary at Arcade, fortunately, just on the Italian side of the lines. He had run out of petrol.[262] The weather over the mountains was very cold and clear with snowstorms all too frequent. In low visibility, it was difficult to discriminate between stratus clouds and the mountain tops. Fog was also a continuous feature over the plains west of the Gulf of Venice.[263] Hardit wouldn't be the last pilot to put down in these conditions, as Norman Macmillan of 45 Squadron remembered:

> [...] weather changes were sudden. At bewildering speed, sunshine might vanish into damp fog, a shallow fog, perhaps no deeper than two hundred feet, but sometimes five hundred, yet always thick enough to enshroud the ground from the view of the pilot flying over it and the aircraft and all else from that of the man on the ground.[264]

---

260. Ralph, W.D., *'Barker VC'*, p. 93
261. AIR-1-1855-204-213-24 & 25, 31 December 1917
262. Ibid.
263. Ralph, W.D., *'Barker VC'*, p. 86
264. Macmillan, M., 'Offensive Patrol', p. 62

It was no mean feat that Hardit was able to make his way the ten miles to the aerodrome at Istrana, the distance, language barrier and terrain making communication with a home base challenging during those early days in Italy. He may have had an extra incentive than usual to do so however. 34 and 45 Squadrons were sharing the base at Istrana and 45's acting commander, Captain Brownell, was throwing a New Year's Eve party, one including those visiting pilots of 28 Squadron.[265] Hardit was given a little teasing no doubt as he entered the villa at Fossalunga, two miles down the road from Istrana, where temporary billets had been found. He was no doubt wet, cold and miserable after his escapade, but was soon warmed by the welcome and the champagne. As he later reminisced, it was no ordinary night:

> It was a fun evening with plenty of Italian champagne – far too sweet for me, making me very sick - when we suddenly heard planes overhead. Shots were fired at us and we rushed to our planes and took to the air. They were Austrians and we were able to shoot down some of them and capture some. We found that members of the Austrian crew who survived were completely drunk! When they sobered up, they told us that they too had been celebrating Christmas when someone suggested that they get into the air and shoot at the British airfield. By then most of them were too drunk but they went up all the same and sadly, for several of them, it was their last Christmas.[266] [267]

As it turned out, Hardit's forced landing on 31 December was representative of what was to be a short stay in Italy. He flew regularly for three weeks or so without incident, until his last sortie on 23 January and then left 28 Squadron for good:

> While in Italy I developed an allergy to Castor Oil used for lubricating our engines. Some of the oil splattered onto our

265. Brownell in later life sent a copy of the signed menu from that evening, including Hardit's signature, to writer Somnath Sapru. See Sapru, S., 'Sky Hawks', pp. 200-201
266. Malik, H.S., 'A Little Work, A Little Play', p. 90
267. Hardit was mistaken here. This party was on New Year's Eve.

faces and kit while we were flying and I would get violently air sick every time I went up. Our Commanding Officer (Glanville) decided to send me back to England with the recommendation that I should be assigned to planes with stationary, as opposed to rotary engines, for stationary engines did not use Castor Oil.[268] [269]

We can only guess at his feelings, leaving behind the formation with which he had gone to war. Little mention is made of the departure in his autobiography, which must have been not without some sadness and regret. 28 Squadron would remain in Italy until returning to Britain in February 1919, though Captain Barker would leave it to join another squadron the previous April. He would go on to become Canada's most decorated soldier, an achievement which stands to this day, earning a Military Cross and two bars, a Distinguished Service Order and bar and the Victoria Cross. He was to be one of the most prolific fighter aces of the First World War with fifty kills credited to his name. Sadly, although Hardit would later be posted to Canada as Trade Commissioner in 1938, he would never meet his former flight commander again after leaving the Grossa aerodrome, for Barker was to be killed in an accident whilst flying in 1930 near Ottawa.

Hardit made his way back through Italy and up through France once more, arriving in Britain in early February to a new RFC posting later in the month. Before taking up the new position, he had some time to visit friends back in Oxford and Eastbourne. As a result, on 10 February 1918, a letter was posted in Eastbourne on his behalf by a retired former High Court Judge of Madras, Samuel Russell. The letter was addressed to an old friend of Russell from his days in India, Sir Murray Hammick, a member of the Council of State, who was based at the India Office. Hammick had been Governor of Madras during 1912, Russell himself having retired to Eastbourne in 1903.

---

268. Ibid., p. 91
269. 11 Squadron was known by some as the 'Castor Oil Squadron' owing to the scale of the low-level poisoning within the unit, a few suffering from constipation apparently. See Bush, J., *'Lionel Morris and the Red Baron: Air War on the Somme'*, p. 98

10 February 1918

Dear Hammick,

There is a young fellow named Malik (North of India Sikh) 2nd Lt. RFC. He was educated at the Eastbourne College and Balliol. He is a great friend of our boys. He is a very good fellow and as straight as they are made.

He is a tip top flying man – flies a "Camel" and has come home from Italy to take out a Dolphin, which I understand is the last word in fighting machines. He is very discontented at the treatment he is receiving from the Financial Department. He has no complaint regarding the pay, but he has a Commission in the British Army and they are not treating him as a British Officer. He says that they are insisting on him introducing from month to month a certificate that he is flying with his unit, otherwise he is not credited by Corps with his flying pay. No such certificate is required from a British Officer and he regards it as an insult – I presume to be treated in this fashion.

He is a splendid young fellow and I believe has done great feats in France and Italy.

It would be such a pity to cause discontent in his mind if it can be avoided. He had tea with us this afternoon and talked a great deal about this matter. He is going to interview the financial people on the subject. He is under the impression that the India Office is consulted in things of this character.

It would be a tremendous pity if such a loyal young fellow as Malik was twisted into a discontented man through "red tape".

If you can do anything in the matter to put things straight, I believe you would be doing a good thing.

With kind regards
S. Russell [270]

---

270. IOR/L/MIL/7/19015: 1917-1920, 10 February, p. 108

Two days later, Sir Murray Hammick brought the letter to the attention of Lieutenant-General Sir Herbert Vaughan Cox, Military Secretary at the India Office, whose primary responsibility was the recruitment of British and other European nationals to the officer ranks of the Indian Army. Hammick told General Cox that Russell was 'level headed and not one to make a mountain out of a molehill. If this officer's feelings can be smoothed down it could be worth doing'.[271]

There is no further reference in the India Office archives about the issue of the document that Hardit was forced to produce each month. The paper itself was likely to have been a 'certificate of identity', which Whitehall encouraged certain classes of Indians in Britain to acquire, as it could play a part in clarifying the evident ambiguities between being a British subject and an 'alien'. Yet, in a situation where he was fighting alongside other British officers, it served only to focus attention on the fact that he was treated differently to his peers.

Nonetheless, this brief correspondence gave a hint of Hardit's state of mind on returning from Italy and was also another illustration of Hardit's capacity to motivate influential connections on his behalf when required.

On 27 February, he reported for duty with 141 Squadron at Biggin Hill in Kent. This unit was newly formed the previous January, in response to increasing bombing raids on London by German 'Gotha' and 'Giant' aircraft. The strategic location of the airfield to the south of London meant that it was ideally placed to defend the capital against attacks from that direction. The Germans were launching an increasing number of sorties at night and combating this threat was to be central to 141 Squadron's role. The site had actually been established at the end of 1916 to develop radiotelephony, which involved experiments with wireless communication, leading ultimately to the first trials of equipment for air-to-air and later ground-to-air exchanges.

During his time at Biggin Hill, which was to last until the following June, Hardit saw the installation of the first long-range transmitter at nearby Aperfield Court, which played a part in the testing processes at various times.[272] The 'Wireless Experimental Establishment' staff occupied

---

271. Ibid., p. 109
272. Caygill, P., *'The Biggin Hill Wing, 1941: From Defence to Attack'* (Pen & Sword Aviation: Barnsley, 2008), p. 3

the South Camp at the airstrip, whilst 141 Squadron occupied the newly constructed North Camp.

The average age of the men of Hardit's new squadron was only twenty-one and many had recently returned from active service on the Western Front. Their numbers included Australians, Canadians, New Zealanders, Rhodesians and very memorably on arrival, an Indian:

> [...] a few days later, an additional pilot arrived, Lieutenant Hardit Singh Malik, a Sikh from Rawalpindi. He turned up late one night, long after the orderlies had gone off duty, and was given an empty room in the requisitioned cottage. In the morning the other officers were woken by piercing yells, and dashed out of their rooms to see what was happening. A batman entered the new arrival's home with shaving water, but had been startled out of his wits by the turbaned and black bearded head on the pillow and fled before streams of Hindustani invective from the indignant Malik. A keen cricketer and golfer, Malik was one of the most popular officers at Biggin Hill. He staunchly refused to part with his turban and somehow managed to fit over it an outsize flying helmet, earning the affectionate name of the 'flying hobgoblin' from the ground crew.[273]

Inevitably, a rivalry developed between the two Biggin Hill camps: on the one side the pilots and the other the 'Wireless Wizards', as they came to be known.[274] Close to the Black Horse pub, in the nearby village of Westerham, was a tearoom with a large teapot shaped advertising sign hanging over the entrance. It became the routine for the occupants of both camps to make off with the sign during nocturnal forays. The increasingly battered sign was then transported to and fro across the site until neither side was certain of its whereabouts. Finally, a truce was called when the increasingly irate owner arrived to retrieve the hoarding and was duly escorted home by a party of officers with teas ordered all round to make amends. In two related photographs, a relaxed looking Hardit posed with

---

273. Wallace, G., '*RAF Biggin Hill*' (Pace Reprographics: Denham, Bucks, 1979), p. 36
274. Ibid.

fellow flyers with the sign, though it's not clear whether he had been a part of the tearoom raiding party![275]

In his letter to the India Office, Samuel Russell had been correct about Hardit flying the single seat Sopwith Dolphin scout with his new squadron. Indeed, it had been the first to receive the plane in January, to join its assortment of other types, which included the B.E.12b, B.E.2s and a solitary Sopwith Pup on the establishment. In his autobiography, Hardit made little mention of his time at Biggin Hill, however, if he thought that the 'Home Defence' role was to be an undemanding one, by comparison to France and Italy, he had initially to think again. The Dolphins had been unmodified or even tested and though the pilots were all experienced they found their new machines very difficult to handle, the aircraft going into a spin when they tried an acute left turn for example and finding that the whole platform lacked stability. The testing of the Dolphins represented a challenging time for the pilots and Hardit was himself almost undone by its notoriously unreliable engine and a cockpit high up between the wings, which could only be entered through the top plane.[276] Having turned sharply close to the ground during one flight, Hardit's machine flipped over and landed on its back with him trapped inside, unable to move and free himself without support from the groundcrew, owing to the cockpit position. Fortunately, the aircraft's fuel did not ignite.[277] In spite of these technical problems, 141 Squadron's airmen came to appreciate the plane's potential for manoeuvrability and all-round vision when flying during daylight hours, though the unit suffered a number of casualties in the process.[278] Nevertheless, its commander in the early months, Major Philip Babington came to the conclusion that the Dolphins were unsuitable for night time operations, their engines often unreliable, rendering the machines impractical for the role required in the face of increasing night-time German bombing raids. As a result, they were replaced by Bristol F.2b Fighters, dependable two-seat aircraft with excellent defensive capacity. Hardit would now be

---

275. The images are in the possession of Mark Haselden, whose grandfather Eric Haselden was a fellow pilot in 141 Squadron. The images can be seen at: www.lwf.it.ox.ac.uk.
276. Wallace, G., 'RAF Biggin Hill', p. 39
277. Ibid.
278. Canwell, D. & Sutherland, J., 'Battle of Britain 1917: The First Heavy Bomber Raids on England' (Pen and Sword Aviation: Barnsley, 2006).

flying with an observer, who was armed with a Lewis Gun and who took on spotting and reconnaissance roles from the rear cockpit. This version of the Bristol Fighter handled like a scout with its single Vickers Machine Gun to the fore, yet with the added benefit of the sting in its tail. To add to the effect, 141 Squadron's Bristol Fighters each sported a bright red cockerel painted on the fuselage following its victory in a Home Defence 'Squadrons-At-Arms' competition later in the year, resulting in the inevitable nickname of the 'Cock Squadron'!

Biggin Hill became a key station in the London Air Defence Area with responsibility for the North Kent sector and 141 Squadron in its night-flying role patrolled a beat between its base and the Thames at Joyce Green. Their Bristol Fighters were equipped with a rudimentary form of wireless telephony, in an early attempt to guide pilots to the enemy in the dark. This scheme worked by feeding information about the enemy supplied by coastguard installations, searchlight and gun platforms, as well as patrolling aircraft, into an operation's room based at the North Camp. The information was then processed and the raiders' positions and courses plotted with increasing degrees of accuracy. The final element was communicating the courses and altitudes required by the intercepting machines and were broadcast via the Aperfield Court transmitter and finally re-laid to the patrolling Bristol Fighters by wireless telephone.[279] This scheme would be the forerunner of the sector control system that played such a decisive part in the Battle of Britain twenty-two years later. It wasn't to be the squadron's only contribution to the development of wireless telephony. In tandem with a company of Royal Engineers based at the North Camp, the Bristol Fighters were employed simulating Gotha bombing raids. These endless hours of formation flying by day and night enabled the engineers on the ground to hone their skills in coordinating searchlight deployment with a revolutionary sound detections system, a frequently tedious, but vital task towards the safeguarding of London.[280] The squadron was called out to combat major German bombing raids on four occasions during Hardit's time with them until early June, yet on none of these occasions did he appear with the crews deployed.

---

279. Wallace, G., 'RAF Biggin Hill', p. 40
280. Ibid.

There *was* evidence of other ways that Hardit was involved during this time at Biggin Hill.[281] He was tasked occasionally with delivering new aeroplanes to replace those lost in the bitter aerial fighting during the German offensives on the Western Front from the end of March 1918 onwards. Along with other pilots, he would deliver a plane to 1 Aircraft Depot at St Omer and then usually return in a Handley Page O/10 transport plane. However, on one occasion, Hardit was uncomfortable with what he saw, as he remembered:

> The Handley Page did not have a good reputation and I did not like the way that the pilot, with whom we were to return, handled the plane. As the officer in charge of our party, I took the responsibility of telling the commander at St Omer that we could not fly back with the pilot as I did not consider it safe [...] At Biggin Hill that evening, our commander Captain Brian Baker [282] informed me that he had received orders from the General to put me under arrest for disobeying orders at St Omer. [...] Baker told me that later that I had done well, for he had just heard that the Handley Page had crashed on landing at Lympne and everyone on board had been killed. In spite of this I was to consider myself under arrest. Baker indicated that this was a mere formality and I was free to go where I liked which gave me a chance for pleasure flying, including a visit to my old golf club at Eastbourne. The old members were excited when I landed on my old school football field alongside the golf course.[283]

It wasn't to be the only opportunity for Hardit to leave Biggin Hill. Early in March, he travelled to Manchester, having been chosen by the RFC to be the recipient of a singular honour. A letter sent on behalf of the

---

281. Canwell, D. & Sutherland, J., *'Battle of Britain 1917: The First Heavy Bomber Raids on England'*.

282. Appointed temporarily to the role on 30 April, owing to Philip Babington's incapacity following a crash. Baker was appointed permanently as commander of 141 Squadron in the days following the night of 19/20 May when he led a patrol against enemy aircraft.

283. Malik, H.S., *'A Little Work, A Little Play'*, p. 95

Air Board to Lord Islington, Under-Secretary of State for India, had confirmed the details:

13 February 1918

Sir,

With reference to telephone conversation regarding Hon. 2nd Lieutenant Hardit Singh Malik, RFC, SR, I am directed to inform you to say that this officer has done most excellent work while with the Royal Flying Corps and is strongly recommended for a permanent commission.

I am to say that he was appointed a temporary Honorary 2nd Lieutenant in the Royal Flying Corps, Special Reserve, on 6 April 1917. He has flown in France where he was wounded and has just returned from Italy, where he has been with a Squadron.

I am to add that he was recommended as the most suitable recipient for the Medallion to be presented by the City of Manchester to the most distinguished flier of the Indian Army. A statement of his service whilst with the Royal Flying Corps is attached.

I am, Sir,

Your obedient servant,
W.W. Warner
Lieut. Colonel, A.A.G.
For Director of Air Organisation.[284]

Although this letter was sent only three days after Samuel Russell had written to the India Office on 10 February, the possibility exists that such a presentation to Hardit might have been part of the 'smoothing down' of his feelings mentioned in Hammick's note to General Cox two days later. Nevertheless, Hardit was a natural choice for the honour, he was back in Britain, had a kill to his name and future ace Indra Lal Roy was yet to claim the first of his ten kills until 6 July that year.

---

284. IOR/L/MIL/7/19015: 1917-1920, 13 February 1918, p. 111

The presentation ceremony took place on Saturday, 2 March at the Athletic Ground at Fallowfield, in Manchester. The event itself was primarily an occasion to present the GOI with a new Sopwith Camel provided by the Manchester Chamber of Commerce.[285] The multiple presentations were made by Mr Stoker of the Manchester Chamber, initially to Lord Desborough, the President of the London Chamber,[286] then to Sahibzada Aftab Ahmad Khan on behalf of the GOI and finally to Colonel Bertram Beor of the <u>Air Ministry</u>. Lord Islington, who had been instrumental in Hardit Singh's award and attendance at the event, sent a telegram from faraway Simla:

> Please convey to the Chamber of Commerce on behalf of the Indian Government my cordial thanks for their generous gift. Under modern conditions of warfare, the importance of the Air Services increases from day to day. In India, the scope of their activity and usefulness has greatly developed and in last year's operations in Waziristan, our airmen showed how aircraft can be utilised to meet the special conditions of frontier warfare. It is very gratifying to us in India, to learn that 2nd Lieutenant Hardit Singh Malik has earned distinction in the Royal Flying Corps and I congratulate him on being selected for distinction. Lord Islington.[287]

In front of a large crowd, Hardit was photographed and filmed with the Camel, which had been named 'Manchester India'. In the short motion picture produced by Pathé, to be shown to cinema audiences, Hardit was to be seen smiling happily atop the Camel's fuselage, pointing to a particular insignia behind the cockpit. He posed more seriously with Lord Desborough and Sahibzada Aftab Ahmad Khan, almost lost among those thronging the ceremonial podium, and then suddenly visible once more, grinning widely for a fleeting moment.[288] In a brief report, which appeared

---

285. 'Chamber of Commerce: Gift of an aeroplane to India', *Manchester Guardian*, 4 March 1918, p. 5

286. Lord Desborough was father to the celebrated poet Julian Grenfell, who was killed in action in 1915.

287. Sapru, S., '*Sky Hawks*', p. 210

288. '*Manchester Aeroplane Gift to India 1914-1918*' – as of 3 August 2020 - Britishpathe. com/video/manchester-aeroplane-gift-to-india.

in the *Manchester Guardian,* a few days later, no mention was made of the commemorative medal, but we must assume that it was presented that day. Hardit made no mention of the event or the medallion in his autobiography, though Somnath Sapru mentioned the occasion in *Sky Hawks.*

It may have been a coincidence, but *The Graphic* of 30 March carried an article entitled 'The Indian as a Flying Man: The latest contingent for our Air Service', which included a tribute to Hardit alongside other Indian airmen - Roy, Sen and Welinkar. The article began with the seemingly salutary story of Mohan Singh (not Hardit's father), another Punjabi Sikh, who having taken up flying in the United States, had 'crossed over to this country in the hope of entering the British Air Service, or at all events, of being sent out to India as an airman. But he found his brown skin a great handicap'.[289] The article continued:

> Several young men belonging to good Indian families and with brilliant records at British Universities and Inns of Court, sought to enter the Royal Flying Corps to serve their Emperor and Empire during a war which required no end of airmen. They had influential friends who did all in their power to assist them. But they all found doors leading to the commissioned rank tightly shut at that time.[290]

The account precisely represented the experience of the other Indians generally and Hardit Singh in particular. The author of the article was journalist Saint Nitar Singh, who was educated at Punjab University, and having travelled extensively in the United States, Canada and Japan, wrote widely for a variety of British publications. The article ended with the following rallying cry: 'Many Indians in Britain, equally as capable of making good airmen as their countrymen in the Royal Flying Corps, are waiting for the chance to serve Emperor and Empire. Now it is hoped that these young men will be given their opportunity!'[291] This was an encapsulation of the position held by Secretary of State for India Edwin Montagu and many, though not all, at the India Office. The publicity surrounding the Manchester presentation and several articles appearing in the popular press

---

289. *The Graphic,* 30 March 1918, p. 394
290. Ibid.
291. Ibid.

about the RFC's Indian pilots during March 1918, can be seen in the light of the renewed appeal for recruits in India and the ongoing discussions about granting King's Commissions to Indians at the forthcoming meetings of the cabinet, as we shall see. The information contained within the articles can only have come from either of two sources – the India Office or the Air Board, such was the detail relating to the circumstances of each of the pilots included. It can be argued that their stories were being used as an opportunity to promote as widely and as positively as possible Indo-British military collaboration in general, and the collective case of Indian RFC officers in particular. Hardit's story was at the forefront of showcasing the part played by Indians in the RFC and it wouldn't be the last time.

Back at Biggin Hill, and with decreasing numbers of enemy sorties to occupy the airmen during the late spring, the time began to pass slowly and Captain Baker was determined to keep everyone in 141 Squadron keen and active. He organised daily rugby matches, paper chases and various forms of airborne challenges. Inevitably perhaps, flying became an increasingly reckless activity and the number of crashes increased as the demands of the contests became ever riskier. It was during this time that Hardit broke his nose in a seemingly low-key accident, which demanded treatment. He was operated on at the Royal Air Force Auxiliary Hospital, at 82 Eaton Square, in a well-heeled part of Chelsea. It was located in a converted mansion and old habits seemed to have persisted, the well-stocked cellars of wine frequently being put at the disposal of the patients! Perhaps while under the influence of the grape, a couple of fellow pilots teased the young and pretty nurse caring for Hardit, telling her that should a Sikh's turban be removed during her care she would have to marry the fellow! Having taken the joke rather more seriously than intended, the startled nurse and the charming flying officer became close friends, dining out and going dancing into the small hours. When Hardit teased her that he was disappointed that she was initially scared of the thought of marrying him, she could only say, 'Well H.S., I didn't know you then!'[292]

Following a brief recuperation, Hardit was reassigned to another unit involved with Home Defence, 78 Squadron based at Sutton's Farm on the north-eastern side of London. Whereas 141 Squadron patrolled south of

---

292. Malik, H.S., *'A Little Work, A Little Play'*, p. 92

the River Thames, 78 was deployed to the north of it, equipped with a full complement of Sopwith Camels. Hardit made no mention of 78 Squadron in his autobiography, but his relocation meant that from 7 June he was to fly a plane powered by either of two versions of a rotary engine which required castor oil, the very lubricant which had caused his sickness and return to Britain from Italy the previous February.[293]

There is no mention of Hardit in the records of the sorties undertaken by 78 Squadron during his posting with it, and indeed, as we shall see, he may well have had a non-flying role with it, which ended early in October, when once more he was transferred to another posting.

---

293. AIR 76/331

Chapter 9

London
1918

'At this time, when the intention of the rulers of Germany
to establish a tyranny, not only over all Europe but over Asia
as well, has become transparently clear, I wish to ask the
government and people of India to redouble their efforts.'
Prime Minister Lloyd George, 2 April 1918

For a year following Hardit's hospitalisation in October 1917, the issue of whether to grant King's Commissions to Indians confronted the cabinet, the India Office, the War Office and the GOI. At its heart, was Lloyd George's desire to recruit a further 500,000 Indian troops to enable the creation of new military formations, the bolstering of understrength battalions and to enable the redeployment of forces to the Western Front. Britain and its allies faced the greatest threat of the war: the initially successful and devastating German offensives of late March, April and May 1918. At their height, German forces drove a forty mile salient into the allied line, almost to the gates of Amiens. For the recruitment campaign in India to succeed, the Viceroy, Lord Chelmsford, believed that to engage the support of moderate Indians in the <u>Imperial Legislative Council</u> and throughout the Raj, only the lifting of the colour bar in relation to the Indian commissions issue would suffice. Even in the event that the additional half a million sepoys were enlisted, Chelmsford knew that there were insufficient officers of the quality required to command these troops and that more would be needed. He saw the granting of King's Commissions to Indians as *the* key concession required by the GOI to enable the most successful recruitment drive possible in the subcontinent, and as such had drawn up final proposals to be debated by the cabinet at two meetings on 25 and 26 April.

During 1918, a common pattern was established: the GOI would set out proposals to be sent to London, which were usually approved by Secretary of State Montagu. The resulting memoranda for each cabinet meeting would then be opposed by the Army Council and by some in cabinet, and an alternative set of proposals would then be sent back to Delhi and the process would be repeated. Agreement proved to be very difficult to find indeed and what follows are the essential moments in the complex and convoluted process to find a satisfactory solution during 1918, one relevant to Hardit's future as a flying officer.

Montagu's visit to India, between 1917 and the following May, couldn't have come at a worse time. The Secretary of State made the trip to hear the views of India's governing classes, and gain support for the shaping of what was to become the Montagu-Chelmsford Report, to be published on 8 July 1918. In his absence, the meetings of the cabinet back in London lacked a truly passionate advocate in favour of granting King's Commissions to Indians. He must have found it particularly galling that opposing views from some military members of his own office were actually to be heard espousing their belief that 'the granting at once of a large number of temporary King's Commissions to Indians would deter British officers from joining the Indian Army', a point of view utterly rejected by Montagu.[294]

In the run up to the two cabinet meetings of April, a conference was convened between officials from both the India Office and the War Office on 14 March. Central to the demands of members of the Army Council, was that any Indian commissioned officers were *always* to be posted to Indian units in India, as this would greatly reduce the possibilities of Indian officers commanding British officers and soldiers.[295] Lord Chelmsford had already made clear the previous November however, that such placements would de facto offer no further benefits to Indian officers than the existing rank of Viceroy Commissioned Officer or an honorary commission. *Only* the principle of granting King's Commissions to Indians in *all* formations of Empire would be acceptable, as was the case when Australian, South African or Canadian officers served with British battalions. Chelmsford and Montagu were looking to establish Indian officers with the same status as their white dominion

---

294. Imperial War Cabinet Agenda and Minutes, TNA, CAB-23-6-22, 26 April 1918
295. CAB-24-49-28, Montagu to Chelmsford, 5 April 1918

counterparts. Lord Chelmsford believed that there were 'serious political objections to emphasising racial distinctions, (and) we deprecate any formal exclusion of Indians from commissioned ranks of the British services'.[296] He represented his case to cabinet in a number of last-minute telegrams from Delhi, some of which did not arrive in time in London to influence the cabinet meeting of 25 April, but were available for the one the following day:

> I trust Prime Minister's personal attention has been drawn to this vital matter of commissions. The proposal we made was put forward by [...] the commander of the Indian Army himself, with full sense of responsibility and its rejections will severely hamper our efforts.[297]

> The alternative you suggest[298] would in no way satisfy the influential classes whose services we are seeking to enlist in recruiting large numbers. We already have power to give temporary commissions in Indian Land Forces and are doing so as a reward for recruiting work. Such commissions possess no novelty and are not sufficiently attractive for present needs.[299]

The GOI's updated proposals to the cabinet were more radical even than those submitted on 20 July the previous year (see Chapter 6):

(a.) Permanent commissions.
   That an announcement of the grant of ten permanent King's commissions yearly through Sandhurst might be made.

   That an announcement of the grant of King's commissions to a maximum of twenty selected Indian officers specifically distinguished in the war might be made.

---

296. CAB-24-49-28, Chelmsford to Montagu, 13 November 1917
297. The Commander in Chief, India was Sir Charles Monro at this time.
298. The idea of granting temporary commissions only to Indians in Indian battalions in the subcontinent, submitted by War Office officials at the 14 March conference.
299. Memorandum: Commissions for Indians. Chelmsford to Montagu. TNA, CAB-24-49-42, 25 April 1918

(b.) Temporary commissions.

That temporary King's commissions should be granted during the war, on the same conditions as apply to British candidates for temporary commissions in the Indian Army, to the maximum number of 200, on nomination by loyal Governments and General Officers Commanding, and approval by the Commander-in-Chief and the Viceroy.

(c.) Honorary commissions.

That an announcement might be made of the grant of honorary King's Commissions to old and distinguished Indian officers still on the Active List, up to an establishment of one per infantry battalion and other arms in proportion, this established number to be filled up gradually.[300]

Following the April cabinet discussions, an amended scheme was agreed upon, the refinements offering reassurance to its opponents. Those resisting change continued to be troubled in particular by the proposal to grant 200 temporary King's Commissions to Indians per year 'on the same conditions as apply to British candidates for temporary commissions in the Indian Army'. They believed that a cautious step by step approach to development was being abandoned and was described on at least one occasion as being 'dangerous'.[301] Concerns were also expressed about the potential problems after the war, by the potential increase in the overall number of permanent Indian King's Commissioned Officers. The responses of the military members of the Army Council were summarised two months later, in a note issued on the matter by the then Secretary of State for War Viscount Milner, who felt initially compelled to clarify his own position on the matter:

I do not feel justified in withholding the subjoined note by the Military Members of the Army Council on the subject. At the same time, my own view is, as I have informed the Military Members, that whatever may be the objections to the grant

---

300. Imperial War Cabinet, Agenda and Minutes, TNA, CAB-23-6-21, 25 April 1918
301. Ibid.

of these commissions on military grounds, the arguments in favour of it, based on the broadest consideration of policy, outweigh them.

The Military Members have no desire to criticise in any way the decision arrived at by the War Cabinet, and they will in future use their best endeavours to carry out the policy determined on. At the same time, they feel that they would fail in their duty as the recognised military advisors of the government if they did not place on record their considered opinion that from a military point of view a grave risk will in the future be run by the contemplated grant of commissions to natives, by which natives will be placed in positions from which they will be entitled to command white officers. A further resulting effect will, in the opinion of the Military Members, be the failure of the supply of British Officers of the right stamp for service with the Indian Army.[302]

The debate continued until the cabinet meeting of 12 June, when a final clarification relating to the main sticking point - the recommendation for up to 200 Indian temporary commissions - was agreed in cabinet and sent by telegram to the GOI. Although what was settled upon was in a diluted form to that desired by Lord Chelmsford, he had something to offer moderates in India. Montagu himself was furious about the opposition to the scheme from the Army Council:

[...] is there an ordinance of nature that cannot be violated with impunity, against placing an Indian, no matter how great his capacity might be, in a position where he commands a British officer? A supposed law of this kind can hardly be distinguished from racial prejudice and must be rejected by those entrusted with imperial responsibilities.[303]

302. Indian Commissions. Note by Lord Milner covering memo by Military Members of Army Council. TNA, CAB-24-55-65, 26 June 1918
303. Memorandum - Commissions for Indians, TNA, CAB-24-57-62, Secretary of State Montagu, 5 July 1918

On 1 April 1918, the RFC and the RNAS were amalgamated to form a new service, the Royal Air Force, under the newly created Air Ministry and its governing body the Air Council. A month earlier, with manpower shortages also affecting the recruitment of suitable numbers of observers and pilots for the RFC, it began to be evident to some officials at the India Office that the granting of commissions to Indians in the embryonic RAF might also be possible, running in parallel to those being debated for the Indian Army. In the lead up to the 14 March conference, the India Office took the initiative to look into the matter. At the beginning of March, its Public and Judicial Secretary, J.E. Ferard wrote to his colleague, the Military Secretary, General Cox, asking for information. Cox would be managing Hardit's case throughout 1918, on behalf of the military department at the India Office. It is worth looking in detail at this ongoing correspondence, for it illuminates how Hardit's status within the fledgling RAF became a unique element in the wider discussions:

> Sir H. Cox,
> Commissions for Indians in the Flying Corps.
> Major Wallinger [304] has shown me this note and letter from Gen. Hogg,[305] in charge of the Flying Corps training, Eastern Command. Do you happen to have considered Flying Corps Commissions in connection with the question of Commissions generally for Indians? Major Wallinger's idea is that they stand on a somewhat different footing and he thought that even if Indians weren't to fly in France they might very well do so in Egypt, Mesopotamia etc.
> What do you think?[306]

---

304. Sir John Arnold Wallinger was a British Indian intelligence officer who led the prototype 'Indian Political Intelligence Office' from 1909 to 1916. He was also the literary prototype of the spymaster of a number of Somerset Maugham's short stories. Wallinger is credited with leading the Indian intelligence missions outside India, notably against the Indian Anarchist movement in Britain. By 1918, he appeared to be based at the India Office in an undefined advisory role.

305. Brigadier-General R.E.T. Hogg was commanding the Eastern Training Brigade until the end of March 1918. He had joined the RFC in 1915, having served in India with Royal Artillery, the 38th Central Indian Horse and the Indian Staff Corps since 1898.

306. Grant of commissions in Royal Air Force to selected Indians, Collection 430/5 Part 1, IOR/L/MIL/7/19010: 1917-1920, 1 March 1918, p. 147

Ferard then wrote to another India Office colleague, Dr Thomas Arnold[307] the following day, requesting his opinion, which brought the following response:

Mr Ferard,

I know of six Indian students who have received Commissions in the Flying Corps (viz, H.S. Malik, Htin Wah, J.P.B. Jeejeebhoy, E.S.C. Sen, S.C. Welinkar and _ _ Roy), and a commission will probably be given to E.P. Sen (a nephew of Mr N.C. Sen). I think that it would be a good thing if it were recognised that Indian students wishing to take part in some form of military service, should have a chance of getting into the Flying Corps.

T.W. Arnold 4/3/18[308]

General Cox's response to Ferard was instructive:

[...] The scheme of the Government of India appears to have overlooked one class of young Indians, possibly because they were unaware in India that such a class existed. I allude to those few who, not contented with sitting with their mouths open waiting for a British Commission to drop into them (as is the case with most), have managed to get taken on in the ranks of British units and have subsequently distinguished themselves and, are now, or have been holding, honorary commissions and are believed to be entirely suitable for a permanent British Commission. Although this class is very small in numbers, yet in my humble opinion it merits favourable consideration.

The grant of British Commissions to the one or two men who have passed successfully through the ranks of our Army, which they entered in the face of many difficulties and from purely patriotic motives, would furnish the most complete reply

---

307. Sir Thomas Walker Arnold was a British orientalist and historian of Islamic art. From 1917 to 1920 he acted as Adviser to the Secretary of State for India.
308. IOR/L/MIL/7/19010: 1917-1920, 4 March 1918, p. 146

to the many who apply to me to be considered for a British Commission, but have not the slightest intention of attempting to do anything to show that they are worthy to obtain it. If men such as the three military careers outlined below, are given a British Commission, it will enable me to say to the rest "Go and do thou likewise".[309]

The three men referred to by General Cox were K.A.D. Naoroji, A.A. Rudra and of course Hardit Singh Malik. 'Kish' Naoroji was the grandson of the aforementioned former Liberal MP for Lambeth North, the late Dadabhai Naoroji. Kish Naoroji rose to the rank of Platoon Sergeant in 16 Middlesex Regiment, until wounded in action in July 1916. Ajit Rudra served with 2 Royal Fusiliers, seeing action at Gallipoli and on the first day of the Somme in front of Beaumont Hamel as a Lewis Gunner.[310] Both men were recommended for training at Sandhurst as part of the GOI's proposed commissions' scheme, but refused, having already completed officer training since leaving their respective battalions, having been initially recommended by their commanding officers. Eventually, both were sent for training in India.[311]

Cox went on to recommend the third candidate for a permanent commission:

> Honorary 2nd Lieut. Hardit Singh Malik, Royal Flying Corps, Special Reserve. The Military Aeronautics Directorate report that this young officer has done most excellent work with the Royal Flying Corps and recommend him strongly for a permanent commission. He was appointed to his present post on 6 April 1917. He has flown in France, where he was wounded, and he has just returned from Italy where he has been with his Squadron. He is the most distinguished flier of the Indian Army. He is the son of an Ahluwalia Sikh landlord of Rawalpindi. I am not sure where he was educated, but he

---

309. IOR/L/MIL/7/19015: 1917-1920, Cox, India Office Minute, 13 March 1918, pp. 105-106

310. Ibid.

311. Barua, P.P., 'Gentlemen of the Raj: The Indian Army Officer Corps, 1817-1949' (Praeger: Connecticut, 2003), p. 47

is well spoken and has a pleasant manner. His record entitles him to consideration equally with the others. He has not been medically examined in the India Office, but there is little doubt that he would pass. He is about 24, I think.

I suggest that, without further loss of time, we represent the case of these three young gentlemen to the War Office and ask them what their view would be of a recommendation made by us that all three should be added to the list of those granted the King's Commission and posted to the India Army.

H.V. Cox 13.3.18 [312, 313]

Although General Cox was complimentary about Hardit, the final sentence suggesting a posting to the Indian Army for *all three* candidates would not have pleased Hardit, who would have wanted to remain a flying officer, now an important part of his identity.

It's worth noting here, that the Indian commissions conference of 14 March had taken place the day before, when it will be remembered, that officials from the War Office had made it clear that any Indian commissioned officers were *always* to be posted to Indian units in India. In this light, and the ongoing policy vacuum on the issue, Cox was looking to resolve the problem of what to do with the commissioning of Naoroji, Rudra and Hardit Singh, by posting all three men to India.

The correspondence continued into the spring and summer, Cox writing this time to the GOI on 5 April, advising that Naoroji, Rudra and Hardit Singh be recommended for King's Commissions in the Indian Army, on condition that all three went through a military college, either at Sandhurst, Quetta or Wellington. Cox made it clear that their attendance would have a 'good political effect, I have seen all three and believe them likely to do well'.[314] Indian Office officials such as General Cox, were guided in this belief by the Secretary of State Edwin Montagu, who was especially keen for the three Indians to succeed. Naoroji, Rudra and Hardit Singh

312. IOR/L/MIL/7/19015: 1917-1920, Cox, India Office Minute, 13 March 1918, p. 106

313. Cox was able to describe Hardit as 'the most distinguished flier of the Indian Army', for by the end of 1917, the RFC had established two squadrons in India. As the RFC was the air arm of the British Army, so the two RFC squadrons based in India were associated with the Indian Army.

314. IOR/L/MIL/7/19015: 1917-1920, Cox to the GOI, 5 April 1918, pp. 102-103

represented test cases for those wishing to grant King's Commissions to Indians, all had been to Oxford or Cambridge, were from 'good' families and had enlisted into British units on their own initiative. If they couldn't graduate from Sandhurst, then few would.

On 15 May, however, the India Office received a less than enthusiastic response to Cox's telegram of 5 April, from the GOI. It indicated that the three candidates were too old to go to military college and in the light of their own scheme proposing to send candidates to Sandhurst, made it clear that:

> To start commission scheme by nominating for Sandhurst a Parsi (Naoroji), a Christian (Rudra) and a Sikh (Hardit Singh), belonging to a class (sic) which has been conspicuously backward in recruiting, would be regarded as most unjust by the leading men of martial classes who have identified themselves with great recruiting efforts of past year and upon whose further assistance we necessarily rely. Your reluctance to grant temporary commissions renders it all the more necessary that Sandhurst cadetships should be given to the sons of landowners and others who have assisted us by loyal service, rather than to young Indians, who, by their accident of being in England at the outbreak of the war, have been able to see active service with British troops.[315]

'Martial classes' referred to here, related to the practice of 'martial race theory', which had underpinned British recruitment practices in India since the Rebellion of 1857. At its heart was the belief that some groups of men were biologically or culturally predisposed to the art of war. Hence Punjabi Sikhs and Nepalese Gurkhas for example, became linked in both military and popular discourse as the British Empire's fiercest, most manly soldiers and men from such groups were enlisted in large numbers.[316] Whilst Hardit was a Punjabi Sikh, as one who was brought up and educated in Britain, it appeared that he was being identified alongside those not considered part of

---

315. Ibid., GOI to India Office, 15 May 1918, pp. 94-95
316. Streets, H., '*Martial Races: The Military, Race and Masculinity in British Imperial Culture, 1857-1914*' (Manchester University Press: Manchester, 2004), p. i

a martial class – a Parsi and a Bengali Christian. Fundamentally, the GOI wanted to select its own candidates in India for officer commissions.

Nonetheless, following the agreement made in cabinet on 25 and 26 April for a scheme granting King's Commissions to Indians, General Cox felt able to find another solution to the management of Hardit's future, namely, that he be transferred to the new RAF on a temporary commission, as would any new British cadet. It was with some relief that Cox wrote to the Permanent Under-Secretary of State for India, Sir Thomas Holderness, that by following such a course of action 'the War Office will then have nothing to do with his case'.[317] In other words, once the Air Ministry had taken over the departmental responsibilities for the running of the new RAF from the War Office, Hardit's case for a commission would be looked on more favourably. Cox knew that there were officials at the Air Ministry who looked upon the granting of commissions to Indians very positively indeed. Even by July however, the War Office continued to be involved, owing to administrative hold-ups within the Air Ministry delaying it fully taking up its responsibilities. Nevertheless, the India Office felt confident enough of success, to request that the War Office grant Hardit a temporary commission.[318] The reply came three weeks later:

> With regard to the case of Honorary 2nd Lieutenant Hardit Singh Malik, a letter was addressed to the Air Council on 16 July last, requesting that this officer might be gazetted to a temporary commission in the Royal Air Force. As no answer has been received up to date, a reminder of this subject has already been despatched.[319]

By the end of August, the Air Ministry confirmed that Hardit had been granted a temporary commission in the RAF at the rank of 'lieutenant', with effect from 1 April 1918.[320] He made no mention of this development in his autobiography, but it was an important moment. From this point on, the Air Ministry would be managing his case, in tandem with the India Office.

---

317. IOR/L/MIL/7/19015: 1917-1920, Cox to Holderness, 16 May 1918, p. 91
318. Ibid., India Office to the GOI, 25 July 1918, p. 74
319. Ibid., War Office to India Office, 16 August 1918, p. 68
320. Ibid., Air Ministry to the War Office, 24 August 1918, p. 67

That same August, General Brancker became Master-General of Personnel within the RAF. As we have seen, Brancker believed himself to be responsible for the 'recruitment of four Indian pilots at the end of 1916 and early 1917.' A month into his new role on 21 September, he wrote to General Cox at the India Office:

> My Dear General,
> You probably know that we have a big training organisation in Egypt for the production of pilots and observers for the Royal Air Force. In all quarters of the world now, we are finding it difficult to obtain good men in sufficient numbers to fill our training establishment. We are drawing to some extent on the armies in India, Mesopotamia, and Palestine, but up to date have taken no Indians for this purpose.
>
> About two years ago, I was instrumental in training I think, 4 Indians, who happened to be in England, for employment with the Royal Flying Corps, and 3 certainly did very well. Personally, I am of the opinion that the well-bred Indian will make a most excellent pilot, and if employed away from his country would be absolutely trustworthy.
>
> I am bringing up the question at the Air Council, but meanwhile I would be very much obliged if you would let me know the official view in the India Office to such a proposal.[321]

General Cox's reply to Brancker on 24 September, began with reference to Hardit Singh Malik:

> [...] who has served as a pilot in France and Italy with some distinction, was then employed as an instructor at one of your schools at home, and now only a week ago returned to Italy as a pilot again.[322]

Cox was mistaken about Hardit returning to Italy, which rather discredited his assertion of Hardit's alleged instructor's role. However, if true, it's likely

---

321. Ibid., Brancker to Cox, 21 September 1918, p. 123
322. Ibid., Cox to Brancker, 24 September 1918, p. 121

to have been whilst serving with 78 Squadron. It will be remembered that this unit operated Sopwith Camels, the same machine responsible for his sickness in Italy earlier in the year and might explain why an instructor's role was appropriate. Hardit had a wealth of experience with the Camel after all. Cox's reply to Brancker continued:

> I agree with you entirely that Indians of the right kind are very likely to make excellent Pilots and Observers. They have extraordinarily good sight, are generally speaking strictly temperate, if not total abstainers, and possess good nerves. I think I may say that the official view of the India Office would be that there can be no objection to the employment of Indians as temporary commissioned officers in the Royal Air Force, provided that they receive equal treatment to young Englishmen selected for the same employment and that the Secretary of State and the Government of India would (given the above condition) be glad to assist the Royal Air Force in the selection of young men from any candidates that they may put forward.

> You will understand that I am only expressing my own opinion, and what I consider probably the opinion of my superiors in this matter.[323]

Cox was correct, but it is worth noting that the end of the war was imminent and policies and opinions could and would change. Two days later Brancker wrote again to Cox, reiterating that he had been 'instrumental in employing the four Indians you allude to'. He continued 'I took them on, I intended to learn from their doings what could be expected in the future'.[324] In other words, Welinkar, Sen, Roy and Hardit Singh had been used as test cases; an experiment to demonstrate that Indians could make the grade as pilots. Finally, Brancker asked Cox his views about using Indians as pilots on the Indian North-West Frontier. The General's reply was an interesting one:

---

323. Ibid.
324. Ibid., Brancker to Cox, 26 September 1918, p. 120

I see no objection whatever to Sikh or Rajput pilots being employed on N.W.F. of India – or in fact any Hindu or Gurkha. Punjabi Mussalmans of good class should be safe also, but *not* Pathans.[325]

Here Cox's beliefs were principally underpinned by martial race theory, many in the British military believing that, although good fighters, 'Pathans' or Pukhtuns or Pashtuns were unruly Muslim peoples and questioned their loyalty at a time when Empire forces were engaged against Muslim Turkish soldiers in the Middle East. This was at a time of course when their Pukhtun tribal areas were part of the ongoing difficulties on the North-West Frontier and their allegiance to the Empire was in some doubt, in the minds of many in the military establishment.

With the granting of commissions to Indians still an ongoing debate at cabinet level, the Air Ministry and India Office began regular communication about the possibility of recruiting Indian pilots with such backgrounds as Hardit. By early October 1918, the Air Council proposed that they would select 100 Indians from 'good families and high physical qualifications for training as pilots or observers at the new establishment in Egypt'. More importantly, the trainees would be enlisted on the same basis as British personnel, be eligible for temporary commissions and for deployment anywhere in the world.[326] It seemed as though the beginning of the end of the colour bar was in sight.

As October 1918 dawned, Lieutenant Hardit Singh Malik was transferred to a new squadron. He was heading back to the Western Front.

---

325. Ibid., Cox to Brancker, 29 September 1918, p. 119
326. Ibid., Montagu to Chelmsford, 7 October 1918, p. 31

Chapter 10

Nivelles
October 1918–April 1919

'The whole Empire pledged its word not to sheathe the sword
until our end was achieved. That pledge is now redeemed.'
King George V, at the Armistice,
11 November 1918

Crichton indicated to Hardit from the rear cockpit the direction their
machine should take through the cloud. Thick fog had descended in the
last half an hour, making what should have been a routine approach to the
aerodrome a rather awkward one. Hardit nodded in reply and pointed the
aircraft towards the long lines of canvas hangars that appeared suddenly
below as the two-seater fell rapidly. His Bristol Fighter was shepherding two
German Albatros D.VIIs to the Belgian city of Nivelles, midway between
Brussels to the north and Mons to the south-west, where the war for the
British had begun in earnest in late August 1914. The captured planes had
managed to keep the Bristol Fighter in sight for much of the short journey,
but as the fog descended, the Germans had dropped out of view and Hardit
was beginning to fret about losing their former adversaries. He needn't
have been concerned. With the Armistice signed a month earlier, many
were war weary, not least the Germans. Yet his observer 'Jock' Crichton
was beginning to be a concern. Since the ceasefire had been announced,
Hardit had noticed an irritability in the Scottish observer that had not been
evident when they had met two months earlier. It hadn't felt personal but
had manifested itself earlier in the day when Crichton's impatience with
the subdued German pilots almost hindered the smooth processing of the
latter's' captive aircraft. Hardit had needed to intervene on behalf of his
exasperated observer, conducting the arrangements in French with the

German fliers, sensing that Jock was becoming ever more agitated and obsessive. That morning, he had noticed that Crichton had been with the engine fitters since dawn, ensuring that the pre-flight checks on their Bristol were done thoroughly. No one wanted to be killed in an accident now that the war was over, there were no medals to be earned, nor kills to be sought. Most wanted just to get home. Some were becoming jumpy, including Jock. Drink and enforced idleness were playing a part.

Hardit put the aircraft down and taxied towards one of the temporary hangars. To his relief, the Germans had followed behind several minutes apart and were now coming to a halt. Almost at once, a reception guard led them away into captivity, giving just enough time for the taller of the two to make a final salute back towards their now condemned machine. With well-rehearsed precision, the process of disassembling the surrendered aircraft was begun by the decommissioning crew. Two hours later, the stripped-down fuselage would be towed away by truck, a process that had been repeated many times during the last month. Hardit and Jock had witnessed the routine several times since their arrival at Nivelles but headed now into the officers' mess. They passed the temporary canvas structures and entered the refectory building, part of what had been a major German aerodrome throughout the war. Having ordered drinks, the two men sat alone, talking desultorily about what to do after the war. Hardit was clear in his mind – he wanted to continue with the RAF in India, or failing that, to join the ICS as he had planned ten years earlier. Jock didn't know what to do, which only seemed to add to his gloom. Inevitably, discussion turned to the previous night's events at dinner.

The two of them had been posted to 11 Squadron in a party of a dozen mixed pilots and observers, among whom were three South Africans, who kept to themselves for the most part when off duty. Since their arrival at Nivelles however, one of them lost no time in whispering racial slurs within Hardit's hearing. He ignored the insults, as was his usual way, the other man's arrogance and demeanour ensuring his unpopularity around the squadron. Hardit thought no more of it until matters came to a head the previous evening. For the first time in a while, almost all the squadron's members were dining together in the officers' mess, when in response to Hardit's declared ambition to continue a career in flying, the South African made it clear that he believed there should be no place for Indians in the RAF. For a moment there was a silence round the table, ended only by an indistinct utterance from somewhere, which was the signal for Jock Crichton to vault the table and grab the astonished Afrikaner opposite by the collar, threatening to kill him if an apology wasn't imminent. Other officers joined in with their own rebukes and having muttered his excuses, the shaken pilot sloped away from the mess hall and out of the squadron, transferred the following day by the respected Australian commander Major Heath.

Lieutenant Hugh Crichton, better known as 'Jock', who hailed from Linlithgow in West Lothian, had been an infantry officer with the Royal Scots, before transferring to the RAF early in 1918. He had met Hardit at 2 Air Supply Depot, Fienvillers, where they awaited posting to a new squadron at the start of October. Having tired of instructing novice pilots with 78 Squadron, Hardit wanted to see action again before the war ended. Following his premature departure from Italy, there had always been a feeling of unfinished business, a sense that he still had aerial ambitions to fulfil. Quite by chance, the two men had been posted together to 11 Squadron late in October, and then paired as pilot and observer.

Outwardly, the personalities of the two men couldn't have been more different. Though a couple of years younger than Hardit, Crichton's dry sense of humour and few words appealed to him, and the two officers formed a close friendship as a result. 11 Squadron was originally based at Bapaume in France, though the front moved eastwards rapidly as German resistance crumbled and the squadron followed them, first to Aulnoye-Aymeries at the Armistice, then Namur in Belgium and finally on 18 December to Nivelles. This aerodrome had been an advanced training centre for the Luftstreitkräfte throughout the war, becoming an assembly point for surrendered German aircraft following the ceasefire, the terms of which required the capitulation of almost 1700 machines.

During their three weeks together until the Armistice, Jock and Hardit flew reconnaissance patrols between Le Cateau and Cambrai, their primary mission to maintain contact with the enemy on a rapidly changing front, one very different from the static lines of 1917. German resistance disintegrated in the face of acute pilot and fuel shortages and on many sorties were not to be seen at all.

11 November 1918 was spent at the aerodrome within the *commune* of Aulnoye-Aymeries, one formerly behind the German lines throughout the war until overrun at the beginning of October. Located in the beautiful Avenois region, the small town was enveloped in forest and bisected by the

River Sambre, an idyllic location and one of the most attractive places at which to be stationed. Yet Hardit's recollection is of a ceasefire of contrasting perspectives:

> When the Armistice was announced there was a tremendous sense of relief. Most of us had come to feel that the war could never end. One of my most moving memories of the Armistice was watching an infantry battalion returning from the trenches marching past our airfield at Aulnoye, totally exhausted, covered with mud, some of them bloody with slight wounds, half asleep as they walked on. They showed no reaction to the Armistice – too fed up and weary to care – a great contrast to the boisterous spirit of the RAF personnel that day. We had a really rough night of it with much shouting, singing, shooting off flares […] We were joined in our celebration by some pilots of a French squadron who landed at our airfield. They shared our dinner and spent the evening with us. The next day, some of us flew over to their airfield to lunch with them and later they presented us with bits of the white flags brought by the German representatives to the Armistice talks.[327]

11 Squadron arrived at Nivelles on 18 December. Despite the occasional sortie with Crichton, there was very little to keep its personnel occupied, in spite of the best efforts of its commander Heath. With time on his hands, Hardit decided to see his old friend from Bournemouth, Clairette Preiss, who was living in Colmar in Alsace. Following the death of her father, she had been imprisoned by the Germans throughout the war (See Chapter 4). Heath could not give permission for such an escapade, and a six-hundred-mile round trip by train was unthinkable, consequently Hardit decided to fly anyway, under the pretext of a flight test.[328] During the last stage of the three-hour trip south, the Bristol Fighter developed a fault, and was forced down close to Commercy, where he was immediately surrounded by American troops billeted nearby. Having shared their hospitality overnight and utilising a team of mechanics to get his machine airborne once more, Hardit

---

327. Malik, H.S., *'A Little Work, A Little Play'*, p. 96
328. Ibid., p. 97

nursed the patched-up plane to Nancy, handing it over to the Independent Wing of the RAF, which was based there under General Trenchard. He was then fortunate to get a lift to Paris via St Dizier, and from the French capital hoped to re-join his squadron at Nivelles. Quite by chance, at the Hotel Chatham, Hardit ran into an equally surprised Major Heath, who, with the war at an end, was in no mood to punish the misdemeanours of one of his flying officers. Laughing off the escapade, he drove Hardit back to Nivelles.

In the last days of December, 11 Squadron was visited by the RAF's Master-General of Personnel, General Brancker. In his autobiography, Hardit stated that Brancker 'happened to visit the squadron'.[329] Yet the visit might not have happened by chance, for a serious threat was now looming over Hardit's future career in the RAF. As we have seen, Brancker had taken a special interest in the Indians who had enlisted in the RFC during 1916-17, and of those, Hardit was the only one who remained on active service. Roy and Welinkar[330] had been killed, Sen had been released as a POW after the Armistice and gone back to Britain, and Jeejeebhoy had returned to a desk job in 1917. General Brancker was to be knighted in the New Year's Honours List of 1919 and due to retire on 13 January. During his final tour of duty visiting a number of squadrons, it may be that he purposely headed for Nivelles to see Hardit. As will be seen, Brancker had cause to find out what his plans were. Hardit recalled his own response at the meeting:

> General Brancker, who had served in India and took a special interest in me [...] asked me what I would like to do now that the war was over. I told him that I would like leave to go home. After that I hoped to continue in the RAF in India.[331]

In addition to this meeting, Brancker had also met Hardit in London, at some point at the end of 1918, as he recalled in a letter to General Cox at the India Office on 3 January 1919:

---

329. Ibid., p. 98
330. When Indian Ambassador to France, Hardit Singh visited the Arras Flying Services Memorial in 1951 and noticed that Welinkar's name was not present on the memorial there. He knew that Welinkar had been recorded as 'missing' after being shot down in April 1918 but didn't know that his grave had been formally identified by 1921. The Commonwealth War Graves were able to inform Hardit that Welinkar was buried at Hangard Communal Cemetery Extension. It's not known if the two men ever met.
331. Malik, H.S., 'A Little Work, A Little Play', p. 98

My dear General,

Thank you very much indeed for your congratulations (about Brancker's forthcoming retirement). I wish you a happy New Year.

I have seen Hardit Singh Malik and am arranging that he does not go back to France at the end of his furlough but proceeds to India on as much leave as we can possibly give him with a view to joining one of the Squadrons in India, if the opportunity arises. I think this should clear matters for him all right. *Thank you very much for sending him over.*[332] (author's emphasis).

It would seem that soon after his meeting with General Brancker at Nivelles, Hardit left 11 Squadron and headed back to London, where he went firstly to the India Office and then to the Air Ministry to meet with Brancker again.

There is no record of what took place beyond what is documented in the above letter, but what both Cox and Brancker knew during their meetings with Hardit, was that as the Armistice had approached the previous November, a pivotal telegram had arrived from the GOI on 1 November (see Appendix B).[333] The telegram utterly rejected the Air Ministry's proposal of a month earlier to recruit Indian flying officers into the RAF, one supported by Brancker and Cox the preceding summer and autumn. Whilst the GOI was willing to contemplate the granting of King's Commissions in the Indian Army, it would now no longer contemplate any such thing, in what it considered to be one of its 'technical and scientific services'. Under the terms of this telegram, Hardit's future career in the RAF was in jeopardy.

The content of the 1 November telegram is self-explanatory, but a couple of points are worth highlighting. Under the conditions set out in the 'Fifth' paragraph, the GOI was again expressing its dissatisfaction with the recruitment of those Indians drafted in Britain like Hardit Singh. It was keen to ensure that both the decisions about who would be enlisted, and where the chosen candidates for commissions came from, were made in India itself. The 'Sixth' paragraph underlined the GOI's belief, that granting commissions to Indians to take command of *sepoys* in the Indian Army was more palatable than awarding them commissions in the RAF, with the

332. IOR/L/MIL/7/19015: 1917-1920, 3 January 1919, p. 58
333. IOR/L/MIL/7/19010: 1917-1920, 1 November 1918, p. 109

possibility of their giving orders to British flying officers. The 1 November telegram was underpinned by racial discrimination as Secretary of State Montagu acknowledged in his formal response to it at the time. He was scathing:

> [...] I regret very much to have to say this, for it is wholly inconsistent with the proclamations and pronouncements of Sovereigns and Ministers, with our assertions against racial discrimination, with our professions and assumptions that we hold India by consent; it is an admission that we hold her by force.

> In this case we are asked by the Government of India when the door is open to us, when of their own free will the Air Ministry makes an offer, we are asked to close it and to bang the door which others have opened in the face of the Indian who wishes to fly.

> [...] a British private or an Indian private ought to be willing and ready, and I do believe *would* be willing and ready, to follow any officer who proves himself capable of leading him. But the question does not arise here. The Air pilot flies by himself as a unit; his incapacity, his failure, his treachery affects himself and himself alone. Of course, this does not apply if he reaches the highest ranks, but that will depend upon his trustworthiness and his capacity [...] [334]

With the war at an end however, support for Indian commissions in the RAF was also beginning to wane within the Air Ministry itself.[335] Although his term as Master-General of Personnel of the RAF ended officially on 13 January, General Brancker's role was de facto occupied by his successor General Fellows, from the first day of the new year. A message sent from the Air Ministry to the India Office, a week after he had taken up his new post, confirmed that Fellows '[...] has promised that Hardit Singh Malik

---

334. Ibid., 14 November 1918, pp. 94-98
335. Richards, C., 'The Origins of Military Aviation in India and the Creation of the Indian Air Force, 1910-1932, p. 31

shall be given leave to India *without* (author's emphasis) any promise to his future posting when his leave expires. He (Fellows) does not think that Brancker has made any promises'.[336] This appeared to be at odds with General Brancker's view that Hardit might be posted to a squadron in India in his communication to General Cox of 3 January. Very aware of the repercussions of the Air Ministry's policy reversal with regard to the granting of commissions to Indians in the RAF, and his recent communications with Brancker, it's evident that Cox himself was becoming a little nervous about the prospect of Hardit heading back to the Punjab to take up a posting there. Correspondence from the India Office to the Air Ministry made clear his concern: 'General Cox is particularly anxious that he (Malik) should not be given any promise about this posting, after his leave'. Indeed, the General went so far as to request that a copy of the telegram granting Hardit leave be sent to him.[337] Finally, Cox was reassured by the Air Ministry that no such promise had been made. Yet, as we shall see, this was not quite true, for someone else within the RAF was intervening on Hardit's behalf.

Hardit's formal period of leave began on 13 January 1919, and after a short interval back in Britain to put his affairs in order, he caught up with friends and made arrangements for the voyage home. He then travelled once more to Marseille, spending a rather frustrating two weeks in a military camp awaiting transportation back to Bombay. When the vessel arrived, Hardit noted that it was the same P&O Royal Mail Ship *Morea* on which he had voyaged to Britain almost ten years earlier. On 5 February, the *Morea* arrived at Port Said, where it remained for a week. On the ship were a good many Indian officers and a few British officers of the Indian Army returning for duty. Hardit developed a friendship with one of them, Captain Keen of 28 Punjabis, who was on the way to re-join his battalion, then stationed in Lebanon.[338] For much of the trip the two got on well, but a difficult conversation ensued one evening, as Hardit remembered:

> We started talking about the Indian Army over some drinks
> and he asked me what my plans were. I told him that after

---

336. IOR/L/MIL/7/19015: 1917-1920, 8 January 1918, p. 57
337. Ibid., 9 January 1918, p. 56
338. The author was unable to trace the records of any Captain Keen of 28 Punjabis. It's likely to be either Captain B.G. Keene of 92 Punjabis or Major G.N.S. Keene of 30 Punjabis who met Hardit.

my leave I intended to stay on in the RAF in India. At that time, of course, we had no Indian Air Force, only some squadrons of the RAF. After a good many drinks he said, "Malik, don't do that!" This surprised and rather annoyed me, and I was more annoyed when, on asking him why he thought it wasn't a good idea, he replied, "You know we don't want Indians in the RAF. You will find one day you will go up and your plane will break up in the air!" I was quite angry and told him that he was talking nonsense, but he persisted to make his point. This made me even more determined to stay in the RAF.[339]

Keen's opinion was one typical of many in the British military establishment of the time, as we have seen. Indeed, Keen might be said to be the personification of the views expounded by the GOI in its telegram of 1 November in response to the Air Ministry's proposals to grant commissions to Indians in the RAF.

As the *Morea* made its way back to India, correspondence about Hardit Singh's future continued to be exchanged, the secretary to the Air Council writing once more to the India Office on 27 February, to reiterate its changed position about the granting of commissions to Indians in the RAF:

[...] I am commanded by the Air Council to say that the policy of employing Indians as pilots in the Royal Flying Corps was proposed at a time when, owing to war wastage, the supply of flying personnel was in danger of running short should the war have been indefinitely prolonged.

In the present circumstances, however, the situation has altogether changed. The wastage in pilots and observers has fallen to normal proportions and considerable reserves of trained flying personnel are immediately available to replace vacancies as they occur.[340]

339. Malik, H.S., *'A Little Work, A Little Play'*, p. 99
340. IOR/L/MIL/7/19010: 1917-1920, 27 February 1919, p. 75

In other words, now that the war was over, Indian pilots and observers were no longer required. But that wasn't the end of it.

Early in March, Hardit arrived back at Bombay and took the train to Rawalpindi. He had not seen his family since leaving as a fourteen-year-old and it can only be imagined what were his thoughts as he travelled back to the Punjab. However, he wasn't to be alone for long, for his return received a good deal of publicity. The return home of a serving RAF officer was not an everyday occurrence, and a large crowd escorted his family to the railway station. Even the District Commissioner Sir Frank Popham-Young was in the reception party, a great honour for a relatively lowly lieutenant. If that wasn't all, Hardit was taken in procession to the local *gurdwara* and officially welcomed at a large public meeting. He was rather embarrassed by the scale of the reception, but his family were of course elated.[341]

What remained of March, and the first two weeks of April, were rather a whirlwind for Hardit and it must have been a culture shock of sorts after his previous life in the military. Much of that time was taken up with the question of his marriage, he was after all an eligible bachelor of twenty-four years old. He was soon engaged to be married to fifteen-year-old Prakash, the younger sister of his brother's wife and a wedding date was set for 13 April, the date of the festival of Baisakhi, one auspicious in the Sikh calendar, for it was on that day in 1699 that the Tenth Guru, Gobind Singh, had created the Khalsa.[342]

A degree of haste was required because Hardit now intended to return to Britain. He stated in his autobiography that whilst back in Rawalpindi, he was persuaded to give up flying by both his own family and prospective in-laws, his ambition to resume with the RAF in India at an end. Yet during the month of March after his arrival in the city, correspondence between Delhi and London about his future continued. A telegram of 14 March from the GOI stated: '...please refer to the telegram of 9 November (clarifying its 1 November predecessor – see Appendix B) from the Viceroy, Lord Chelmsford to the Secretary of State for India. The Government of India do not wish Lieutenant Malik taken on the strength of the Royal Air Force in India for the reasons stated therein'.[343] Five days later, Montagu intervened

---

341. Malik, H.S., *'A Little Work, A Little Play'*, p. 100
342. Ibid., p. 101
343. IOR/L/MIL/7/19010: 1917-1920, 19 March 1919, p. 61

on Hardit's behalf, writing a telegram back to Lord Chelmsford himself to make a last-minute appeal:

> Private and Personal. Please see your Army Department telegram of March 14th addressed to me about a Commission for Lieutenant H.S. Malik in the Air Force in India. I very much regret that this should have arisen, but I beg of you to reconsider most carefully your policy with regard to the exclusion of Indians from the Air Force [...] My present view is that, however, very strongly that there is no military danger in allowing Indians the use of aeroplanes and that if you put up for this new Service a new racial bar which is unwarranted by military danger, you will as flying proceeds and develops, give to our successors an infinite amount of unnecessary trouble. I should be very glad if you would consider the matter personally.[344]

Lord Chelmsford would not reply to this telegram until over a month later, on 22 April. What became evident though in the weeks that followed, was that another person, this time unknown, had interceded on Hardit's behalf back in January and that his case continued to be active with the RAF in India. On 27 March, General Cox was forced to write to the Air Ministry again, doubly frustrated no doubt, as he had openly advocated for Indian officers within the RAF back in September, but was now having to do an about-face. He referred to his previous January correspondence:

> [...] you will see that we made a special request that Malik should not be given any promise regarding his ultimate posting, and that he should not be posted to a squadron in India until the policy regarding the employment of Indians in the RAF in that country had been settled. It appears from the attached telegram (sadly missing – author) that within a week of your promise *somebody* (author's emphasis) within the Air Ministry wrote officially to the Director of Aeronautics

---

344. Ibid., 14 March 1919, p. 60

in India proposing that Malik should be taken on the strength of the Air Force out there.

It is difficult to understand how this can have happened, and it has resulted in a misunderstanding which has now to be cleared up.[345]

That 'somebody' was most likely General Brancker, a man who believed sincerely in Indians taking their place as equals with British officers in the RAF. It's likely to have been one of Brancker's last acts before retirement. The 'misunderstanding' referred to, may have resulted from Hardit reporting for duty with 31 Squadron at one of its bases on the North-West Frontier where it had been deployed since late 1915. We know this because when returning to Britain in July 1919, the unit from which he was given leave to do so was 31 Squadron, as his service record testified.[346] Hardit made no mention of this in his autobiography.

By 9 April, the matter had been resolved, though the final communication from the Air Ministry in response to Cox's 27 March correspondence posed another question:

> Dear Sir Herbert Cox,
> I have looked up the case of Lieutenant H.S. Malik and find that a letter was sent to say that he would be posted to a Unit in India.
> We have now heard that he himself wishes to join a Unit at home which we are going to agree to, and therefore the question as far as he is concerned will be settled to your satisfaction. [347]

Prior to his wedding on 13 April, it appeared that Hardit had been in communication with the RAF in India and had subsequently declared himself willing to return to a unit back in the UK. It is worth surmising what had taken place: Hardit's attempt to take up a posting with 31 Squadron had been declined, following that squadron's correspondence with the Air Ministry. In spite of Hardit stating in his autobiography that he had been

---

345. Ibid. 27 March 1919, p. 69
346. AIR 76/331
347. IOR/L/MIL/7/19010: 1917-1920, 9 April 1919, p. 64

persuaded to leave flying altogether during this time, he was in actual fact still a member of the RAF on his return to Britain in July.

The timeline of these events isn't entirely clear. What is clear is that during the first two weeks of April, Hardit had other things on his mind, not least his impending nuptials. He was conscious too of the unrest in the Punjab, which would reach its violent conclusion on the very day of his marriage.

Chapter 11

Amritsar
April 1919–July 1921

> 'As the clock struck five on thirteenth April
> They all gather in the Bagh, my friends.
> Seeking justice fair and honour, they stand
> Sikhs, Hindus, Muslims together, my friends.'
>
> Nanak Singh, *The Gathering in*
> *Jallianwala Bagh*

Hardit was in a buoyant mood as he turned down Horse Guards Parade from the Mall towards the India Office buildings in Whitehall. Well-groomed with a crisp white shirt, though donning a rather worn Balliol tie under a dark wool flannel suit, the warm weather seemed to reflect his contentment. Nevertheless, as he turned into King Charles Street, mounting the 'Clive Steps' two at a time, his smile hid some residual nerves. He barely gave Robert Clive's bronze statue a second glance, focusing instead on the great edifice of George Gilbert Scott's gothic architecture towering above him. He had been to the India Office many times before of course, first as a teenager with his brother Teja Singh all those years ago, and then as a student and flying officer, but this time was different. Normally, he would resolve business with the desk secretaries, but today he had an appointment with the Secretary of State himself, Edwin Montagu, at 1030 hours.

It was the summer of 1920 and having been nominated by the GOI for the prestigious ICS, Hardit knew that under the terms of his successful application, a probationary year in Oxford was necessary at the Indian Institute there. Since his arrival back in Britain with new bride Prakash in August the previous year, their ambition had been to return to India as promptly as possible once entry to the ICS had been secured. Having already spent three years at Balliol and secured a good honours degree in Modern History, Hardit was keen to take up a role back in India after spending so long away from his family and friends. There were worse things than another year at Oxford, but he decided to request special dispensation to return to the subcontinent immediately, rather than undertake the probationary year. So it was that Hardit made an appeal to the authorities and to his surprise was granted an interview with Montagu himself.

He passed through the magnificent Durbar Court, at the heart of the building, its four sides surrounded by three storeys of marble columns. Led by one of the secretaries, he was taken to a narrow antechamber outside the Secretary of State's office and waited there. Half past ten came and went, so too eleven o'clock. Finally, the office door opened and Hardit wasn't sure if the tall monocled man with the large bald domed head who had answered it was yet another official, having seen the Secretary of State only in grainy photographs in *The Times*. Montagu introduced himself, apologising for his tardiness and instantly putting Hardit at ease. By reputation, he had an open, relaxed manner and many Indians with whom he came into contact noted an absence of snobbishness, prejudice or elitism, which was not always true when meeting British officials.[348] The office was a regal one, furnished magnificently with thick oriental rugs, an elegant hand-carved desk and chair, and oak panelled walls decorated with Indian miniatures and the portraits of former Secretaries of State.[349]

Montagu knew a good deal more about Hardit than anticipated – small details of the latter's marriage, sporting interests and education all seemed familiar to him, he was evidently on top of his brief, though his acquaintance with the details seemed to imply a more personal interest. Hardit pondered later whether such charm merely reflected his skill as a politician. His own father had profited from a similar attribute, able to convey warmth and empathy to any new acquaintance with whom he came into contact. Though he may not have admitted it to himself, Hardit exhibited the same qualities in his interactions. The two talked on about his future plans and the abandonment of his RAF career a year earlier, for which Montagu expressed some regret. He explained that, although he would look into the matter of withdrawing the requirement for Hardit's probationary year in Oxford, he could make no promises.

---

348. Levine, N.B., '*Politics, religion and love: the story of H.H. Asquith, Venetia Stanley and Edwin Montagu*' (New York University Press: London, 1991), p. 460
349. Ibid., p. 450

Having parted outside the Locarno Suite, Hardit looked back at the slightly stooping figure walking away down the corridor. The weight of responsibilities had borne down on the Secretary of State since the middle of 1917, the time of the greatest challenges the Raj had known since 1857. Faced by the demands of a series of political events in 1919: the reform movements in India; the Paris Peace Conference; the aftermath of the Jallianwala Bagh Massacre and the failure of his marriage, Montagu's health had broken down and he had entered a nursing home for several months. Some days before his appointment with Hardit Singh, he had been turned down for the role of Viceroy of India by Prime Minister Lloyd George. He would die prematurely four years later at the age of only forty-five. Inevitably perhaps, not long after their meeting, confirmation came that Hardit would be returning to Oxford, albeit this time with his beloved Prakash.

Almost eighteen months earlier, on 13 April 1919, the couple were married in Rawalpindi. A grand occasion was planned, though the wedding was overshadowed somewhat by familial and political upheavals. The ceremony itself caused some difficulties, as Hardit remembered:

> My father-in-law, Bhagat Ishwar Das, a prominent lawyer in Lahore, a brilliant man, known in his day as one of the first men in the Punjab to acquire an MA degree, was active in the somewhat aggressive Hindu Reform Movement, the Arya Samaj. He was a very keen student and admirer of the Vedanta, and he wanted our wedding ceremony to be according to the Vedic rites. My mother-in-law was a Sikh and therefore both religions, Hindu and Sikh were followed in my wife's family. My father was acknowledged as a leading figure in the Sikh community. As far as my family were concerned, the wedding had to be according to Sikh practices – the Anand Karaj ceremony. Controversy over this question arose. I found all this very distressing as instead of the atmosphere being one of rejoicing, it grew embittered, with feelings running high. I therefore suggested a compromise: we would have both ceremonies. Happily, this was accepted and peace was restored.[350]

---

350. Malik, H.S., *'A Little Work, A Little Play'*, p. 102

Prakash was having preparatory problems of her own. She was not able to prepare her trousseau, a critical part of any wedding ceremony. At one stage it was even suggested that a postponement would be necessary, but she would countenance no delay. Her difficulties resulted from the imposition of martial law in Rawalpindi, part of the wider shutdown across the Punjab by the colonial authorities. The problems would come to a head in Amritsar on the very day of the wedding, a day of infamy in Indo-British relations.

Following the visit to India by Secretary of State Montagu between November 1917 and the following May, the Montagu-Chelmsford Report was published. The report built upon the Montagu Declaration and would be officially implemented by the Government of India Act of 1919, effective from December of that year. Historian Kim Wagner succinctly summarises the essence of the Montagu-Chelmsford Report:

> The carefully worded announcement described the aim of British policy in India towards "increasing association of Indians in every branch of the administration and the gradual development of self-governing institutions with a view to the progressive realisation of responsible government in India as an integral part of the British Empire". At the more practical and immediate level, the reforms introduced a system known as "dyarchy", which divided the functions of government between the centre, in the newly established colonial capital in Delhi, and the provinces, where new legislative bodies were established for Indian electorates (though still less than ten per cent of the male population). Greater responsibilities were devolved to the provinces, where Indian officials would play a greater role and have responsibility for raising local taxes and control over areas such as education and agriculture. The British Government at the centre nevertheless retained tight control over those areas considered vital to the safety of the Raj, and Indians would accordingly have little say over state finances, law and order, or military matters – let alone foreign policy.[351]

---

351. Wagner, K.A., *'Amritsar 1919 – An Empire of Fear and the Making of a Massacre'* (Yale University Press: London, 2019), p. 23

Indian nationalists, who had been hoping for a substantial transfer of power and greater steps towards full independence, were disappointed with the Montagu-Chelmsford Report to say the least. The watered down proposals relating to the Indianisation of the Raj's military, administrative and governmental structures could not conceal the entrenched attitudes of racial and cultural bias underpinning them, no matter how hard Montagu, in particular, had challenged them.[352] Yet from the point of view of those leading the home rule movements in India, the country's role in support of the Empire had deserved so much more. If the Montagu-Chelmsford Report was cause for dissatisfaction in India as the First World War ended, there was worse to come, for the British were also introducing parallel legislation, which was 'completely contradictory and incompatible with the spirit of reform'.[353]

Another report, this time published by the Rowlatt Committee in August 1918, recommended the continuation of emergency legislation deemed necessary by the British to maintain control and defend the Raj. Based on the Defence of India Act of 1915, the resulting Rowlatt Acts necessitated the suspension of the rule of law, reaffirmed sweeping powers to crack down on political activities, detainment without trial and trials without juries. The committee's members believed that without the continuation of the principles of the 1915 Act, prisoners and political detainees would have to be released into a potentially febrile atmosphere anticipated by the return of thousands of demobilised *sepoys*, particularly into the Punjab. In addition, ruthless over-recruitment, new forms of taxation, growing inflation and yet another flu epidemic, had all reduced the province to breaking point. The Rowlatt Acts were also a sop, intended to soothe the nerves of those many officials of the Raj, and in parliament back in Britain, who had been opposed to the Montagu-Chelmsford Reforms. The Acts were aimed at ensuring that the British remained firmly in control and had the means required to stave off any future challenges to their authority.[354]

As Hardit returned to the Punjab in the spring of 1919, the Rowlatt Acts were the cause of widespread opposition, prompting Gandhi to lead those feeling betrayed by the British after their steadfast support of

---

352. Ibid.
353. Ibid., p. 41
354. Ibid., pp. 42-44

Empire, and particularly recruitment during the war. He recommended the tactic of _satyagraha_ and proposed that _hartals_ take place across India. The Punjab was already under martial rule owing to the Ghadar revolutionary outbreaks of 1914-17, and on 8 April, Gandhi was prohibited from entering the province in support of the anticipated _hartals_ there, for fear of triggering further unrest. The following day, two prominent Punjabi congressmen, Satyapal and Kitchlew were deported by the British authorities. Violence erupted as a result, and when news reached Amritsar on 10 April, three Britons were killed and a number of others attacked. British officials imposed a curfew and embarked upon severe punishments right across the Punjab.[355] The severe repression in Amritsar culminated in the massacre at Jallianwala Bagh on 13 April following the prohibition of meetings and gatherings within the city. As Hardit was mounting a grey horse on which he would lead the wedding procession in Rawalpindi that day, over a hundred and fifty miles away in Amritsar, the festival of Baisakhi was attracting large crowds. The main events of the massacre there are well known. A market was taking place in the Jallianwala Bagh, a square enclosed on three sides and it was there that a meeting was convened during the late afternoon to discuss the Rowlatt Acts and other repressive measures. The officer in charge, General Dyer ordered his soldiers to fire into the crowd, which had formed to listen to the speakers and was made up of men, women and children, many of whom were in the Bagh for motives other than political ones. As Dyer made clear to the Hunter Commission which followed, the shooting was essentially a punishment for the crowd disobeying the gatherings prohibition, which had been issued earlier. As a result, 379 people were killed and 1,200 wounded according to the official casualty estimates. Other approximations of the number of victims that day are far higher still. The following day, the RAF flew further sorties over villages surrounding Gujranwala killing a further eleven people. The machines of 114 Squadron had been seen throughout the unrest flying over the province in a number of different roles.

The impact of the Amritsar Massacre had an almost instantaneous effect. The following week, a telegram was sent by Lord Chelmsford to Montagu, in response to the latter's previous communication a month earlier:

---

355. Bates, C., _'Subalterns and Raj'_, pp. 130-131

Private. Your private and personal telegram of March 19th. Case of Lieutenant Harditt (sic) Singh Malik can now be settled satisfactorily, transferred at his own request to the Home establishment Royal Air Force as a Flying Officer and passage to England is being arranged for him about May 23rd.

Recent disturbances emphasise the importance of strict adherence to policy laid down in the telegram quoted above (see Appendix B), at any rate for the present.[356]

In summary therefore, Hardit had returned home to India to join the RAF, but the volte face by the Air Ministry brought about by the GOI's change of policy regarding Indians becoming commissioned officers, meant that was no longer possible. The unrest in the Punjab and the massacre at Amritsar undoubtedly played a part in the decision making. 31 Squadron in particular, and the RAF in India in general, did not welcome the arrival of a Sikh pilot into its ranks in March and April 1919. More importantly though, we learn from Chelmsford's telegram above, that Hardit had decided to return to Britain to continue his flying career. We know from his autobiography that his immediate family and in-laws persuaded him to give up flying, which was certainly owing to the inflammatory atmosphere in the Punjab from the time of his arrival back in India. Both the families were aware of the terrible position into which he would have been placed, with the possibility of being asked to bomb protestors, his own compatriots, in his own country. His willingness to travel back to Britain to continue with the RAF demonstrated however, that his ambitions as a pilot were not over when he left India. He also had a backup plan – to obtain a place in the ICS for which he would need to be in London.

The Jallianwala Bagh Massacre piled the pressure on an already embattled Secretary of State Montagu, emboldening the opponents of his Indian reforms even further. He found time to issue a telegram to Lord Chelmsford on 5 May. The telegram reflected his exasperation:

Private. Your private telegram of April 22nd about Indians and aviation. As Malik has returned to this country (owing to delays

---

356. IOR/L/MIL/7/19010: 1917-1920, 22 April 1917, p. 59

Hardit wouldn't actually leave until the end of July - Author's note) the question is not for the moment urgent and in the situation caused by your adherence to your Military Department's view, the most I can hope for is that it will not become urgent so long as I am Secretary of State [...] I cannot agree to your views and will not consent to any new racial disqualification. Such a disqualification is in my opinion out of date and would be indefensible after the use that we were prepared to make and did make during the war of Indians who could fly.[357]

Nevertheless, the tide was turning against Montagu and later that month the Air Ministry once and for all agreed to adhere to the principles laid down by the GOI of 1 November 1918. The time of granting commissions to Indians in the RAF was over, for the time being at least.

Immediately after their wedding, the newlyweds headed into the beautiful province of Kashmir for a honeymoon lasting several weeks, Hardit finding time to play golf and with Prakash visiting the renowned Shalimar Bagh Mughal Garden in Srinagar. There then followed an abortive attempt to return to Britain at the end of May, when having left Prakash in Kashmir, Hardit travelled to Calcutta to board a ship, only for it to break down a short way down the Hooghly River. He returned to Kashmir for the rest of June and July, whilst awaiting the sailing of another vessel on which to return to Britain.

When the opportunity came, Prakash and Hardit took the train from Rawalpindi once more bound for Bombay, permission having been obtained from the RAF for his wife to accompany him on the journey. On the train, which had originated in Peshawar and which was congested with British Army officers coming back from the North-West Frontier, Hardit was embroiled in a confrontation. Having settled Prakash into a first-class women's compartment, he struggled to find a seat himself. The only berth available apparently was to be found in a two-seater compartment which was already occupied by a senior officer:

I could not tell his rank as he was in his shirtsleeves, and in those days, officers did not wear badges of rank on their

---

357. Ibid., 5 May 1919, p. 57

shirts. He was standing at the doorway and I asked him if he could kindly move to one side so that I could get in. He replied very rudely, "There is no room for you in here. Go and look somewhere else!" "I am getting in here!" I said and pushed him back rather violently. As he was a little man and taken by surprise, he fell down. Picking himself up, furious, he said, "What is your name and your regiment?" Equally furious, and not giving a damn who he was, I told him, "My regiment you can see!" and I pointed to my uniform, "As for my name, I will tell you mine when you have told me yours!" He did not reply but picked up his pipe and papers from the seat and I sat down. When I had calmed down, I looked up to the peg where his tunic was hanging to discover that he was a Brigadier-General. It was just as well that he was not wearing his uniform when I pushed him. I would of course have been in serious trouble – a Flight Lieutenant knocking down a Brigadier-General! And an Indian Flight Lieutenant to a British Brigadier at that![358]

At Bombay, the couple boarded His Majesty's Indian Ship *Dufferin* back to Britain. A torrid voyage, blighted by inclement weather, sea sickness and the absence of air conditioning was worsened by the fact men and women were segregated – the ship was a military transport. As a consequence, the fifteen-year-old Prakash had a torrid time sharing a cabin with other British women, a couple of whom were particularly unpleasant to her. The journey was only made palatable by the presence also of a more sympathetic English woman. They were more than ready to come ashore at Southampton when the voyage came to an end.

According to his service record, Hardit officially left the RAF on 16 August 1919, which cannot have been too long after his disembarkation. During the voyage back to Britain, Hardit made up his mind what to do with his future. It's feasible that he had wanted to take advantage of complimentary transportation for the two of them courtesy of the RAF, whilst always intending to embark on an ICS career, only permissible back in London. If that was the case, no-one would have blamed him. A flying

---

358. Malik, H.S., *'A Little Work, A Little Play'*, p. 106

career that had begun with the RFC in the freezing cold of Aldershot in the spring of 1917 was over.

Hardit turned now to the business of gaining a place with the ICS. In the normal course of things, entrance was by annual competitive examination every August. Yet these weren't normal times and the war had changed the application process. Before 1914, it was very difficult for Indians to gain places, but during the war and after, it was problematic to interest young Britons in a career in India and the India Office therefore had to abandon its efforts to maintain a set ratio of Indian and European candidates, admitting a 'disproportionate' number of the former. Greater employment opportunities for Indians had been part and parcel of the constitutional reforms implemented by Montagu and Lord Chelmsford, but the government was forced to go further than it had intended because it simply could not get sufficient young Britons to fill ICS posts.[359]

Owing to the delays in returning to Britain, Hardit had missed the chance to submit an application that August of 1919. We must assume therefore, that having made a successful application in the summer of 1920, he then returned to the University of Oxford for the Michaelmas term that October and spent the probationary year there until the summer of 1921.

Having saved up a significant amount of money during his leave from the RAF, Hardit and Prakash were able to live a relatively comfortable life during 1919-20, staying initially in the Coburg Hotel in London. Prakash found the green splendour of the capital's parks and the surrounding countryside as attractive as Hardit had done all those years before. Thereafter, the couple were able to call on many individuals and families Hardit had befriended over the years, both in Britain and France. Following a golfing holiday with Indian relatives at the Boar's Hill Hotel, near Oxford, in September, they took a holiday to Devon and Cornwall with Harold Boston, with whom he had undergone flight training at Reading and Vendôme, the two having kept in touch throughout the war. In the photographs taken during the trip, Prakash can be seen with Boston's wife Lucy, almost overwhelmed with the size of her fur coat, attempting to keep out the cold.

---

359. Ewing, A., *'The Indian Civil Service'*, - as of 12 September 2020 - britishempire.co.uk

The couple then sought out warmer climes, traveling to Paris and the south of France to stay with friends, and from there rented a beautiful villa on the Côte d'Azur to escape the British winter.[360]

During the spring of 1920, increased amounts of time were spent back in Oxford, inevitably on the golf course. Determined not to be a 'golf widow', Prakash took up the game and taught by her husband, she created a sensation wherever she went, a splendid sight in an improvised sari, complete with a double fold to prevent it blowing up in the wind.[361] There are charming photographs of the couple taken at this time, which bear witness both to their happiness and to the quality of both of their golf swings! There was also time to return to Bournemouth to meet with Mademoiselle Specht who had taught Hardit French. The couple stayed with her for several months, finding a motherly figure in their lives away from home on the south coast.

In the summer of 1920, Hardit successfully applied to the ICS under a scheme whereby former military personnel of officer rank were encouraged to fill up vacancies in the service. He was actually nominated from the list of applicants by the GOI which had resorted to direct appointments when confronted with acute personnel shortages, and so it was to Oxford that the couple proceeded in the autumn of 1920.[362] Hardit studied criminal law and languages, believed to be relevant to an aspiring civil servant, at the Oxford Institute, on the corner of Catte Street and New College Lane. Under the watchful eye of Arthur Macdonell, he consolidated his knowledge of Sanskrit, Persian and Arabic, taking advantage of the dedicated library and museum there.

Away from his Oxford studies, he spent an idyllic summer of 1921 playing golf for the university, taking a blue for the second time, and was part of the record-breaking team which thrashed Cambridge at Hoylake.[363] There was time for cricket too, playing for the university First XI which must have delighted him, not having had the opportunity between 1912 and 1915. He also played for a second spell with the Sussex County Club again at that time, scoring a century against Leicestershire in the county championship at the end of June. In the club's current archives at Hove is

360. Malik, H.S., *'A Little Work, A Little Play'*, p. 109
361. Ibid., p. 111
362. Potter, D.C., *'Manpower Shortage and the End of Colonialism: The Case of Indian Civil Service'*, in Modern Asian Studies (1973), pp. 47–73
363. Malik, H.S., *'A Little Work, A Little Play'*, p. 110

an autograph book signed by Hardit during the match with Surrey at the Oval in the middle of July. The signatures of the Sussex and England fast bowling legends Arthur Gilligan and Maurice Tate also adorn the page – fine company indeed. In the museum at Hove is a tribute to Hardit Singh, who had made his debut with the club in 1914.

At the end of the academic year, he passed his examinations and was duly posted to India as he recalled:

> My examiner for the Viva Voce, a distinguished judge, asked me the difference between "culpable homicide" and "murder", but when he realised that I didn't know the answer, he said with a twinkle in his eye, "Never mind. How are Sussex doing this year?" He obviously knew that I had been playing county cricket for Sussex and I passed![364]

Hardit and Prakash returned to India at the end of 1921. He began his ICS career as Assistant Commissioner to Sheikhupura, near Lahore on 6 January 1922. It was to be the start of a long and illustrious career.

While the couple departed for India, Edwin Montagu was still battling with the military and political establishments in Britain and India for granting commissions to Indians in the RAF. The degree of his frustration was written into his various memoranda:

> I am absolutely opposed to asking Indians to risk their lives in aeroplanes during the war, then, after the war, refuse to allow them to get Commissions; and I will never consent to agreeing with any Government department who (sic) objects to putting Indians in command over British personnel. I cannot for the life of me understand why I am being continually asked by my colleagues in the Government to assent to a proposal which violates every pledge and every understanding about racial discrimination that has been given in the name of his Majesty's Government from Queen Victoria downwards.[365]

---

364. Ibid., p. 111
365. IOR/L/MIL/7/19010: 1917-1920, 8 December 1921, p. 7

Chapter 12

Conclusion

'I know that I shall meet my fate
Somewhere among the clouds above;
Those that I fight I do not hate
Those that I guard I do not love…'

W.B. Yeats, *An Irish Airman*
Foresees His Death

What then was the future for Indians wishing to serve as officers in the RAF? Following the end of the First World War, the passing of the Government of India Act in December 1919 and the emboldened calls for greater Indian autonomy, change was in the air once more. Discussions about the place of the RAF in the Indianisation reforms continued when the 'Army in India Committee' led by Lord Esher, was appointed by Secretary of State Montagu to inquire into the administration and organisation of the Indian Army. In their final report, the Esher Committee called for a series of reforms including:

> The superior ranks of every branch of the army, including the Artillery, Air Force, Engineers, Transport and Supplies, etc. should be freely open to qualified Indians, and for this purpose the number of King's commissions to be given to Indians should be materially increased every year.[366]

The Esher Committee Report was considered, not only by the Westminster parliament, but also by the Indian Legislative Assembly in Delhi that passed 'Resolution 7' on 28 March 1921. The resolution began, 'That the King-

---

366. Esher Committee Report, Annexure II, pp. 103-104

Emperor's Indian Subjects should be freely admitted to all arms of His Majesty's Military, Naval and Air Forces in India and the Ancillary and Auxiliary Services'.[367] In effect, the resolution called for RAF recruitment restrictions to be lifted for units in India. Ironically, from this time on, the GOI argued *in support of* these proposals, citing the Air Ministry's own propositions of three years earlier, which had called for 100 Indians to be selected for pilot training in Britain and to serve as RAF officers. This *volte face* by the GOI was in stark contrast to its previous sober rejection of the case, it now tried to justify:

> It is true that our acceptance of this proposal is diametrically opposed to the views stated in November 1918. We have, however, examined the question afresh, and are satisfied that the time has come for making a distinct step forward and for recognising the rights of Indians to serve in all branches of the naval, military and air forces of their own country, subject only to their attainment of the requisite standard of efficiency.[368]

In spite of this change of heart, the transformation was decidedly slow from an Indian perspective. Not long before his resignation in March 1922, Edwin Montagu took up the cause once more and restated the appeal that Indians should be allowed to take commissions in the RAF. He continued to face opposition at home and in India, the main stumbling block to progress remaining the anxiety of many in the military establishment of allowing Indians commissions in the 'technical services' which included the RAF.

Nevertheless, as heels were dragged in London and Delhi, the idea of forming a separate 'Indian Air Service' was mooted by the then Air Marshal Trenchard, along with the concept of offering places at Cranwell to small numbers of Indian cadets.[369] Notwithstanding the impediments to change, the granting of commissions to Indians in the RAF was firmly on the table once more. The opportunity for real change though, was presented by the establishment in March 1925 of the 'Indian Sandhurst Committee' under the chairmanship of

---

367. Telegram from the Viceroy's Army Department, to the Secretary of State for India, TNA, WO 32/5079, 30 March 1921, p. 2
368. Ibid.
369. Richards, C., *'The Origins of Military Aviation in India and the Creation of the Indian Air Force, 1910-1932,* p. 38

Lieutenant-General Sir Andrew Skeen. Essentially, the Sandhurst, or 'Skeen Committee', as it came to be known, was formed to investigate the supply of Indians into the commissioned ranks of the Indian Army and to decide whether the establishment of an 'Indian Sandhurst' was a workable idea.[370] The committee was made up of predominantly Indian members and although its conclusions were wide ranging, specific reference was made to the failure of the RAF to accept Indian candidates for commissioning:

> The refusal of commission (sic) in the Air Force in our opinion is singularly indefensible because a number of Indians were actually employed as officers in the Royal Flying Corps during the Great War. They rendered efficient service. One was awarded the Distinguished Flying Cross (Indra Lal Roy - author) and he and another of the officers referred to (Welinkar - author) were killed in action.[371]

Convened at Simla, the Skeen Committee called hundreds of witnesses, the vast majority associated with the Indian Army. Having been educated at an English public school, nominated by the GOI for the ICS, interviewed by the Lytton Committee and being the last of the Indian airmen to be active on duty with the RAF, Hardit Singh was an obvious choice to be called before the committee. He was able to attend the hearings in person, while in the role of Deputy Commissioner of Gujrat on 21 December 1925. The committee that day was made up of the Chairman, Lieutenant-General Sir Andrew Skeen; Mr Muhammad Ali Jinnah,[372] a member of the Central Legislative Assembly; Mr E. Burdon, Secretary to the Army Department of the Government of India; Major Zorawar Singh, representing the Indian States; Mr Diwan Bahadur Ramachandra Rao, an ICS lawyer; Sir Phiroze Sethna, Member of the Council of State and Captain Hira Singh, late of 16 Rajput Regiment.

Hardit's responses to the committee are recorded in full in Appendix C and are worthy of further scrutiny for the light that they shed on his

---

370. Deshpande, A., *'British Military Policy in India, 1900-1945'* (Manohar Publishing: New Delhi, 2005), pp. 100-104
371. Omissi, D., *'The Sepoy and the Raj: The Indian Army, 1860-1940'* (Macmillan: London, 1994), p. 85
372. The founder and future first Governor-General of Pakistan.

opinions, education, and career.[373] The transcript illustrated that his responses to the committee were always measured, demonstrating a degree of self-awareness relating to the limitations of his knowledge, yet aware also of those specialisms which had brought him before it in the first place. Exhibiting his skills as an embryonic diplomat, he occasionally qualified his answers, offering equal weight to both sides of a line of reasoning. In the following instance, for example, he was asked to reflect upon the question of Indian students' 'feelings of unhappiness' at their treatment whilst studying in Oxford:

> *Mr Malik*– I think there was a feeling. That feeling did not exist before. It is possibly due to the fact that there is an increasing number of Indian students at the Universities, which fact is resented now by the Universities and by the British boys. I can't say to what extent the authorities resent it, but there is always a certain amount of friction between the English and Indian students as a body. Indian students keep a good deal to themselves. At the same time, you will find lots of cases in which Indian and English students get on extraordinarily well together. Even people who don't play games and are only interested in study, form study circles and so on.

In this illustration, his reply had the ring of authenticity, yet also bore witness to his other qualities: the capacity of seeing good in people and a desire to promote harmony, which were written large throughout his autobiography. They were also necessary attributes in an Indian Civil Servant. Thus, in spite of the underlying 'tensions' described, Hardit wanted the committee to know that both Britons and Indians had the capacity to get on well, even outside the sporting arena, important though he believed that was. It is worthy of note, that this was the first documentary evidence of Hardit making reference to friction between British and Indian students while at Oxford, although he had hinted at it when submitting a response to the Lytton Committee at the end of 1921.

---

373. Indian Sandhurst Committee, Volume V – Evidence, IOR/V/26/280/17: 1927, 21 December 1926, pp. 62-70

Throughout the interview, Hardit Singh drew upon his experiences in Europe and more recently upon his various roles as Deputy Commissioner, which were of special relevance to an interviewing panel considering courses of instruction at Sandhurst for Indian cadets. He was after all western educated, had a wartime military career in the British armed forces and recent knowledge of Indian educational institutions. Here was a man uniquely placed between east and west, able to comment upon some of the military and educational characteristics of both cultures with knowledge and understanding. It's apparent that the committee members were most interested in his opinions, not about his flying career, as might have been expected, but about his reflections on the most effective educational system for preparing young men for a life in the Indian armed forces. The committee cross-examined the Deputy Commissioner about the features of the best types of schools and the desirable personal qualities and backgrounds of suitable personnel able to make a successful martial career. In response, Hardit referenced his own education, upbringing and training throughout – emphasising the value of learning abroad, of the importance of a public school education and the requirement for the highest quality of teaching. In this regard, Hardit's opinions echoed his father's views a quarter of a century before, relating to the alleged poor quality of education provided by Rawalpindi's local schools, his sons having benefitted from alternative tuition of a high calibre as a result.

Hardit's vision for an effective regime for producing Indian cadets, as set out for the committee, might best be summarised as: transplanting to India the benefits of the English public school ethos as he saw them; the recreation of quasi-military British institutions such as university Officer Training Corps, junior and senior cadets and the boy scout movement; along with the development of specialist military training institutions such as Dehra Dun.[374] When submitting evidence to the Lytton Committee four years earlier, Hardit had commended the introduction of a British style public school institution to India. In doing so once more before the Skeen Committee, he was underlining the widely held belief in Britain that there

---

374. The Prince of Wales Royal Indian Military College (Today the Rashtriya Indian Military College) at Dehra Dun in Uttarakhand, was established in 1922. The purpose of the school was to provide an education and training for Indian boys being sent to the Royal Military Academy Sandhurst, as part of the policy to make the officer cadre of the Indian Army more indigenous.

was a direct connection between the ethos of public schools and the ability to lead men into battle.[375] The witness's referral to the importance of that very British military concept of 'efficiency' was an indicator to the committee, if ever they needed one, that they were in the presence of a former member of the British military establishment.

It may be inferred that Hardit believed such a public school style education inspired attitudes of leadership, independence, inquisitiveness and self-confidence. Similarly, many British parents believed that such an ethos promoted the playing of team games and endowed their sons with the status of a gentleman.[376] Many, though not all of these values sound familiar. They reflect the character of the type of education that Mohan Singh Malik had provided for his son as we have seen. It is equally unsurprising, that Hardit emphasised to the committee on several occasions, the value that he placed on sporting participation, and by implication, its perceived advantages in enabling integration and the breaking down of barriers between people. Sport had opened doors for him throughout his life and those doors were to stay open.

It became evident as the interview continued that Hardit believed that rather than send Indian cadets to Sandhurst, a new educational infrastructure was required based on the Dehra Dun model. The price to be paid for recreating this entire military training organisation in India would be the forfeiture of the gains of foreign travel from which Hardit had himself profited. Yet on the credit side, it removed the potential for 'tension' between Indian and British students, referred to at the University of Oxford, and those related to the problems encountered by Indians wishing to enlist in Britain in 1914.

Also worthy of mention is Hardit's expressed belief to the Skeen Committee of the importance of a recruit coming from a military background: 'tradition is a very great help. I believe in it tremendously'. He was referring here both to a recruit's familial background, (although his own immediate family were not from a military upbringing) and also whether a potential recruit belonged to one of the martial classes. Again, and again, the committee explored the importance that the interviewee

375. Sheffield, G., 'Officer-Man Relations: Morale and Discipline in the British Army 1902-22' (Macmillan: London, 2000), pp. 119-120
376. Halstead, T., 'The First World War and Public School Ethos: The Case of Uppingham School', War & Society (2015), 34:3, pp. 209-229

attached to the value of 'tradition' and 'class'. Hardit's attitude was nuanced to a degree, believing that although ideally a boy would come from one of the martial classes, or from a family with a military tradition, an excellent military school or academy could mitigate the perceived deficiencies of background, in order to produce cadets of the highest standard and efficiency. In doing so, he was expressing the conventional military thinking of the age relating to martial race theory, as has been seen in Chapter 9. It will be remembered that General Cox espoused similar doubts about the recruitment of a 'Pathan' as did Hardit here when referring to a 'Punjabi Mussalman'.

The report of the Indian Sandhurst Committee had the potential to break the long impasse which existed in the formulation of military policy in India, as is evident from its main recommendations.[377] The bulk of these referred to the Indian Army, including the raising of the number of places for Indians at Sandhurst to twenty in 1928 and the establishment of an equivalent military college in the subcontinent. Indians were also to be eligible for employment as King's Commissioned Officers throughout the Army and the Prince of Wales College at Dehra Dun was to be developed as a preparatory school for Sandhurst.[378] But what of the RAF? The roles played by Hardit Singh and the other Indian pilots during the war and referred to in the report, can be said to have had an impact on the committee, though the inclusion of the RAF in the deliberations seems to have resulted from the ongoing misconception by its members that the RAF in India continued to be a specialist arm of the Army.[379] Nonetheless, two places were to be allocated to cadets at Cranwell upon the publication of the report in 1927, with the number rising to six the following year, and the prospect of further increases in the years ahead.

The backlash against the unanimous report's findings began almost at once, particularly from within the ranks of the Conservative Party in Britain, the net result of which was to consign it to cold storage.[380] However,

---

377. Guptha, P.S., 'The Debate on Indianisation, 1918-1939', in Deshpande, A. & Guptha, P.S., *'The British Raj and its Indian Armed Forces, 1857-1939'* (Oxford University Press: Oxford, 2002), p. 255

378. Ibid.

379. Richards, C., *'The Origins of Military Aviation in India and the Creation of the Indian Air Force, 1910-1932*, p. 42

380. Guptha, P.S., *'The Debate on Indianisation, 1918-1939'*, p. 258

the political realities in India drove forward the concept of an 'Indian Air Force' which was approved by the then Secretary of State for India in December 1927. Even this concession was to be granted by creating India based squadrons, to be manned entirely by Indian personnel with the intention therefore of avoiding the situation where Indians might be placed in command of British personnel.[381] Such discriminatory thinking was beginning to be unsustainable however, and when Gandhi initiated the Civil Disobedience Movement on behalf of the Indian National Congress during March 1930, Ramsay Macdonald's Labour Government was driven to hold the Round Table Conferences in London between 1930-32. Here the Skeen Report became a useful tool of reference for nationalists during the negotiations, with the result that the first Indian Air Force unit – 1 Squadron was formed on 1 April 1933. It would be the basis of the Indian Air Force in existence today.

When Hardit Singh arrived in Britain in the spring of 1909, his future success was by no means certain. Many young Indians were sent to Britain for an education, which it was hoped would enable them to better themselves socially and financially. Some would return to their homes in the subcontinent disgruntled and disenchanted, however, with no definite qualifications for any type of employment and often to become alienated from their friends and families back home.[382] Oftentimes, their disillusionment resulted from their experiences in Britain – the sense of alienation they had felt in a foreign culture, in addition to feelings of isolation and loneliness. Racial discrimination frequently played a part. Yet Hardit's experiences, from being tutored at home in Rawalpindi to his first ICS posting in 1922, can be seen in hindsight to have laid the foundation for a rich and rewarding life. Why was that?

In 1946, a contemporary of his at Oxford, Professor Roy Bailey, wrote him a letter which Hardit cherished throughout his life. Bailey was a Fellow and Chaplain at Balliol, a writer and poet whose friendship Hardit had valued. Bailey's letter referred to the exchanges between Indians and the English:

---

381. Richards, C., '*The Origins of Military Aviation in India and the Creation of the Indian Air Force, 1910-1932,* p. 42
382. Mukherjee, S., '*Nationalism, Education and Migrant Identities*' (Routledge: Abingdon, 2010), p. 114

What I do always expect to find is a difference, and probably more differences than with a foreign European, which makes inter-communications of ideas difficult. But I always felt that you, years ago, contributed to, and have contributed since, more to the Anglo-Indian understanding than any man I've known, not in the least by being "de-Indianised" which would have wrecked everything as much as the de-Americanised and stupid Anglophile Rhodes scholar does, but by simply being yourself, Indian through and through, and yet not only understanding, but being understandable, by the English.[383]

Hardit referred to Ridley's letter when interviewed by Charles Allen in 1983, two years before his death.[384] It is interesting to speculate why Hardit valued this letter and felt impelled to reproduce it in his autobiography. On the face of it, the letter particularly emphasised Hardit's integrity and powers of communication, for although in the Allen interview, he described himself as becoming 'westernised' in those early years in Britain, he was nevertheless, a proud patriot and a believer in the cause of Indian independence. How had he managed to maintain this integrity in the eyes of others, able to be meaningfully understood and accepted in both cultures? Hardit himself believed that Sikhism and the values inculcated in him at an early age by family were at the heart of the maintenance of his single-minded adherence to faith, country and culture. This is all true, yet there may be more to it than that.

The British politician Thomas Macauley's educational directive of 1835, which emphasised the importance of Western education for Indians was intended to 'create classes of persons Indian in blood and colour, but English in taste, in opinions, in morals and intellect'.[385, 386] By encouraging

---

383. Malik, H.S., '*A Little Work, A Little Play*', p. 112
384. '*Hardit Singh Malik, 1894-1985*' – as of 30 October 2020 – empirefaithwar.com, interview with Charles Allen in 1983 (Courtesy of Somnath Sapru).
385. Thomas Babington Macaulay, (25 October 1800 – 28 December 1859) was a British historian and politician. He played a major role in the introduction of British and Western concepts to education in India, and published his argument on the subject in the 'Macaulay's Minute' in 1835. He supported the replacement of Persian by English as the official language, the use of English as the medium of instruction in all schools, and the training of English-speaking Indians as teachers.
386. Mukherjee, S., 'Nationalism, Education and Migrant Identities', p. 8

those from the subcontinent to study in Britain, his ultimate goals were to enable the spread of Western Civilisation to India and the creation of a class of Indian 'collaborators' able to service the needs of the Empire.[387] By becoming westernised, Hardit Singh might be said to be the personification of these objectives, yet Macauley's policy ultimately failed, for numerous Indians who were educated in Britain became central to the eventual success of the home rule movements in India, whilst others like Hardit, personified the cause of Indian freedom in their diplomatic roles around the world when representing their country, both before and after 1947. He became one of many British educated diplomats, who were not agents of imperial 'collaboration', but representatives of an aspiring independent country, the personification of India at its best, what it could and would be in the future.

That's not to say there weren't inconsistencies or ambiguities in serving the British Empire, its armed forces or the ICS, there were. How was Hardit able to rationalise such service whilst fundamentally disapproving of imperialism and imperialists? Like many Indians of his generation who studied in Britain, he made a distinction between a Britain of 'two nations', not Disraeli's rich and poor, but one at the same time *both* liberal and imperialist. As he himself acknowledged, it was the liberal education at school and university in Britain which instilled in him the importance of an appreciation of the different beliefs and values of others, of the meaning of tolerance, and faith in the rule of law. In doing so, he was able to accommodate an aesthetic and idealistic attachment to Britain while opposing its imperialism in India.[388] He was able to thus hold two seemingly contradictory perspectives, whilst at the same time, exploiting the imperial relationship for himself, extracting intellectual and social resources and creating international connections.[389]

From the outset, Hardit assumed British customs, both in dress and manner, influenced by his environment and the better to enable him to fit in and be more readily accepted in society. He was not alone, many students coming to Europe adopted what became known as the 'cuff and collar cult' mentality, enabling them to adapt to the new culture at best, whilst coping

---

387. Wainright, A. M., *'The Better Class of Indian': Social rank, imperial identity and South Asians in Britain 1858-1914'* (Manchester University Press: Manchester, 2008), p. 195
388. Lahiri, S., *'Indians in Britain, 1880-1930'* (Cass: London, 2000), p. 211
389. Mukherjee, S., 'Nationalism, Education and Migrant Identities', p. 4

with a potentially hostile environment at worst.[390] Compared to the vast majority of Indian students, Hardit's early tutoring in Rawalpindi gave him a head start, endowing him with an excellent knowledge of the English language, a degree of cultural awareness and some understanding of the demands of the education system. He enjoyed other advantages too, which would allow him to adapt relatively smoothly into the privileged society in which he would find himself. Many of these benefits came from his association with members of the British middle and upper classes during his time at Eastbourne, Oxford and in the RFC. In early twentieth century Britain, the social elite's definition of 'class' tended to incorporate 'race' when classifying a newcomer as a means of establishing and reinforcing their identity.[391] These judgements were based on their *own* understanding of Indian society and interactions with Indians as individuals. So, while some Indian students were embraced in the social groups in which they began to move with Britons, others were left out on the basis of class.

In Hardit's case, there were a number of reasons for his inclusion, an obvious one was wealth. British institutions responded to Indians with financial means more favourably than those without. Hardit's father could afford to pay for his son's public school education, which gave rise to Hardit possessing a certain demeanour, and wealth also guaranteed a degree of financial security and therefore status within society. Similarly, at a time when one's 'class' and 'family' were important descriptors of identity, his father's various positions of authority and responsibility in Rawalpindi were eminently reassuring to his son's adopted institutions in Britain. In documents relating to Hardit's RFC career produced by the GOI and the India Office, for example, reference was made consistently to his father's position and standing in the Punjab, alongside other facets of Hardit's own identity important to the British establishment: his schooling, university and of course that he was an Indian who played team sports.

While many Indian students coming to study in Britain lacked the necessary social background similar to the one enjoyed by Hardit Singh, they also lacked the skills and interests that British school and undergraduate culture prized most highly, particularly competitive team sports. Conversely,

---

390. Wainright, A.M., *'The Better Class of Indian': Social rank, imperial identity and South Asians in Britain 1858-1914'*, p. 160
391. Ibid., p. 8

Hardit took an active part in such games, making friendships as a result, and treating university life, as did many of his indigenous peers, almost as a finishing school for 'membership in the old-boy' network.[392] Such an environment was instrumental in preparing him for a wartime career in the RFC and as a member of the ICS.

The most significant part of those early years in Britain were those spent at Eastbourne College, which enabled Hardit to acclimatise in a public school setting where leadership, individuality, curiosity and self-assurance were prized equally as highly as academic and intellectual achievement. It was here he learned to look after himself, manage relationships with significant adults and to make meaningful friendships. It was here also that he discovered, and began to understand, the social and cultural norms of Britain's governing classes, for attendance at even a minor public school such as Eastbourne, was the surest way of achieving gentlemanly rank and therefore access to the circles of the social elite. It's not surprising that Harold Macmillan questioned Hardit about his former school at their preliminary Balliol meeting in 1912. The future prime minister was making an assessment of Hardit's social status and although he may not have been overly impressed, what mattered were the benefits that Hardit accrued in British schools from the age of fourteen. For many Indians arriving fresh at a British university at the age of eighteen or more, their sole interest in academic study and intellectual pursuits would prove disadvantageous, often resulting in isolation, loneliness and inhibited social development. Their backgrounds were also a drawback in this context because they came from secondary schools of which few British students had heard and therefore their prior experiences carried no identifiable social markers with which British undergraduates could assess them as they assessed one another. In addition, the newly arrived Indians often had no friends to accompany them, they were alone, making their way in university society as best they could.[393]

Hardit too had been alone initially, but he was able to make a virtue of the fact as a young teenager, able to draw social capital from his recent British style tuition, family background, relative wealth and sporting prowess. As a result, he had no alternative but to assimilate and forge friendships with

392. Ibid., p. 205
393. Ibid., p. 204

British boys at Eastbourne, gaining knowledge of public school codes of behaviour and the resulting self-confidence, independence and resilience which ensued. Similarly, Motilal, the father of the future first Prime Minister of India Jawaharlal Nehru, advised his son *not* to live with his two cousins when studying at Cambridge for fear that all three would seek out only their own company and not British society.[394]Although for Hardit this was never a choice, the end result was the same, both men at ease in western society for the rest of their lives.

A central theme of this book highlights how challenging it was for an Indian to serve in Britain's armed forces faced with racial discrimination, be it 'institutional' or 'interpersonal'. In his autobiography, Hardit gave occasional glimpses of some of the difficulties and obstacles he faced during the war, always described in a dignified manner, without rancour or resentment.

Recent scholarship of Indian students in Britain, has emphasised the alienation and bigotry that many faced, often at the hands of British students. Yet, in relation to his school and university years, Hardit mentioned only the attempt to remove his turban on the first night at Eastbourne as an example of any such discrimination. It stands to reason that there must have been other instances, for in the period before the First World War, racial prejudice was rife at Oxford in particular, the halcyon days of Master Jowett during the nineteenth century having long gone.[395] He made mention of only one other illustration of having received interpersonal racism, by the South African pilot at Nivelles. Yet, whilst living in Britain and a member of the RFC and RAF, he described a number of instances of institutional acts of discrimination.

There may be so few descriptions of personal bigotry against him recorded in his autobiography for several reasons: firstly, he was so well assimilated into British society at an early age. Secondly, as a well-adjusted and educated person of faith, he managed any instances of prejudice against him, able to control his emotions and responses effectively. Thirdly, his liberal attitude to life gave him a viewpoint which attached little blame to the vast majority of British society for the political agendas

---

394. Lahiri, S., *'Indians in Britain, 1880-1930'*, p. 40
395. Ibid. p. 55

of the Empire, so enabling him to depersonalise acts of discrimination.[396] He summed up his attitude to racism during his 1982 interview with Trevor Fishlock: 'There was occasional petty prejudice [...] Incidents like that did not make me bitter. I had so many British friends.'[397] It was the instances of institutional racism inherent in imperialism that he found most infuriating.

Before leaving for Britain in 1909, an uncle warned Hardit: 'when travelling by train in England...never to let yourself to be left alone with a young girl in the same compartment!'[398] Hardit made light of the advice when giving a speech in London about Anglo-Indian relations as Indian Ambassador to France in the early 1950s, telling the audience: 'I spent many years at school and college in England, but in spite of all my efforts, I never succeeded in finding myself alone with a young lady in a railway compartment!' This charming ice-breaker enabled the Ambassador to speak openly about relations between the two countries.

Yet his uncle's words were a constant reminder to the young Hardit of the cultural complexities of interracial interactions with members of the opposite sex. Such concerns related to the restrictions that Indian society placed on men and women outside of their families in the subcontinent. Moreover, many middle-class Indian parents believed that the socially conservative upbringing of Indian youths 'prepared them poorly for the licentious openness of British society'.[399] Such stereotyping played a part, with many Indian families believing that British working-class women were unfettered by any moral restraints. There was a small degree of reality in this perception, for it was not unknown for Indian students to be singled out for attention by women of many backgrounds in Britain, attributed to the fact that the men were often regarded as princes, as Hardit discovered when arriving in Cognac.[400] [401] Moreover, many British administrators of the day, also believed the stereotype of British working-class women being detrimental

---

396. Mukherjee, S., '*Nationalism, Education and Migrant Identities*', p. 69
397. Fishlock, T., 'When a child of the Raj could find an ever-open door', *The Times* (London), 16 October 1982
398. Malik, H.S., '*A Little Work, A Little Play*', p. 27
399. Wainright, A.M., '*The Better Class of Indian': Social rank, imperial identity and South Asians in Britain 1858-1914*', p. 213
400. Ibid.
401. Lahiri, S., 'Indians in Britain, 1880-1930', p. 122

an influence on Indian middle and upper-class men.[402] The substance of his uncle's words may also have reflected Indian anxieties about another British stereotype prevalent before the First World War, which portrayed Indian men as sexual predators.[403] At the heart of these cross-cultural categories and labels, was the very great fear at the time of interracial marriage. This became so great in official circles during Hardit's period of study at Oxford, that the India Office distributed a circular to all registry offices in Britain 'warning of the risks attendant in such marriages.'[404]

In view of the prevailing conditions therefore, it was not surprising that romance seemed not to have blossomed for Hardit whilst in Britain. There were opportunities of course, with the London boarding house keeper's daughter Cissie; with Clairette Preiss, with whom he later acknowledged to being in love, and perhaps even with the nurse in the hospital in Chelsea.[405] As he made clear however, having acknowledged having strong feelings for Clairette in 1915, he had decided not to 'marry outside my own country'.[406] There were too many obstacles to any such long term association, too many voices counselling to the contrary and no one was better placed between the two cultures to understand fully the implications of an interracial marriage. During the impressionable years of his youth therefore, he was able to live amongst the British, enjoying the benefits of their friendships, faith, history and traditions, without compromising his own beliefs and heritage.[407] He was guided by the spiritual and ethical beliefs inherited from his faith, the words of Sant Attar Singh and the support of his family.

Hardit Singh Malik went on to have an illustrious diplomatic career in many parts of the world. It began as Assistant Commissioner of Sheikhupura District on 6 January 1922, before being continued in the role of Deputy Commissioner from 1926. He then completed periods of duty in other provinces, until returning to London in 1930, serving as both Deputy

402. Wainright, A.M., *'The Better Class of Indian': Social rank, imperial identity and South Asians in Britain 1858-1914'*, p. 212
403. Ibid.
404. Lahiri, S., 'Indians in Britain, 1880-1930', p. 122
405. Malik, H.S., *'A Little Work, A Little Play'*, pp. 52, 56 & 111
406. Ibid., p. 53
407. Ibid., p. 13

and Acting Trade Commissioners to Britain until 1934.[408] The following year, Hardit was appointed as Deputy Secretary in the Indian commerce department, and spent the succeeding years in India, before his selection as Trade Commissioner to Canada and the United States in 1938. [409] He served in New York, Washington and Ottawa until 1943, and had the honour of being awarded the Order of the British Empire (OBE) in 1938, before his appointment as a Companion of the Order of the Indian Empire (CIE) in 1941.[410] [411]

In 1944, Hardit Singh became the Prime Minister (dewan) of the powerful principality of Patiala, under the rule Maharaja Yadavindra Singh, carrying out that role until Indian independence in 1947 and the dissolution of the ICS.[412] After Partition, he joined the new Indian Foreign Service and was appointed as the first High Commissioner to Canada. He then went on to serve as the Ambassador to France and was also the leader of the Indian delegation at the United Nations General Assembly held in Paris. In 1956, he was decorated as a Grand Officer of the Legion of Honour by the President of France.

Hardit Singh's final engagement with the RAF took place at the Diamond Jubilee of British military aviation in 1972, hosted by the British Government. Former members of the RFC and RNAS were invited, with Hardit the only surviving Indian airman of the Great War transported back to Britain for the final time, courtesy of the Indian Air Force. There was time for a mini reunion of 28 Squadron at the reception and an opportunity to revisit old friends in Britain in the two months that followed.

Throughout his life and into old age Hardit continued to play golf as often as possible, though the opportunities for cricket dwindled. His innate modesty and sense of fun enabled him to maintain, and continue to form friendships, arguably the greatest source of joy in his life, after his family.

Having retired in 1957, he moved to New Delhi, remaining active until the age of eighty-eight. He suffered a stroke in 1984 and passed away a

---

408. '*The India Office and Burma Office List: 1945*' (Harrison & Sons: London Ltd, 1945) p. 263
409. Ibid.
410. '34469', *The London Gazette* (Supplement), 31 December 1937, p. 14
411. '35184'. *The London Gazette* (Supplement), 6 June 1941, p. 3286
412. '*The India Office and Burma Office List: 1945*', p. 263

year later, on 31 October 1985, three weeks before his ninety-first birthday. He was survived by his wife, Prakash; two daughters, Harsimran and Veena, and a son, Harmala Singh. His autobiography, *A Little Work, A Little Play*, was published posthumously in 2010.

To the end, he carried with him the two bullets which Lieutenant Paul Strähle's Albatros had put there. Occasionally, they gave him discomfort, yet in many ways, it was appropriate that they had accompanied him on life's journey, constant reminders of that foggy day over Flanders in October 1917:

> My miraculous escape had a profound effect on my life. It convinced me that one dies only when one's time comes, a conviction which led to a kind of fearlessness which has given me strength throughout my life in facing several crises in the years to come.[413]

The period before and during the First World War had been the making of him and was the time of his life.

---

413. Malik, H.S., *'A Little Work, A Little Play'*, p. 89

Appendix A

During the academic year 1920-1921, Hardit was back in Oxford, having been required to undergo another year's study as part of his ICS entrance requirements. Members of the Lytton Committee arrived in the city at the end of May 1921, having earmarked him as a potential witness. (The written submissions from witnesses to the committee were typed up in the third person singular, though the handwritten originals are no longer available. Inconsistencies of grammar and spelling have been left as in the original.)

Corrected summaries of the oral evidence taken at Oxford, 31 May to 03 June 1921, IOR/Q/10/4/2, Hardit Singh Malik's testimony, 3 June 1921, pp. 1-3

Friday June 3rd. The third witness to be called was Mr Malik of Balliol College. Now a probationer for the I.C.S.

He said that what was generally agreed among the Indian students to be their chief grievance was that comparatively so few of them could get into college. He did not think that the non-collegiate students derived so much benefit from Oxford as did the College men, and it was only the latter who had any real chance of social intercourse with Englishmen.

He thought that the two types of Indian men who got most out of university were:
  a) Those who were up with the purpose of doing serious work. i.e., Research or any serious branch of study.
  b) Those who had been to a British Public School.

He thought that the record, both at Oxford and subsequently in India, of the men who had received a Public School education had been a good one.

As regards the selection to be exercised in India, he did not advocate a Government body for the purpose. He thought that it was necessary to have men on the Selecting Council who had experience of English universities; but it should not necessarily be composed of Indian university authorities.

He thought that the Delegacy for Oriental students (in Oxford and headed by Sir Stephen Montagu Burrows - author) worked very well, and that apart from the inherent distaste for guardianship, that the Indians at Oxford respected it.[414] His own relations with Mr Burrows had been very happy.

The witness said that he had come to England in 1908, (sic) had spent a year in a Preparatory School in London and had been at a Public School for three years (sic), coming to Oxford in 1912.[415] He had served in the Army (sic) during the war and since then had spent 9 months in India. He thought that a man, if he had come over here to school and intended to go to university, should go home at least once during that time. He thought that it was essential for the Indian boy who came here to school to be placed in the care of a family in England, otherwise he was opposed to their coming at this early age.

Speaking of the difference in temperament between the Indian and English students he thought that the Indian was on the whole, more serious, both

---

414. In essence, guardianship involved taking charge of a student's education and welfare needs. In return, parents were required to pay a fee and ensure that the guardian's counsel and directions were adhered to. With the establishment of an institutional framework in the wake of the Lee-Warner Report, guardianship was no longer left to unofficial associations. Oxbridge students were virtually forced to accept guardianship as admission would otherwise prove impossible. Arguably its most important function was to provide a report on the conduct and progress of the students' studies. Inevitably, many Indian students resented any form of guardianship, which it was alleged was operated to offset seditious influences and often to create conditions favourable to the formation of friendships with English persons. At Oxford, guardianship was managed by the Delegacy for Indian Students led by Sir Stephen Montagu Burrows.

415. It is the author's contention that Hardit Singh travelled to England in April 1909 (see Chapter 1). He was actually at Eastbourne from the end of May 1910 to July 1912, two years and two months approximately.

in his games, possibly his work and in his general outlook on life than the average English boy. It was because of this difference that the Indian, without the Public School preparation finds himself in a totally strange atmosphere when he comes to this country.

He would welcome the introduction of the Public School system to India, though there would necessarily have to be a few modifications to make it suited to the Indian genius.

He thought that in the promotion of social intercourse the various social clubs that existed were very useful as long as they did not tend to become political; he felt this to be a danger common to a great many college and University clubs. He did not know of any club which included in its membership Englishwomen and Indian men, though as regards the women's colleges, he said he had received invitations to tea which showed that Indians were not ignored.

Mr Malik said that his life outside work was purely athletic. He had been captain of the Balliol Cricket XI; he played golf for the university and this brought him into contact with many Englishmen with whom he was on very good terms.

The witness said that he did not think that there was any truth in the statement that many Indians did not get enough scope in athletics at the University. He felt convinced that if an Indian showed skill in a game he would have a perfectly good chance of getting into a team, either college or University. Indians were potentially very good athletes but many of them were too lazy to take the trouble to become good at games: their reluctance to take part in games was less due to physical activity than to a constitutional laziness. He had made some effort to organise clubs and games for the Indians but he had not met with much response.

He was a member of the Medjlis, and considered it to be a valuable body, provided that its present tendency to become a political society did not increase. He did not think that complaints should be levelled against it on account of political utterances which emanated from it, as similar complaints might with justice be alleged against any society with definite views, such as the Socialist/Labour Societies. He would be in favour of admitting Englishmen to the Medjlis. He did not want to break up the Indian social traditions but he thought that any form of Indian clique at Oxford was inadvisable.

As regards the cost of living at the University, in a way that, without any extravagance, would enable a man to take part in college life, he said that in his view £400 a year was the minimum, but to be really comfortable he would put the amount at £550.

He had been in the French Army (sic) from 1916-17 and subsequently in the Flying Corps in the English Army and had experienced no difficulty in getting on well with the other officers. They lived together in the closest and most friendly of terms. He had been in his school O.T.C. (Officer Training Corps) and the English boys had shown no objection to his presence there. He did not think that the reason that the Oxford University O.T.C was closed to Indians was a social reason, he thought that it was political. He considered the restrictions unfair, and that Indians greatly resented it. He did not think that there was, partly at least, any feeling amongst ex-service men that Indians should not be admitted to the corps.

He thought that the only way for the Indian to get into social intercourse with Englishmen was by being at one of the Colleges. He felt that the Indians in the Non-Collegiate body were inclined to congregate together and to nurse their grievances until these grievances, real or supposed, became exaggerated.

Appendix B

Grant of commissions in Royal Air Force to selected Indians, Collection 430/5 Part 1, IOR/L/MIL/7/19010: 1917-1920, 1 November 1918, p. 109

Copy of telegram

From   Viceroy Army Dept.,
Dated   1. 11. 18.
Received 10am, 5th.
14591. Your telegram of the 7th ultimo. No. 2588.

Employment of Indians in Royal Air Force.

We are unable to support the proposals of Air Ministry for reasons:

They contemplate grant to Indians of permanent commissions in the Air Force. Indian officers granted such commissions would almost certainly elect to serve in India after the war. Effect of this would be that the Air Force in this country would then be largely officered by Indians, a result which we regard as undesirable.

Secondly, in our despatch of 2nd March, no.16, we affirmed importance of retaining Artillery and Machine Gun Companies in British hands. We consider that this policy applies equally to Royal Air Force. Prior to receipt of your telegram under reply, we already had under preparation a despatch recommending that, in technical and scientific services of the Army, including the Air Force, all positions allotted to officers and those assigned to skilled NCOs and men, other than workshop ratings, should be filled exclusively by Europeans.

Thirdly, we are aware that this principle has not been strictly adhered to in certain theatres of war, but we consider that it should be upheld as part of our post bellum policy in India, and on these grounds, we are opposed to granting of permanent commissions in Air Force to Indians.

Fourthly, grant of temporary commissions in the Air Force is also open to serious objections. To bestow such commissions on Indians while debarring them from permanent commissions for which their British comrades will be eligible, would constitute legitimate source of grievance as it would deprive them of reward which they might reasonably expect besides creating racial difference which it would be difficult to justify, especially in the case of those who had rendered good service in the field.

Fifthly, it is true that a few honorary and temporary commissions in the Air Force have been granted to Indians since the beginning of the war, but this was done without consulting us, and we consider for reasons stated no more commissions of this kind should be granted. As it is, the suitable disposal of these officers after the war is likely to prove a difficult matter.

Sixthly, proposal to admit Indians to Air Force seems to us at variance with the principle laid down by the War Office and accepted by War Cabinet that Indians granted commissions should always be appointed to Indian Army. We presume that objections raised by the War office…are as applicable to case of Air Force as they are to that of Army. With regard to your suggestion that volunteers for Air Force might be drawn from candidates now being selected in India and at home for temporary commissions, we would observe that our objections are as applicable to them as to cadets who would be recruited under Air Ministry's scheme. In no case, however, would we recommend course of instruction at Indore be dispensed with, as we regard this as indispensable in order to render candidates socially and professionally for commissioned rank.

Eighthly, (sic) we would add that from experience gained in selection of candidates for Sandhurst and temporary commissions we are of opinion that it would be very difficult to secure candidates of good family to the number required by Air Ministry possessing the knowledge of English and high physical qualifications demanded.

Appendix C

Oral Examination of Special Witnesses – Indian Sandhurst Committee hearings – 21 December 1925, Hardit Singh Malik.

Indian Sandhurst Committee, Volume V – Evidence, IOR/V/26/280/17: 1927, 21 December 1925, pp. 62-70

The interview panel: The Chairman, Lieutenant-General Sir Andrew Skeen; Muhammad Ali Jinnah, a member of the Central Legislative Assembly; Mr E. Burdon, Secretary to the Army department of the GOI; Major Zorawar Singh, representing the Indian States; Diwan Bahadur Ramachandra Rao, an ICS lawyer; Sir Phiroze Sethna, Member of the Council of State and Captain Hira Singh, late of 16 Rajput Regiment.

Mr Burdon – Would you mind giving the Committee a brief account of your career. At what age did you go to England?

Mr Malik – At the age of between 13 and 14.

Mr Burdon – What was the school you went to?

Mr Malik – I first went to a preparatory school in London, and then to Eastbourne College.

Mr Burdon – From Eastbourne you went to Oxford?

Mr Malik – I did.

Mr Burdon – Did you get a scholarship there?

Mr Malik – No.

Mr Burdon – What was your college?

Mr Malik – Balliol.

Mr Burdon – What did you read there?

Mr Malik – I read History.

Mr Burdon – What examinations did you take first?

Mr Malik – I took Responsions[416] first and then I took the Honours Course in History.

Mr Burdon – How old were you then?

Mr Malik – I must have been about 22.

Mr Burdon – When did you join the army?

Mr Malik – I joined up in that very year. I went out first of all with the French Red Cross.

Mr Burdon – How did you manage to get into touch with the French Red Cross?

Mr Malik – Through my tutor at Oxford.

Mr Burdon – You first served as a volunteer?

Mr Malik – I served as a volunteer with the French Red Cross. Then I got a letter from my tutor at Balliol saying that the GOC Flying Corps, General Henderson, would probably be prepared to consider me for

---

416. 'Responsions' was the first of the three examinations formerly required for acceptance for an academic degree at the University of Oxford.

a commission in the Royal Flying Corps, if I went to see him. I took leave and went and saw him, and he made me an offer. Then I went back to France and finished up with the French Red Cross. I came back to England and was appointed a cadet in the Royal Flying Corps. I was a cadet for about 10 or 15 days at Farnborough before I got my commission. After getting the commission I went to Reading for a two months' course of technical training before starting flying. There they asked us where we wanted to go for our preliminary flying, and I with a batch of three or four others chose a place in France where the Royal Naval Air Service had a Flying School. I did my preliminary flying there, and after a month or six weeks I returned to England and got my pilot's certificate. We formed a squadron from the school and I went over to France as a pilot. That was No.28 Squadron which is now at Quetta. I was wounded in France with them in October 1917.

Mr Burdon – You were in action with the Flying Corps?

Mr Malik – Yes. We were doing what they call fighting patrols. Our aeroplanes were single-seaters with two Vickers guns. Our job was fighting and nothing else. I was wounded in the air, but not very badly.

Mr Burdon – You came back after you got fit?

Mr Malik – I went back to my squadron which had moved to Italy in December of the same year. In about March or April 1918 I came back to England on night flying on the defence of London and after spending three or four months in England, I went out again to France with No.11 Squadron and I was with them at the time of the Armistice. After the Armistice I applied for eight months' leave and came out to India. I then went back to England in August 1919 and got myself demobilised. I did so because I had got married in 1919, and I was anxious then to be demobilised.

Mr Burdon – Was there a talk at any time of your remaining in the Flying Corps permanently?

Mr Malik – When I got my leave, I was told at the Air Ministry that at the end of my leave I was to take up an appointment with a squadron in India.

Mr Burdon – Did they raise any difficulty about demobilising you?

Mr Malik – No.

Mr Burdon – How did you enter the Indian Civil Service?

Mr Malik – I got in on the nomination of the Government of India while I was in England.

Mr Burdon – Immediately after being demobilised?

Mr Malik – No, sometime after. I got my appointment to the ICS in 1920, and I was then sent back for a year to Oxford. I came out to India at the end of 1921. I am now at Lahore on special duty. I was Deputy Commissioner at Sheikhupura and then of Gujrat, and I have recently been on special duty in connection with the Northern Command manoeuvres.

Mr Burdon – How did you like service in the Flying Corps?

Mr Malik – I liked it very much.

Major Zorawar Singh – Do you think that if the Flying Corps (sic) was opened up to Indians it would be popular among them, and they would make a success of it?

Mr Malik – I think it would attract only a limited class. I see no reason why they should not make a success of it.

Major Zorawar Singh – What are your views about the establishment of an Indian Sandhurst?

Mr Malik – I think the idea is to have a military training institute in India. It will have only one disadvantage, that is, that a young man instead of going out to a foreign country, which I personally believe will be good for him, will not think of going; he will stay in his own country, because our young men are naturally inclined to stay in their own country.

Major Zorawar Singh – But suppose that in order to get over that difficulty, after the course at an Indian Sandhurst, you provided for a post-graduate course abroad?

Mr Malik – I don't think a mere tour would do. They would have to stay with a British Regiment in England. I think a year's stay would do. That would get over the difficulty of foreign travel and association and would certainly help.

Major Zorawar Singh – What do you think about the pace on Indianisation? How soon do you think the whole army should be Indianised?

Mr Malik – It is impossible for me to answer that question because I am not sufficiently in touch with the Indian Army. I am at present a civilian.

Major Zorawar Singh – As an Indian and as a patriot, how soon would you like the Indian Army to be Indianised?

Mr Malik – I should say as soon as possible consistently with efficiency. I can't say the exact time, because I am not really in touch with modern military requirements.

Major Zorawar Singh – Do you think that we have enough material in the country in our schools and colleges? We have got a lot of schools and colleges in our country and there is also one school at Dehra Dun, which specially prepares boys for the army. Do you think that we can get enough candidates for Sandhurst?

Mr Malik – I don't think that you can get enough. I think that you will need many more Dehra Duns. The existing educational institutions do not turn out really the type of man that the military authorities require, I mean the type of man who will be successful at a place like Sandhurst. I should have thought that you could certainly get 10 men suitable for Sandhurst in the whole of India.

Major Zorawar Singh – If you think our education is defective, what improvements would you suggest?

Mr Malik – The Dehra Dun college is an excellent institution and has made a very good beginning indeed. I should suggest a multiplication of Dehra Duns.

Major Zorawar Singh – We have been given two alternative schemes. One is the multiplication of Dehra Duns, and the expansion of the present institution, if necessary, and another is to improve the education in the ordinary schools and colleges and to add army classes there, so that the supply from Dehra Dun may be increased?

Mr Malik – I think that you will find it very difficult to do that in the ordinary schools. It is not so much a question of improving the training of the boys as of improving the staff. Unless you improve the staff, it is very difficult to give the necessary training.

Major Zorawar Singh – There are some colleges in India which approach the English Public Schools. For instance, there are four or five Chiefs' Colleges[417]. If army classes were attached to them, don't you think that the number of candidates would improve?

Mr Malik – I think by the institution of army classes you might get boys to become keener on that side of the training. The University Training Corps in the various Universities will also help.

Diwan Bahadur Ramachandra Rao – I think you were one of the students who appeared before the Lytton Committee in 1921?

Mr Malik – Yes. I gave evidence. I was in England from 1908 (sic) practically continuously to the end of 1921. I was brought up in the traditions of the English Public Schools. I took a good deal of part (sic) in games, and I played golf for Oxford. My view is that those who do well in games get on much better in the English Universities than those who do not play games.

---

417. 'Chiefs' colleges' in India were founded to provide education for the princely and aristocratic families of India.

Diwan Bahadur Ramachandra Rao – Is it a fact that during the war many Indian students offered to serve in the army in various capacities in Great Britain?

Mr Malik – Yes, a good many did. I used to meet students and talk over things with them. There was a considerable amount of resentment on the grounds of having been excluded from serving in the army.

Mr Jinnah – You offered yourself?

Mr Malik – Yes, but I was unsuccessful in the India Office, and I therefore went to the French Red Cross. I offered to serve in any capacity and several students did the same thing, but their offers were all refused by the India Office. At that time there was a good deal of feeling on this question among Indian students. I do not know if there was any definite rule to exclude them.

Diwan Bahadur Ramachandra Rao – They were also debarred from joining the O.T.C., and that formed the subject of a representation to the Lytton Committee.

Mr Malik – I was in my school O.T.C.

Diwan Bahadur Ramachandra Rao – Did you know that several students tried to get into the O.T.C. in England and could not?

Mr Malik – No.

Diwan Bahadur Ramachandra Rao – Was there a feeling among the Universities that Indian students were not desirable?

Mr Malik – Do you mean among the University authorities or among the Indian boys?

Diwan Bahadur Ramachandra Rao – Was there a feeling among the Indian students?

Mr Malik – I think there was a feeling. That feeling did not exist before. It is possibly due to the fact that there is an increasing number of Indian students at the Universities, which fact is resented now by the Universities and by the British boys. I can't say to what extent the authorities resent it, but there is always a certain amount of friction between the English and Indian students as a body. Indian students keep a good deal to themselves. At the same time, you will find lots of cases in which Indian and English students get on extraordinarily well together. Even people who don't play games and are only interested in study form, study circles, and so on.

Diwan Bahadur Ramachandra Rao – Barring the individual cases, you mean as the number increases there is a greater tendency for the Indians to keep together?

Mr Malik – Yes, that is so.

Diwan Bahadur Ramachandra Rao – What was the number of Indians at Oxford and Cambridge? 70 or 80?

Mr Malik – I think it was more than that, but I could not say definitely.

Diwan Bahadur Ramachandra Rao – Do you think that, if military education is to be imparted to Indians, we ought to have training institutions in this country as early as possible?

Mr Malik – Yes, I do think so.

Diwan Bahadur Ramachandra Rao – And that any reliance on British institutions can only go up to a certain stage, and that, as the number of Indians at these institutions increases, there will be trouble? Supposing the number of Indians to be admitted to Sandhurst is increased to 100 or 150, do you think that the authorities at Sandhurst or the British cadets will resent it? Will there be any friction between the Indian cadets and the British cadets or the authorities?

Mr Malik – I think that you would arrive at the point which I have just mentioned, at which the Indians would be inclined to keep together more and more, and there would be the same kind of friction as at the universities.

Diwan Bahadur Ramachandra Rao – From that standpoint you believe that we should make a very early beginning here?

Mr Malik – I believe that you should begin early. That is why I favour the Dehra Dun institution and other institutions of that sort.

Diwan Bahadur Ramachandra Rao – Since you returned to India have you seen any of the educational institutions in this country? Have you been to any of the colleges?

Mr Malik – I am constantly in Lahore and I meet a lot of college students. There is plenty of material in this country for Sandhurst, but you have not the means of training that material at present.

Diwan Bahadur Ramachandra Rao – From that standpoint would you suggest any change in our secondary schools or colleges to prove this material?

Mr Malik – I would suggest the institution of military classes, O.T.C.s., junior cadets and senior cadets, the boy scout movement has also done good work. All these should be encouraged in our schools. And I think that if you can afford to have some special institutions like Dehra Dun for training boys for a military career, you will not need army classes in your secondary schools.

Diwan Bahadur Ramachandra Rao – Supposing the multiplication of Dehra Dun in the provinces becomes somewhat difficult from the financial point of view, then is it your idea that we should adopt this alternative method of preparing the material?

Mr Malik – I won't suggest it as an alternative. I don't think it will be effective as an alternative method. I think a special institution is absolutely necessary.

Diwan Bahadur Ramachandra Rao – But assuming that there are difficulties in increasing the number of special institutions, would you keep open another door for the present?

Mr Malik – I think the institution of army classes in the Punjab in the present secondary schools would only be a very small step towards the training of a boy for a career at Sandhurst, whereas if you send him to a special institution like Dehra Dun, you will be able to give him the best possible training and prepare him for a military career.

Diwan Bahadur Ramachandra Rao – You have to consider the question of cost. Don't you think that the question of cost arises in the case of Dehra Dun? There are not many parents who can afford it, but would you wish for that reason that the sons of the comparatively poorer classes should be kept out of the army?

Mr Malik – I think it is up to Government to see that if a boy is selected from a poorer class he is helped to get along. I would suggest subsidising pupils in a number of schools.

Diwan Bahadur Ramachandra Rao – Would you limit your recruits to special institutions like Dehra Dun only?

Mr Malik – From the point of efficiency, I would. I think it would be a good thing in the long run, because after all, when you have got your institutions for training boys for the army, you would want boys to take advantage of those institutions, and the boy from an ordinary school, no matter how good he may be, will I think, suffer some sort of disadvantage as compared with a boy trained at Dehra Dun.

Diwan Bahadur Ramachandra Rao – Dehra Dun cannot accommodate more than a certain number. Are we to wait until we get more Dehra Duns? Are we to stop our progress in the meantime if we can get boys from other sources, even though they may be a little inferior?

Mr Malik – As it is the commencement, I think that keeping up the highest standard is most important.

Mr Jinnah – Supposing we want 50 or 100 boys every year and Dehra Dun can only give us 8, are we to confine ourselves to Dehra Dun until we can get many more Dehra Duns?

Mr Malik – I think that you should confine yourself only to efficient officers.

Mr Jinnah – Then do you think that we should wait until Dehra Dun gives us the right number of men?

Mr Malik – If those 100 vacancies have to be filled up, they must be filled somehow.

Mr Jinnah – We don't want worthless stuff, but suppose the material is selected with care and trained properly?

Mr Malik – I have no objection provided the selection is very, very careful.

Mr Sethna – Are you aware that Dehra Dun boys at Sandhurst have not done as well as other boys from Universities and colleges?

Mr Malik – I have never heard that.

Mr Burdon – That is only an allegation by certain people and not an established fact.

Diwan Bahadur Ramachandra Rao – Do you consider boys at the Intermediate stage of the Punjab University suitable material for sending to Sandhurst?

Mr Malik – I think you will find boys of that class suitable for Sandhurst.

Diwan Bahadur Ramachandra Rao – Could you get a fairly good number?

Mr Malik – In the Punjab University you could pick out 10.

Diwan Bahadur Ramachandra Rao – Do you know the present methods of publicity adopted for obtaining recruits? I should like to know the grounds on which rejections are made.

Mr Malik – As Deputy Commissioner I personally have a look at the boy's physique, though that is really for the doctor to decide about. I look to his family connections to see whether he is likely to make a good soldier. I also observe his carriage, personal demeanour and so on.

Diwan Bahadur Ramachandra Rao – Do you mean by family connection whether he belongs to a family with military traditions?

Mr Malik – Yes.

Diwan Bahadur Ramachandra Rao – What is the publicity given?

Mr Malik – A Government *communique* is published in the papers in Lahore.

Diwan Bahadur Ramachandra Rao – How often?

Mr Malik – I could not say that. I only know what publicity is given in the district.

Diwan Bahadur Ramachandra Rao – You are not responsible for publicity?

Mr Malik – No.

Diwan Bahadur Ramachandra Rao – Who does it?

Mr Malik – I do not know.

Diwan Bahadur Ramachandra Rao – How many applications have you had in your district?

Mr Malik – I have only had to deal with applications once, and then I had only two.

Diwan Bahadur Ramachandra Rao – Did you see the insertion of the local *communique* in the local press?

Mr Malik – Yes, in the "*Civil and Military Gazette*", "*Tribune*" and other papers.

Diwan Bahadur Ramachandra Rao – What other methods are adopted?

Mr Malik – I cannot say.

Diwan Bahadur Ramachandra Rao – You have not done anything yourself?

Mr Malik – No. But as a Deputy Commissioner I am naturally supposed to know the people in my district and would naturally know what suitable candidates are available.

Diwan Bahadur Ramachandra Rao – Government never asked you to find out other recruits?

Mr Malik – I got no orders to do so.

The Chairman – How did you get those two applications?

Mr Malik – The people came to see me.

The Chairman – Is it a fact that only people who know the Deputy Commissioner are allowed to see him?

Mr Malik – Any man can come in and put in his application. I invite petitions and I get 40 to 50 a day.

Mr Sethna – A European Deputy Commissioner would not have the same opportunities as you have?

Mr Malik – I think so.

Mr Sethna – You said that you knew of people who would provide suitable material for Sandhurst. Do you think a European Deputy Commissioner has the same means of finding out?

Mr Malik – Yes.

Major Zorawar Singh – Have you any definite instructions as to what boys to send up?

Mr Malik – I could not say without making a reference to the papers. The orders are rather lengthy.

Mr Jinnah – Is it not one of the instructions that boys from the so-called martial classes are to be given preference?

Mr Malik – I could not say. My memory is not good enough for that.

Mr Jinnah – These two boys that you selected were from the martial classes?

Mr Malik – One was the son of a local Civil Surgeon; the other was the son of a <u>Zemindar</u>. I do not think that he had any military traditions.

Mr Jinnah – You said you joined the Air Force from the Red Cross? Were there any other Indian (sic) who joined the Air Force?

Mr Malik – There were three boys, Velinkar from Bombay, Roy from Calcutta and Sen.

Mr Jinnah – Did they do well?

Mr Malik – Yes.

Mr Jinnah – Where are they now?

Mr Malik – Velinkar and Roy were killed in action. I do not know where Sen is now.

Mr Jinnah – You think that in India you could get boys for the Air Force?

Mr Malik – Yes, I am an Indian myself.

Mr Jinnah – Do you think that Roy and Velinkar belonged to the martial classes?

Mr Malik – Velinkar was a Mahratta and Roy was a Bengali.

Mr Jinnah – Do you think Bengalis are a martial race?

Mr Malik – I have not sufficient experience of them.

Capt. Hira Singh – If the boys are caught young and sent to Dehra Dun, do you think they will do better than boys who come through the ordinary schools and colleges?

Mr Malik – Yes.

Capt. Hira Singh – You think that it is essential to find out the military tradition behind a boy?

Mr Malik – Tradition is a very great help. I believe in it tremendously.

Capt. Hira Singh – Do you think that if officers are recruited from the non-martial classes, they will command the same confidence as those who have looked to the army as a career for a long time?

Mr Malik – That question might suitably be answered by officers of the Indian Army. I have no experience as a soldier.

Major Zorawar Singh – Given character and proper training, you see no reason why any man should not make good?

Mr Malik – That is so.

Capt. Hira Singh – Do you think those who have no military tradition will prove better than those who have?

Mr Malik – It is a question of very careful selection at a suitable age. I do not see why they should not make good officers.

Capt. Hira Singh – Do you refer to exceptional cases or are you speaking generally?

Mr Malik – I refer to exceptional cases.

Diwan Bahadur Ramachandra Rao – Would you select any Punjabi Mussalman without examining his traditions?

Mr Malik – I would not.

Diwan Bahadur Ramachandra Rao – There seems to be a distinction between martial and non-martial classes. In recruiting would you leave out the non-martial classes altogether?

Mr Malik – I would not leave them out altogether.

Mr Burdon – You are keen on games?

Mr Malik – Yes, I got my 'blue' for golf and hockey at Oxford. I also played cricket for the University, but I did not get my 'blue'.

Mr Burdon – Did you find that proficiency in games carried one a long way in England?

Mr Malik – Yes.

Glossary

Aéronautique Militaire	French air force
Air Board	governing body of the RFC and RNAS during 1916-1917
Air Council	governing body of the Royal Air Force advising the Air Ministry
Air Ministry	department of government responsible for the RAF from 1918
Albatros	German bi-plane fighter aircraft
All India Muslim League	political party established in 1906
Anglo-Indian	British person born or settled in India
ardas	set prayers in Sikhism
Army Council	governing body of the British Army advising the War Office
Arya Samaj	Hindu reform movement
batman	airman assigned to an officer as a personal servant
cantonment	permanent military station in British India
Civil Lines	residential neighbourhoods for senior civilian officers and their families
commission	official document confirming rank of an officer in the armed forces
Croix Rouge Française	French Red Cross
fagging	younger pupils acting as personal servants to the oldest boys at a public school

gali (s) *galiaan* (p)	passageway/s
Ghadar movement	founded by expatriate Indians to overthrow British rule in India
Gnome	French engine manufacturer
Government of India (GOI)	body headed by the Viceroy and the Imperial Legislative Council
guardianship	taking charge of an Indian student's education and welfare needs
gurdwara	temple
Guru Granth Sahib	central religious scripture of Sikhism
hartal	traditional form of strike action
Imperial Legislative Council	governing council for British India from 1861 to 1947
Imperial War Cabinet	British Empire's wartime ruling body during the First World War
Indian Civil Service (ICS)	elite civil service of British India during the period between 1858 and 1947
Indian National Congress	political party of India, which dominated the home rule movement
Indianisation	process promoting Indians to more senior positions in government services
Jasta	German air force squadron
Jemadar	equivalent to a lieutenant in the Indian infantry or cavalry
Khalsa	highest order of the Sikh religion
King's Commissioned Officer	one with the authority to serve as an officer in the British Armed Forces
kirpan	sword or a dagger carried by Sikhs
Luftstreitkräfte	air service of the Imperial German Army
Majlis	Arabic and Persian term meaning "council"
mohalla	area of a town or village; a neighbourhood
non-commissioned officer	personnel with rank of corporal, sergeant etc

Officer Training Corps (OTC)	training units similar to a university club, but operated by the British Army
permanent commission	awarded to an officer intent on a long-term professional career
rigging	ropes and wires supporting the structure of a biplane
sant	holy person of exalted status, especially in Sikhism
satyagraha	act of nonviolent resistance
scout	fighter plane
sepoy	Indian soldier
Singh Sabha movement	Sikh opposition to the proselytising activities of other religions
sticky	drying cricket pitch which favours the bowler
Swadeshi movement	begun in 1906 by Indian nationals opposed to the Partition of Bengal
temporary commission	one awarded to an officer for the duration of the war only
Vedanta	branch of Indian philosophy
Vedic	ancient rituals and rites of passage
Viceroy's Commissioned Officer	commissioned officer, but with authority only over Indian troops
vilayat	foreign land; especially England, Britain, or Europe
War Office	department of government responsible for the British Army
Zemindar	a landowner, especially one who leases his land to tenant farmers

Bibliography

Ashworth, C., '*Action Stations: Military airfields of the Central South and South-East*' (Patrick Stephens: Yeovil, 1985).

Bailey, C., '*Francis Fortescue Urquhart: A* Memoir' (Macmillan: London, 1936).

Barua, P.P., '*Gentlemen of the Raj: The Indian Army Officer Corps, 1817-1949*' (Praeger: Connecticut, 2003).

Bates, C., '*Subalterns and Raj*' (Routledge: New York, 2007).

Boston, W.H., '*Some Memoirs of An Unknown Pilot in The Royal Flying Corps and Royal Air Force 1917-1918*' (Barbara Boston: Shropshire, 1991).

Brown, J.M., '*Gandhi's Rise to Power: Indian Politics 1915-1922*' (Cambridge University Press: London, 1972).

Buckerfield, L. & Ballinger, S., '*The People's Centenary – Tracking public attitudes to the First World War Centenary 2013-2018*' (British Future: London, 2019).

Bush, J., '*Lionel Morris and the Red Baron: Air War on the Somme*' (Pen & Sword: Barnsley, 2019).

Canwell, D. & Sutherland, J., '*Battle of Britain 1917: The First Heavy Bomber Raids on England*' (Pen and Sword Aviation: Barnsley, 2006).

Caygill, P., '*The Biggin Hill Wing, 1941: From Defence to Attack*' (Pen & Sword Aviation: Barnsley, 2008).

Chandra, B., '*India's Struggle for Independence*' (Penguin Books: Delhi, 1989).

Das, S., '*India, Empire and First World War Culture*' (Cambridge University Press: Cambridge, 2018).

Deshpande, A., '*British Military Policy in India, 1900-1945*' (Manohar Publishing: New Delhi, 2005).

Doabia, H.S., *'Life Story of Sant Attar Singh* Ji' (Singh Brothers: Amritsar, 1992).

Gandhi, M.K., *'An Autobiography – The Story of My Experiments with Truth'* (Penguin Books: London, 2001).

Graham, M., *'Oxford in the Great War'* (Pen and Sword Military: Barnsley, 2014).

Grey, P., & Thetford, O., *'German Aircraft of the First World War'* (Putnam: London, 1970).

Gupta, P.S., & Deshpande, A., *'The British Raj and its Indian Armed Forces 1857-1939'* (Oxford University Press: Oxford, 2002).

Guttman, J., *'Sopwith Camel'* (Osprey Publishing: Oxford, 2012).

Halstead, T., *'The First World War and Public School Ethos: The Case of Uppingham School'*, War & Society (2015).

Hunter, W.W., *'Imperial Gazetteer of India'* (Clarendon Press: Oxford, 1908).

Jones, M.J., *'British Nationality Law and Practice'* (Oxford University Press: Oxford, 1947).

Kirpanali, S.K., *'Fifty Year with the British'* (Sangam: London, 1993).

Lahiri, S., *'Indians in Britain, 1880-1930'* (Cass: London, 2000).

Levine, N.B., *'Politics, religion and love: the story of H.H. Asquith, Venetia Stanley and Edwin Montagu'* (New York University Press: London, 1991).

MacKail, J.W., *'James Leigh Strachan-Davidson - A Memoir'* (Clarendon Press: Oxford, 1925),

Macmillan, N., *'Offensive Patrol'* (Jarrolds Publishers: London, 1973).

Malik, H.S., *'A Little Work, A Little Play'* (Bookwise: Delhi, 2011).

Mazunder, R.K., *'The Indian Army and the Making of Punjab'* (Orient Longman: Delhi 2003).

Mittal, S.C., *'Freedom movement in Punjab, 1905-29'* (Concept Publishing: Delhi, 1977).

Mukherjee, S., *'Nationalism, Education and Migrant Identities'* (Routledge: Abingdon, 2010).

Omissi, D., *'The Sepoy and the Raj: The Indian Army, 1860-1940'* (Macmillan: London, 1994).

Pardon, S., (Ed.) *'Wisden Almanac, 1915'* (John Wisden & Co: London, 1915).

Pati, B., *'India and the First World War'* (Atlantic Publishers: New Delhi, 1996).

Rai, L.R., *'The Story of My Deportation, 1908'* (Digital Library of India: Delhi, 2015).

Ralph, W.D., *'Barker VC'* (Grub Street: London, 1997).

Ranasinha, R., (Ed.) *'South Asians and the Shaping of Britain, 1870-1950'* (Manchester University Press: Manchester, 2012).

Sapru, S., *'Sky Hawks'* (Writers Workshop Books: Calcutta, 2006).

Satthianadhan, S., *'Holiday Trip to Europe and America'* (Varadachari & Co: Madras, 1897).

Seton, M.C.C., *'The India Office'* (Putnam & Sons: London, 1926).

Sheffield, G., *'Officer-Man Relations: Morale and Discipline in the British Army 1902-22'* (Macmillan: London, 2000).

Sik, K.S., *'Nationality and International Law: An Asian Perspective'* (Nijhoff: Dordrecht, 1990).

Smiles, S. *'Self-Help with Illustrations of Conduct and Perseverance'* (John Murray: London, 1859).

Streets, H., *'Martial Races: The Military, Race and Masculinity in British Imperial Culture, 1857-1914'* (Manchester University Press: Manchester, 2004).

Van Wyngarden, G., *'Jasta 18. The Red Noses'* (Osprey: New York, 2011).

Visram, R., *'Asians in Britain: 400 Years of History'* (Pluto Press: London, 2002).

Wagner, K.A., *'Amritsar 1919 – An Empire of Fear and the Making of a Massacre'* (Yale University Press: London, 2019).

Wagner, K.A., *'The Skull of Alum Bheg'* (Hurst: London, 2017).

Wainright, A.M., *'The Better Class of Indian': Social rank, imperial identity and South Asians in Britain 1858-1914'* (Manchester University Press: Manchester, 2008).

Wallace, G., *'RAF Biggin Hill'* (Pace Reprographics: Denham, Bucks, 1979).

Index